ADVANCE PRAISE

Navigating Relationships in the Modern Family

"The edited volume "*Navigating Relationships in the Modern Family*" is timely, provocative, and important in terms of pushing the boundaries of communication in different kinds of families not often studied by scholars. The volume features well-established scholars who provide state-of-the-art reviews of knowledge claims in a range of areas and then advance recommendations for scholars and practitioners. The book sharpens voices and perspective on family communication in order to understand how diverse modern types of families live out their lives in interconnected ways."

Jeffrey T. Child, Professor of Communication,
Kent State University

"This book will be a major contribution to the area of family communication. It covers an extraordinary range of family forms. Even the traditional family forms are brought up to date by including current research."

Kathleen M. Galvin, Professor of Communication Studies,
Northwestern University

Navigating Relationships in the Modern Family

Children, Families, and Aging

Thomas J. Socha
General Editor

Vol. 15

The Lifespan Communication series
is part of the Peter Lang Media and Communication list.
Every volume is peer reviewed and meets
the highest quality standards for content and production.

PETER LANG
New York • Bern • Berlin
Brussels • Vienna • Oxford • Warsaw

Navigating Relationships in the Modern Family

Communication, Identity, and Difference

Edited by
Jordan Soliz and
Colleen Warner Colaner

PETER LANG
New York • Bern • Berlin
Brussels • Vienna • Oxford • Warsaw

Library of Congress Cataloging-in-Publication Data

Names: Soliz, Jordan, editor. | Colaner, Colleen Warner, editor.
Title: Navigating relationships in the modern family: communication, identity, and difference / edited by Jordan Soliz and Colleen Warner Colaner.
Description: New York: Peter Lang, 2020.
Series: Lifespan communication: children, families, and aging; Vol. 15
ISSN 2166-6466 (print) | ISSN 2166-6474 (online)
Includes bibliographical references and index.
Identifiers: LCCN 2019052564 (print) | LCCN 2019052565 (ebook) |
ISBN 978-1-4331-6237-4 (hardback) | ISBN 978-1-4331-6238-1 (paperback) |
ISBN 978-1-4331-6239-8 (ebook pdf)
ISBN 978-1-4331-6240-4 (epub) | ISBN 978-1-4331-6241-1 (mobi)
Subjects: LCSH: Families. | Communication in families. |
Interpersonal relations.
Classification: LCC HQ728.N38 2020 (print) | LCC HQ728 (ebook) |
DDC 306.85—dc23
LC record available at https://lccn.loc.gov/2019052564
LC ebook record available at https://lccn.loc.gov/2019052565
DOI 10.3726/b14764

Bibliographic information published by **Die Deutsche Nationalbibliothek**. **Die Deutsche Nationalbibliothek** lists this publication in the "Deutsche Nationalbibliografie"; detailed bibliographic data are available on the Internet at http://dnb.d-nb.de/.

The paper in this book meets the guidelines for permanence and durability of the Committee on Production Guidelines for Book Longevity of the Council of Library Resources.

29 Broadway, 18th floor, New York, NY 10006
www.peterlang.com

Printed in the United States of America

To our families and loved ones: biological, biological, legal, and chosen.

Jordan: Thank you "Bobbi."

Colleen: For Seth, Essie, and Camille. You are my home.

Table of Contents

Preface

Colleen Warner Colaner and Jordan Soliz

Despite evidence to the contrary (Coontz, 1993), families are still conceptualized in idealized ways in popular discourse. Such depictions often reflect mainstream ideologies and put forth a view that families are homogenous entities in terms family members' social identities, worldviews, and value orientations. In reality, families are a collective of individuals that often vary in their values and beliefs as well as social positions and identities (e.g., socio-economic status, age groups, political affiliation). Moreover, the last few decades have seen a dramatic increase in family compositions in which so-called "traditional" social boundaries are transcended (e.g., interfaith families, multiethnic families) as individuals marry outside of and/or select out of these social boundaries. For instance, marriages and families that cross traditional racial-ethnic divides have been growing drastically over the last decade in the United States (Pew Research Center, 2014). As such, discourses about family are changing within and outside of the family (Galvin, 2006). Families are not only more diverse than what is depicted in popular perception and traditional discourse, but one could argue that it is in the family where most of our more in-depth interactions with those with different worldviews and social identities occur (Soliz & Rittenour, 2012). Further, formative processes in families (e.g., marriage) by their very nature can create differences with and across family relationships. In fact, much of the popular discourse on step-families and in-law relationships tend to overemphasize the negative consequences of these "new" families formed through marriage (e.g., the "evil" stepmother, the contentious mother-in-law and daughter-in-law relationship). In short, family relationships are far from homogenous.

Because families are salient, instrumental, and influential ingroups (Sani, 2012; Soliz & Rittenour, 2012), understanding how families balance individuality, salient differences, and collective familial identity not only provides insight into family communication processes, but it can also shed light on how to communicatively manage difference outside of the family (i.e., can we apply collaborative communication skills learned from diverse family relationships to other situations?). Although family communication scholars and practitioners recognize complicated family structures and the implications thereof, our textbooks and edited volumes are often void of an explicit focus on differences in families, especially as it relates to salient social identities such as race-ethnicity, religion, political affiliation (Soliz & Phillips, 2018; Turner & West, 2018). Thus, the central purpose of this edited volume is to provide an overview of family forms and relationships in which divergent social identities or identities related to family formative processes (e.g., stepfamilies, adoption) are part of the family culture. The specific focus of the volume involves discussion of the challenges these differences can pose for maintaining positive, healthy relationships as well as demonstrating how families communicatively manage these differences in a manner that both promotes relational solidarity while enabling individuality and wellbeing. In doing so, the chapters in this volume speak to family forms, relationships, and dynamics that characterize the modern family experience. Further, the edited volume illuminates the manner in which families can influence attitudes both through what happens in the family (e.g., under what conditions can interfaith marriages in the family change perceptions of religious groups outside of the family?) as well as how families socialize the worldviews of its members toward other social groups.

Defining the Modern Family

Implicit in the focus of this edited volume is the very nature of what constitutes the modern family. Family conceptions and definitions vary widely among communication scholars. Many scholars advocate for inclusive family definitions that recognize that families exist beyond the boundaries of household, blood, and law (Baxter, 2014). The modern family is more complex than ever before, requiring elaborated discourse to create, sustain, and support divergent identities with the coherent whole. The modern family involves distinct identities (e.g., religious, racial, ethnic, political, sexual orientation, health/ability, and social class) as well as structures (e.g., adoptive, foster, stepfamily, in-law), as the current volume details. The family of the future will be increasingly complex, with technological advancements changing the course of reproduction, longevity, and connection (Galvin, 2013).

As the family changes over time, it becomes increasingly difficult to create inclusive definitions of the family. Complex definitions are needed to reflect complex relationships, identities, and experiences. With so many families falling outside of clear biological and legal connections, more reliance is needed on communication processes to understand the reality of modern families (Galvin, 2006). Many scholars rely on the role lens for family definitions—family relationships are considered familial to the degree that individuals act like and feel like family (Floyd, Mikkelson, & Judd, 2006). The role lens pulls in a number of relationships into the family realm, such as voluntary kin, families lacking legal guardianship (e.g., foster parents, stepparents who have not adopted the child), and relationships that remain after legal connections dissolve (e.g., relationships maintained with the spouse's family after the death or divorce). Although these relationships do not receive the legal sanctions provided by other bases of commitment, they play an important role in many individuals' lives and are at times the most meaningful relationships we have.

At the same time, we must be cautious about who is included in our family definitions. There is reason to consider limiting family definitions to a small range of personal relationships. Floyd and colleagues (2006) remind us that overly broad definitions of family put the discipline at risk of conceptual obfuscation—if family definitions are too inclusive, then we conflate the experiences and communication processes relegated to family units. Even with the complexity of family relationships in the present era, it is important to consider how families are unique and distinct from other non-family relationships. Thus, we offer the following definition:

> We define families as groups of individuals who are connected through legal statute, biological relatedness, or prolonged commitment. Families are characterized by interdependence, long-term investments, and enduring ties that remain over time and generations. These unique features differentiate families from other relationships.

The interdependent nature of family is embedded in the legal, biological, and commitment-based pathways of family connectedness. As family systems theory demonstrates, individuals in the family system are affected by what happens to other members of the system, for better and for worse. Long-term investments of financial support, affection, and expectations of care are primary functions of family relationships. Family relationships are enduring and are often the longest relationship of our life, such as siblings who are connected cradle to grave or the considerable anticipated future shared by parents of newborns and newly married couples. Family legacies—both positive and negative—connect individuals across generations. These unique features converge as hallmarks of family relatedness.

This volume highlights the myriad differences that emerge in the family, which at times can be hard to navigate given the uniqueness of the family form. Family relationships are difficult if not impossible to dissolve due to the involuntary nature (e.g., parent-child relationships, in-law relationships) and the interdependence of family relationships. The fact that diverse identities occur in the family is exactly what makes these relationships complicated. This complexity requires that we put guardrails on our definitions. If family relationships could easily be entered and broken, the differences highlighted in this volume would not be so difficult to navigate.

We also need to be cognizant of the internalized beliefs inherent in broad, role-based definitions of the family. Many students in our classroom discussions, for example, initially define families as places where you receive comfort, care, and support. This assumption of family as exclusively positive spills over into other close, satisfying relationships, such as when we suggest that a workplace is "like a family" or a close friend is "like a brother." These relationships are positioned as family because they are close and satisfying. Such positioning implies that families are by and large healthy, safe, and comfortable relationships. Defining family according to positive communication practices has ties to the role lens, insomuch that nonfamily members can be considered family when they meet a certain threshold of closeness and support. Indeed, many families offer considerable love and support to one another, maybe even ideally so. However, positive communication processes fall short of explaining the range of family experiences that characterize this unique relationship.

In reality, using the term family in exclusively positive ways may cover a multitude of sins. When we overemphasize family relationships as positive, we depart from the realities that many families face. As the family forms detailed in this volume suggest, families face a number of deep identity differences, which at times prove to be challenging and, other times, provide a rich and diverse family life. We also see trauma, abuse, and neglect in the family system, perhaps seen most clearly in the 400,000 children in the foster care system after their biological families were deemed unable to provide care (Petrowski, Cappa, & Gross, 2017). Relationship violence and conflict in the family clue us in to the darker elements of family interactions. When these unpleasant, unhealthy, and damaging patterns take root in family relationships, the interdependent and enduring nature of these relationship complicate matters. We cannot easily discard or dissolve many family relationships. Even when families opt for estrangement, relationship distancing involves ongoing and active communication practices (Scharp, Thomas, & Paxton, 2015). The current volume cautions against a trend toward toxic positivity of family definitions, revealing that differences are imbued in the family system, and it is the nature of the communication that often differentiates the positive and negative outcomes of these differences.

The fact that families are enduring, even in the face of such difficulty and difference, is exactly what makes family worthy of studying. If family relationships were easy to discard or simple to navigate, there would not be such an opportunity to understand the complex communication practices that families engage to maintain connectedness and solidarity in the face of competing identities and experiences. And importantly for this volume, navigating those differences within the family through communication practices has important implications for relationships outside the family in ways that promote inclusion, difference, and equity.

Organization of the Edited Volume

Chapters in this book center on a focused family purview in which issues of identity and difference stem from one of two sources: either social identities (e.g., ethnic-racial, political) or formative processes (e.g., step-families, adoption).

The first several chapters focus on social identity difference in the family: age, race and ethnicity, religion, politics, sexual orientation, and social class. Although not often considered a salient social identity, Fowler and Zorn provide an overview on the role of age identity in family relationships—specifically intergenerational family relationships (IGFRs: e.g., grandparent-grandchild relationships)—in the initial chapter. In doing so, they demonstrate how many intergenerational and age-based barriers and opportunities exist in our family relationships.

As we mentioned in our introduction, both multiethnic-racial families and interfaith families are increasing in many parts of the world. Yet, perceptions of families being fairly homogenous in terms of race, ethnicity, and religion are still pervasive in popular discourse. Thus, in the second chapter, Harris, Young-Heil, and Huong discuss the nuances of identity and identity development for individuals with mixed ethnic-racial backgrounds, highlighting the role of communication in the family—primarily with parents—as well as other social contexts (e.g., friendships, schools). In Chapter 3, Ting-Toomey and Martinez address the complexities of religious and faith-based differences in the family, focusing on both romantic couples and parent-child relationships. Both chapters provide theoretical and applied considerations for advancing scholarship and/or programs and resources that can serve these families.

Although political differences have always been a part of family life, today's political climate and media landscape lead many to claim we are more polarized than ever, which leads to profound impacts on the time families choose to spend with one another. Whereas a great deal of the discussion on political differences focuses on strangers or non-intimate relationships, Warner and Park detail in the fourth chapter how political (dis)agreement takes shape in the family system. They argue that attitude congruence is the most likely outcome in the nuclear family, yet political disagreement occurring mostly with extended family members can reduce family communication and connectedness.

In Chapter 5, Manning synthesizes the research on queer families including partners, parenting, and trans identity, emphasizing how this research continues to challenge heteronormative understandings of family. In doing so, Manning calls for innovative theoretical and methodological approaches that not only account for and give voice to queer family experiences, but also advance family communication scholarship in general.

Social class is relatively absent in research on family communication. Dougherty, Ferguson, and Williams address this gap in Chapter 6, emphasizing the role of social class in influencing family culture, relationships, and family functioning. In doing so, they also highlight the barriers and opportunities related to social mobility with important considerations for family communication and family relationships.

Chapters 7 and 8 focus on how voluntary and forced migration shapes family dynamics and individual well-being. In Chapter 7, Kam, Murillo Mendez, and Cornejo highlight the family communication process in immigrant families, with particular attention to family separation-reunification and the impact on well-being of family members. Chapter 8 shifts to research on and insight into refugee experiences in Australia. Hebbani and MacKinnon summarize how the process, and often trauma, associated with refugee displacement and resettlement plays out in family relationships, including identity development of family members.

Whereas illness identity may bring to mind issues related to health and health care, illness identity shapes and is shaped by family dynamics. As such, in Chapter 9, Palmer-Wackerly and Voorhees delineate the relational nature of illness. They demonstrate the profound effect illness has on family. Importantly, they explain how family can influence how patients and others understand and experience their illness in ways that extend beyond individual diagnoses.

The volume then shifts to address family changes related to formative processes: adoption, foster care, in-laws, and stepfamilies. Colaner and Kilgore discuss adoptee difference and belonging regarding birth and adoptive families in Chapter 10. Confounding factors such as complex developmental trauma as well as transracial adoption may exacerbate differences in the adoptive family network. Repositioning adoptees as collaboratively centered between biological and adoptive families may promote belonging and help alleviate feelings of differences in the family system.

In Chapter 11, Nelson and Thomas review family communication scholarship centered around the foster care system and foster families. They utilize a critical lens to reveal the limitations of the ideology of family-as-biology which falls short to reflect foster family experiences. They argue that communication within and about foster care troubles this cultural ideology, creating space for new, emergent understandings of family.

Recognizing the many salient issues related to identity and difference that emerge from marriages, the next two chapters focus on in-law relationships and stepfamilies. In Chapter 12, Mikucki-Enyart and Heisdorf acknowledge how in-laws occupy a liminal space in family life, simultaneously seen as "insiders" and "outsiders." They illuminate causes and consequences of in-law difficulty and advance practical tools for intervention to assist families in positively navigating their in-law relationships.

In Chapter 13, Schrodt reviews how stepfamilies achieve family solidarity, a process that can be difficult given that stepfamilies most often form in the wake of a romantic breakup, a divorce, or a parent's death. He specifically identifies and describes communication related to the personal, relational, and familial identities that promote wellness in stepfamily relationships.

Each of the preceding chapters includes a synthesis of literature on the family context that highlights current research and theorizing. Following the synthesis of literature, we asked each of our contributors to include a section labeled "Beyond the Family" in which they discuss how family communication can influence attitudes, behaviors, and discourses outside of the family and/or how cultural and social discourses play a role in family interactions. For instance, how does grandparent-grandchild communication influence attitudes toward older adults and aging? Can we improve interfaith dialogue in general by understanding communication in interfaith families? How do ideologies of social class influence family functioning? How do adoptive and foster children help us understand children as connected to multiple caregivers, asking who belongs to the child rather than to whom the child belongs? Finally, each chapter concludes with a section on implications for both scholars and practitioners.

The final chapter concludes our volume by offering a synthesis of family difference with an eye toward future possibilities. Rather than focus on a specific type of family or family relationship, the final chapter by Rittenour emphasizes the role families play in shaping our attitudes towards self and others. She reemphasizes that although there are considerable differences in the modern family, the family is the "ultimate ingroup," consequential for socializing children into appreciation and acceptance toward others or more prejudiced attitudes. She highlights the important practices parents employ to produce more prosocial orientations toward outgroups.

Family Communication: Moving Forward

The complexity of the modern family requires complex and nuanced research practices. Responding to the complexity requires that we consider the underserved role of children in family communication scholarship and the need to engage families in communication education. We discuss each of these in turn below.

A Call for Children's Perspectives

Despite a robust literature on parent-child communication, surprisingly few communication studies actually consider children's experiences. Miller-Day, Pezalla, and Chesnut's (2013) meta-analysis of research articles published in communication journals revealed that only 3.7% of articles included children's perspectives. Of the communication literature that does solicit children's perspectives, Miller-Day and colleagues noted that the majority of these studies (63%) utilize informants over the age of 12. Even more, about half of communication literature that examines children's perspectives focuses on media and technology, with only 35 articles examining family communication. Resultantly, there is a dearth of research representing children's communication perceptions and capacities, especially young children's point of view, and especially children's perceptions of family communication. It is clear that very little communication research seeks to understand how children receive communication, how children's communication abilities develop over time, what children offer in the interaction, how children's responses shape the interaction, and how children view family relationships and interactions.

Scholars have critiqued communication scholars' lack of attention to children's perspectives over the last decade (Miller-Day et al., 2013; Miller-Day & Kam, 2008; Socha & Stamp, 2009; Socha & Yingling, 2010;), encouraging more empirical research with children. The lack of research on children's communication is detrimental to the field because it truncates our ability to speak to a full range of family experiences. Children are active agents in society, co-creating their worlds, reality, and relationships via social interaction, in line with all human behavior (Freeman & Mathison, 2008). Until scholars include children in family communication research, our discipline is unable to stake our claim as family experts. This lack of attention to children's experiences will inhibit the ability for family communication scholarship to speak intelligently to holistic family dynamics in the modern family experience across the range of human development.

The future of family communication research should expand and adjust to make room for children's voices in order to understand children's experiences in their own words and worlds. As families continue to diversify in social identity and formative processes, children will increasingly have perspectives and experiences that differ from their parents. Continuing to rely on parents' perceptions of family communication—as has been the long-standing practice in our discipline—will not be sufficient to fully explain family dynamics. Family communication scholarship will be inadequate to address family differences in the modern era unless children's voices are honored and included in our research.

A Call for Family Communication Education

As the family becomes increasingly complex, identity differences create opportunities to support families with resources to better navigate difference. Family communication processes naturally lend themselves toward intervention (Kam & Miller-Day, 2017). Communication skills can be taught, adapted, and improved to promote individual and relational well-being, which may be vital to highly functional complex families in the modern era. Although the communication discipline has roots in practical responses to social problems, family communication scholars have been somewhat reticent to work directly with families. Galvin (2013) notes that researchers in psychology, social work, and family studies have pursued these family educational efforts vigorously. Disciplines such as psychology which has a clinical arm or family studies that has a family life education approach may seem better routes for research application. However, family communication scholars have important knowledge to contribute to such programs. Chapters in the current volume takes up practical implications, with important and valuable suggestions for communication education outlets pertinent to the family difference context at hand. There is great potential for impactful communication education and intervention programs.

Existing family education models show promise for family communication education work. Gottman, Shapiro, and Parthemer's (2004) *Bringing Baby Home*, Purvis' (2013) *Empowered to Connect*, Hecht and colleagues' (2003)

Keepin' it REAL, and Webster-Stratton's (2006) *The Incredible Years* are examples of research-based, evidence-tested educational programs that target relational and/or communicative processes to promote individual and relational health. Gottman and colleagues's work in particular targets important communication practices that produce positive outcomes, such as improved marital quality (Shapiro, Gottman, & Fink, 2015) and maternal mental health (Shapiro & Gottman, 2005). Intervening at the communication level provides an important target with actionable steps and research-based positive outcomes. The future of the family requires that communication scholars attend to nuanced differences and the communication processes that contribute to solidarity in the face of relationship difference. Thus, it compels family communication researchers to engage research and service models that create, distribute, and test family education programs to support the modern family.

Working directly with families provides one outlet, but practitioner training offers another important avenue to promote attuned communication practices. Marriage and family therapists, social workers, physicians, family lawyers, and policymakers work with families to solve practical problems and promote better quality of life for individuals and families. These practitioners have highly specialized skill sets that allow them to target specific layers of family interaction to promote wellbeing. Many of these practitioners, however, are not abreast of the complex communication processes central to diverse family forms and experiences. Educating and partnering with mental health practitioners and family service providers offers an important intervention point to distribute our scholarship to families who may need the information the most.

Conclusion

We hope this book provides further reconsideration of the diversity of family forms and structures, acknowledging the pleasant function of family relationships (e.g., solidarity, support, wellbeing) while being mindful of the complex differences inherent in the modern family form. Considering identity and formative differences points our attention toward the interplay between the individual, relational, and social identities that drive family communication processes. Combining these communication processes with an understanding of the social structures in which they exist has implications for illuminating family functioning and the role family plays in shaping attitudes and vice-versa. We hope this volume provides a platform for considering family complexity in the current and future era.

References

Baxter, L. A. (2014). *Remaking "family" communicatively.* New York: Peter Lang.

Coontz, S. (1993). *The way we never were: American families and the nostalgia trap.* New York: Basic Books.

Floyd, K., Mikkelson, A. C., & Judd, J. (2006). Defining the family through relationships. In L. H. Turner & R. West (Eds.), *The family communication sourcebook* (pp. 21–42). Thousand Oaks, CA: Sage.

Freeman, M., & Mathison, S. (2008). *Researching children's experiences.* New York: Guilford Press.

Galvin, K. (2013). The family of the future: What do we face? In A. L. Vangelisti (Ed.), *The handbook of family communication* (pp. 675–697). Mahwah, NJ: Lawrence Erlbaum.

Galvin, K. M. (2006). Diversity's impact on defining the family: Discourse-dependence and identity. In L. H. Turner & R. West (Eds.), *The family communication sourcebook* (pp. 3–20). Thousand Oaks, CA: Sage Publications.

Gottman, J. M., Shapiro, A. F., & Parthemer, J. (2004). Bringing baby home: A workshop for new and expectant parents. *International Journal of Childbirth Education, 19,* 28.

Hecht, M. L., Marsiglia, F. F., Elek, E., Wagstaff, D. A., Kulis, S., Dustman, P., & Miller-Day, M. (2003). Culturally grounded substance use prevention: An evaluation of the keepin' it REAL curriculum. *Prevention Science, 4,* 233–248.

Kam, J., & Miller-Day, M. (2017). An introduction to the special issue on family communication and substance use prevention and intervention. *Journal of Family Communication, 17,* 1–14.

Miller-Day, M., & Kam, J. (2008). Investigating communication in families: Children, parents, and grandparents. In W. F. Eadie (Ed.), *21st century communication: A reference handbook* (Vol. 1, pp. 303–312). Thousand Oaks, CA: Sage Publications.

Miller-Day, M., Pezalla, A., & Chestnut, R. (2013). Children are in families too!: The presence of children in communication research. *Journal of Family Communication,* 13, 150–165.

Petrowski, N., Cappa, C., & Gross, P. (2017). Estimating the number of children in formal alternative care: Challenges and results. *Child Abuse & Neglect, 70,* 388–398. doi:10.1016/j.chiabu.2016.11.026

Pew Research Center. (2014, March 6). The next America. Retrieved from http://www.pewresearch.org/packages/the-next-america/

Purvis, K. B., Cross, D. R., Dansereau, D. F., & Parris, S. R. (2013). Trust-Based Relational Intervention (TBRI): A systemic approach to complex developmental trauma. *Child & Youth Services, 34,* 360–386.

Sani, F. (2012). Group identification, social relationships, and health. In J. Jetten, C. Haslam, & S. A. Haslam (Eds.), *The social cure: Identity, health, and well-being* (pp. 21–38). New York: Psychology Press.

Scharp, K. M., Thomas, L. J., & Paxman, C. G. (2015). "It was the straw that broke the camel's back": Exploring the distancing processes communicatively constructed in parent-child estrangement backstories. Journal of Family Communication, 15(4), 330–348.

Shapiro, A. F. & Gottman, J. M. (2005). Effects on marriage of a psycho-communicative-educational intervention with couples undergoing the transition to parenthood, evaluation at 1-year post intervention. *The Journal of Family Communication, 5*, 1–24.

Shapiro, A. F., Gottman, J. M., & Fink, B. C. (2015). Short-term change in couples' conflict following a transition to parenthood intervention. *Couple Family Psychology, 4*, 239–251.

Socha, T., & Stamp, G. H. (2009). *Parents and children communicating with society: Managing relationships outside of home.* New York: Routledge.

Socha, T., & Yingling, J., (2010). *Families communication with children: Building positive developmental foundations.* Malden, MA: Polity.

Soliz, J., & Phillips, K. E. (2018). Toward a more expansive understanding of family communication: Considerations for inclusion of ethnic-racial and global diversity. *Journal of Family Communication, 18*, 5–12.

Soliz, J., & Rittenour, C. E. (2012). Family as an intergroup arena. In H. Giles (Ed.), *The handbook of intergroup communication* (pp. 331–343). New York: Routledge.

Turner, L. H., & West, R. (2018). Investigating family voices from the margins. *Journal of Family Communication, 18*, 85–91.

Webster-Stratton, C. (2006). *The incredible years: A trouble-shooting guide for parents of children aged 2–8 years.* Seattle, WA: Incredible years.

1. *Age Identity and Intergenerational Relationships in the Family*

Craig Fowler and Andrea Zorn

Intergenerational family relationships (IGFRs) represent a distinctive inter-age bond, comprising as they do both an intragroup element (deriving from shared family status) and an intergroup dimension (resulting from parties to the relationship having divergent age identities) (Soliz & Rittenour, 2012). Although a sense of shared family identity may partially protect IGFRs from intergroup-based communication challenges that can buffet non-familial inter-age relationships (Soliz & Harwood, 2006), IGFRs remain a context within which ageism occurs (Pecchioni & Croghan, 2002).

In this chapter we first discuss demographic trends that shape and contextualize ties between parents and children, and between grandparents and grandchildren. Second, we highlight theoretical perspectives that inform our understanding of whether divergent age identities pose a barrier to congenial IGFRs. Third, we examine how IGFRs may influence cross-generational relationships occurring in *non*-family settings. Finally, we identify implications for scholars and practitioners.

Weedkiller on the Beanpole: Dampening Overexcitement about the Familial Benefits of Increased Longevity

An intriguing claim regarding how demographic trends affect family structures is that the combination of increased life expectancy and declining birth rates has increased the prevalence of "beanpole" families that have relatively few branches (horizontal, intra-generational ties), but a lengthy trunk (vertical, inter-generational ties; Dykstra & Komter, 2012). Thirty years ago, in fact, it was noted that because of the verticalization of families, "a growing number of women may spend a few years when they are both grandmothers and granddaughters" (Hagestad, 1988, pp. 406–407), and the suggestion that families would soon more frequently consist of four or five generations gained acceptance (Matthews & Sun, 2006).

We had hoped to offer a contemporary assessment of the number of persons living in four- and five-generation families. However, although Uhlenberg (1993) suggested that it should be straightforward to gather data that could establish how common four- and five-generation families actually *are*, asking the right questions of the right people is sufficiently challenging that Herlofson and Hagestad (2011) consider "How common are four-generational structures in a given society?" an "unanswerable question" (p. 348).

Certain facts of family life *can* be stated confidently, however. First, the prospect of more numerous four- and five-generation families seems not to have come to fruition. Indeed, some data suggests their incidence has declined in recent years (Grünheid & Scharein, 2011; Lundholm & Malmberg, 2009) because of reduced fertility and delayed childbirth (Margolis & Wright, 2017; Matthews & Sun, 2006), and that the norm is for families to run "three generations deep" at a time (Dykstra & Komter, 2012). Second, increased life expectancies let contemporary families sustain IGFRs over periods of time that would have been unfathomable a century ago. According to Hagestad and Uhlenberg (2007), for example, the probability that a ten-year old would have all four (biological) grandparents alive increased from 6% to 41% over the twentieth century. Grandchildren can also expect to have at least one grandparent alive well into adulthood. For instance, whereas just one-fifth of 30-year-olds had a living grandparent in the year 1900, this figure is expected to increase to four-fifths in the near future (Hagestad & Uhlenberg, 2007). Regarding these changes, Silverstein and Long (1998) observe that "an unprecedented number of grandparents…live long enough to see their grandchildren reach adolescence, young adulthood, and middle age, thereby allowing the possibility of long-term relationships between them" (p. 912).

Comparable trends characterize parent-child relationships: From U.S. data, Uhlenberg (1996) concluded that the probability of having both parents alive at the age of 40 increased from 22% to 59% during the twentieth century, whereas the probability of having *neither* parent alive at that age fell from 28% to 5%. Cheeringly, Uhlenberg also determined that by the age of 50, more than 80% of individuals are likely to have at least one living parent, and European data is similarly encouraging (Lundholm & Malmberg, 2009; van Gaalen & Deerenberg, 2014). Thus, although the rise of four- and five-generation families has not materialized, people *are* likely to have living parents and grandparents for much longer than was previously the case.

Theorizing Intergenerational Family Ties

How Do Age Identities Affect IGFRs?

A person's age identity encompasses not only awareness of chronological age, but understandings of how old they *feel*, of how old they are perceived as being by others, of the labels attached to them by others on the basis of age, and the social significance of these labels (Logan, Ward, & Spitze, 1992). Although age identities are influenced by factors such as one's actual age, life-cycle stage, and health status (Logan et al., 1992), they are also socially and discursively constructed (Harwood, 2008). Rather than being a fixed "thing," our age identities are "dynamic and interactionally achieved…constructed by and for individuals, often bilaterally" (Coupland, Coupland, Giles, & Henwood, 1991, p. 87). As Taylor (1992) asserts, conversations (between younger and older persons) "can be read as collaboratively authored documents that reveal who and what the participants think they are…Conversation is an arena for performance and contest in which actors create, maintain, and challenge representation of their identities" (p. 495).

Interactions between persons with different age identities are often thought to be fraught with difficulty, particularly when the parties involved are highly aware of their discrepant group identities (Harwood, Raman, & Hewstone, 2006). In this section, we discuss the impact that differing age identities (and mindfulness of the same) may have on parties to IGFRs.

According to the *intergenerational stake hypothesis* (IGSH), parents often evaluate the parent-child relationship more positively with respect to intimacy and enjoyableness than do their children (Bengtson and Kuypers, 1971). The IGSH proposes that older family members (who are conscious that they are comparatively close to the end of their lifespan) view intergenerational continuity and connectedness to (grand)children as extremely important and thus have a vested interest in prioritizing (and claiming) harmony and consensus in their IGFRs. Conversely, younger generations are often more concerned with establishing autonomy, making the most of (perhaps newfound) personal freedom, and establishing who they are independently of their family, and therefore have less incentive to perceive IGFRs through the rose-tinted lenses that color the gaze of (grand)parents. In fundamental ways, then, awareness of one's age identity and related developmental tasks affects perceptions of IGFRs.

Age identities have other important implications for IGFRs. Because family members of different generations may have different values and norms, and have likely experienced transitions and events that non age-peers either cannot understand or cannot remember, there may be little common ground on which to build relationships. Fingerman (2003) labels this generational divide a "developmental schism." The schism may be most problematic when the youngest generation are still children, adolescents, or emerging as adults. This is because gains in longevity permit a lengthy period of co-living[1] during which children and parents interact on a peer-like basis. Objectively, a child born when their mother is 25 will continue to be 25 years younger than their mother for as long as both are alive. Subjectively, however, that 25-year gap becomes less meaningful over time: Being the five-year-old child of someone who is 30 (or even the 25 year-old child of someone who is 50) is a very different experience from being the 70-year-old child of someone who is 95, for in the latter case, the child and parent have more comparable experiential repertoires. This argument coheres with the *role similarity hypothesis*, according to which increases in closeness and reductions in conflict are expected as parents and children come to share a greater number of social and familial statuses (Aquilino, 1997; De Goede, Branje, & Meeus, 2009). Moreover, as adult children enter middle age, they attain "filial maturity," and are able to see their mother and father not merely as *parents*, but as individuals with their own "past histories," their own flaws, and as people with whom they can have an "empathetic, compassionate, and reciprocal…relationship" (Birditt, Fingerman, Lefkowitz, & Kamp Dush, 2008, pp. 1–2).

As members of IGFRs grow older and live alongside one another for longer, age salience in day-to-day interactions may decrease. Nonetheless, certain events may bring consciousness of age identities to the fore, which can influence IGFRs. An older relative might become increasingly mindful of their age as they experience transitions such as surrendering their driver's license or entering residential care. Such recognition of one's advancing years may be accompanied by the realization that one has relatively little time left to live. And, per socioemotional selectivity theory (Carstensen, 1992), this sense of whether one has an expansive versus constricted future time perspective influences prioritization of emotional versus knowledge-based goals: When an individual believes they are "running out of time," (s)he is expected to place greater weight on maximizing emotional well-being, manifest through choices of interactional partners and prosocial behavior with those partners. Of course, the same events that render age salient for older relatives may also make age salient for younger kin who know of them. From the perspective of a child or grandchild, for example, when a (grand)parent stops driving or moves into a care facility, such events make age salient and force them to acknowledge their relative's mortality. The term "relational time perspective [RTP]" (Fingerman, Miller, & Charles, 2008, p. 401) captures a person's sense of whether another person (and thus their relationship with that person) has a foreshortened or extended future and helps account for "the behaviors...[older persons] evoke from their social partners" (Fingerman & Baker, 2006, p. 196): When a person perceives only a limited RTP, they may modify their behavior towards a others in order to "enhance...positive experiences and minimize tensions...rather than risk ending the relationship on a sour note" (Fingerman et al., 2008, p. 400). Thus, when awareness of age identity is accompanied by foreshortened (future or relational) time perspective, people may be particularly motivated to work at maintaining or restoring the emotional quality of IGFRs.

How Do IGFRs Affect Age Identities?

Although the preceding discussion highlights the potential for age identity to affect IGFRs, the relationship between age identity and family communication is likely reciprocal. That is, family relationships may also affect (or *effect*) age identities. Here, we examine how the communication of younger family members can induce or entrench among older kin age identities that conform to ageist stereotypes, discuss how older family members' communicative choices can shape age identities ascribed to them by younger kin, and argue that family communication teaches young and old alike the meaning of age at different points in the lifespan.

Young-to-old Family Communication and the Inducement of Ageist Age Identities. Intergenerational communication is one means by which older adults—via reflected appraisal—develop a sense of self who they are, and grasp how much they are (or are not) valued by younger people. This way of thinking reflects an intergroup perspective on communication (Giles, 2012), because it presumes that individuals place themselves (and others) into social categories, attribute meaning to these categories, and interact partly on the basis of these social categories. Perhaps no single perspective from our discipline has shed as much light on intergenerational relationships as communication accommodation theory (CAT; Giles, 2016), which describes and explains the communicative modifications people enact during conversations with individuals belonging to other social categories.

Interactions (and behaviors occurring within them) can be labeled accommodative or *non*accommodative. Accommodative communication is perceived as prosocial and appropriately adapted. Older adults are likely to perceive as accommodative younger communicators who are respectful, complimentary, attentive, and supportive (Williams et al., 1997). *Non*accommodative interactions are those construed as negative, or as featuring inappropriately adjusted (or unadjusted) talk. Young-to-old nonaccommodation typically involves patronizing communication in the form of overly nurturing or controlling speech (Giles & Gasiorek, 2011). A prominent account of the interplay between communication accommodation and age identity is found in the Communication Predicament Model of Aging (CPM) (Ryan, Giles, Bartolucci, & Henwood, 1986).

According to the CPM, when people encounter older individuals, physiological, environmental, behavioral, and contextual cues render age salient and "activate" negative old-age stereotypes. Once triggered, these stereotypes prompt negative expectations for the interaction (e.g., that it will be unsatisfying; that the older adult will be a difficult conversationalist, see Ryan, Kwong See, Meneer, & Trovato, 1992). These expectations, in turn, lead younger interactants to overaccommodate the older adult by engaging in excessively nurturing or directive speech, which curtails the communicative and behavioral autonomy of the older person. Rodin and Langer (1980), for example, report an experiment in which participants elected to ask simpler interview questions to 71-year-old targets rather than 42-year-old targets, thereby limiting the older adults' presentation of self. That a limited conversational playbook may be employed during conversations with older adults (familial or otherwise) is problematic, because "If someone is talking to you as if you are a 4-year-old, it's pretty difficult to display intellectual prowess or sparkling wit!" (Harwood, 2007, p. 79).

Receivers and observers of patronizing communication tend to "blame the victim" (La Tourette & Meeks, 2000; Ryan, Bourhis, & Knops, 1991). Consequently, older recipients of patronizing talk may perceive such talk as having being *earned* and come to redefine themselves as "old." The toll taken by overaccommodative speech is particularly striking given that older adults frequently report not only *feeling* younger than their actual age, but expect others to believe they are younger than their actual age (Kaufman & Elder, 2002). In fact, this may help account for why older persons often experience younger interlocutors' communication as overaccommodative: One can imagine an exchange in which (1) an older adult demands that a younger interlocutor explain "Why are you talking to me as though I'm 90?", (2) receives the response "Because you *are* 90!" and (3) replies huffily "Well, I only *feel* like I'm 70."

Ultimately, the CPM holds that recipients of stereotype-driven overaccommodation experience a loss of agency and self-esteem (O'Connor & Rigby, 1996) that can render them fatalistic about age-related decline (Rodin & Langer, 1980), prompt withdrawal from social interaction, and elicit the very age cues the younger interactant assumed were present from the start (Ryan et al., 1986). For example, Coudin and Alexopoulos (2010) concluded from their experiments that "the mere activation of negative stereotypes can cause older adults to adopt a condition that is reminiscent of dependent states, where the elderly complain about their loneliness and remain passive, avoiding any behavioral initiative or risk taking" (p. 519). Similarly, Eibach, Mock, and Courtney (2010) found that when older persons were primed with negative age stereotypes—particularly when they also encountered youth-oriented linguistic codes that emphasized their own agedness—they adopted more age-typed moral positions. Thus, the stereotypes that were held by the younger interactant now comprise part of the older person's internalized age identity, resulting in external behaviors that may restart the CPM cycle during subsequent interactions with younger persons.

Although research on the CPM is often conducted in healthcare contexts, the paradigm also furthers our understanding of how, through communication, younger generations may harm the age identities of older family members. As one group of scholars explained, "Interaction with family members can...demoralize older adults by communicating too much care and concern and promoting excessive dependence" (Nussbaum, Pitts, Huber, Raup Krieger, & Ohs, 2005, p. 292). Likewise, Taylor (1992) argues that the most integral members of older people's social networks may be the very people whose communicative behaviors disempower them and instill in them a sense of agedness. This is problematic, for Kaufman and Elder (2002) suggest that "feel[ing] younger relative to their age...may be a strategy for resisting old age and approaching death" (p. 175). Overaccommodation, therefore, is not merely a minor irritant. Rather, by signaling that a person is perceived as elderly, it provides an unwelcome reminder of one's mortality and undermines cognitive resistance to the existential threat posed by death (Martens, Goldenberg, & Greenberg, 2005).

Old-to-Young Talk Prompts Ascription of Age Identities and Increases Age Salience. Whereas CPM-related studies speak to the possibility that—through their age-based accommodations—younger persons coerce older persons into assuming subjectively negative age identities, other research shows that older persons have agency to create for themselves particular age identities via their linguistic and communicative behaviors. In any intergenerational encounter, older adults' disclosure of age, references to age roles or categories, discussion of historical events, and commentary regarding their health trajectory can make age salient and emphasize the intergroup nature of the conversation.

In the specific context of IGFRs, Harwood et al. (2006) documented the potential for grandparents' communication to render age salient and modify the age identities presented to grandchildren. In particular, the content, topic, and style of grandparents' communication often reinforced the age-based intergroup component of grandparent-grandchild (GP-GC) relationships by increasing age salience. For example, grandchildren were more conscious of their grandparents' age when grandparents revealed painful information; talked about their age, health, or the past; or demonstrated a lack of understanding regarding contemporary society. Contextual features of grandparent communication, such as appearing deaf or speaking in ways that implied a cognitive impairment (e.g., forgetfulness and repetitiveness) also reinforced age salience, as did stylistic feature of talk such as appearing condescending. Many of these communicative characteristics could—from a CAT perspective—be characterized as ***underaccommodative*** because they show insufficient awareness of (or adaptation to) the conversational preferences of grandchildren. Moreover, by eliciting increased recognition of agedness and emphasizing the intergroup element of interaction, these underaccommodative behaviors predict decreased closeness in the GP-GC bond and inhibit the development of a sense of shared family identity (Soliz & Harwood, 2006).

Family Talk Guides Understandings about the Meaning of Age and Age Identity. Family communication guides individuals' expectations regarding ageing and development, and thus shapes the implications of ageing for identity—and perhaps the "possible selves" (Ryff, 1991; Smith & Freund, 2002)—that family members internalize. For instance, the communication young adults experience during their interactions with older family members can constitute ***memorable messages*** (Holladay, 2002) and ***environmental chatter*** (Gasiorek, Fowler, & Giles, 2016) that establish and transform understandings of aging and age identity.

To some extent, young adults come to understand what it means to grow older (and thus what age identity might "look like" at different life stages) via explicit, memorable messages about aging from older persons, and, in particular, older family members (Holladay, 2002). Interestingly, Holladay's sample of young adults recalled about one and a half unequivocally "positive" message about aging per unambiguously "negative" message, and believed that older persons thought carefully about the messages they sought to convey about aging. Nonetheless, younger people also encounter countless unspoken or incidental messages about aging from family members. For instance, simply observing one's older family members likely shapes younger persons' expectations for aging, and their routine interactions with older relatives surely contribute to their understanding of what it is (and will be) like to be an older person (Carstensen, 2009; Harwood & Anderson, 2002). Older relatives are important role models for young persons, demonstrating through their behavior and demeanor what it means to be old and offering insight into whom one's "future self" might be.

Whereas older persons might think carefully about the messages they want younger persons to take on board about aging, younger persons may habitually say things and act in ways that make it clear to older relatives that they consider being old problematic. Birthday celebrations of older persons, for instance, often involve teasing (Ellis & Morrison, 2005) that both inhibit the recipient's ability to construct a positive (age) identity (Ryan et al., 1986), and entrench ageist stereotypes in the sender's own mind (Levy, 2009).

Beyond the Family: Family Communication and Society

Although recent findings and reviews are equivocal (Mendonça, Marques, & Abrams, 2018), some studies suggest young children recognize signs of aging, can distinguish between images of people representing different age groups, and perceive older adults in negative stereotypic ways (e.g., Burke, 1982). Further, even though very young children have a limited grasp of how age is measured and expressed in years, they nonetheless recognize that sketches of a person at four different "stages of life" represent the aging process. For example, Seefeldt, Jantz, Galper, and Serock (1977) presented children with four pictures showing the same man at approximately 30, 45, 64, and 77 years of age. Despite the fact that the 3- and 4-year-old children in this sample never estimated the man's age at higher than 10 years, they were reliably able to identify the picture that depicted the oldest man. Recent, large scale studies suggest that older children (aged 10–11 years) have multi-faceted notions of aging and older adults, but reinforce that negative stereotypes relating to older people's mobility, capacity for independence, and cognitive impairment are pervasive (Lloyd, Devine, & Carney, 2018).

Given that relatively few young children have contact with older people outside the family (Page, Olivas, Driver, & Driver, 1981), it is understandable that researchers have examined how communication in the GP-GC relationship may influence not only the quality of relationships between family members, but shape attitudes towards older people in general. Harwood, Hewstone, Paolini, and Voci (2005) grounded their examination of GP-GC communication in intergroup contact theory, and tested the hypothesis that grandchildren's contact with grandparents (who represent members of the age-based outgroup) would predict attitudes towards older people in general. These authors found grandchildren's high-quality contact with frequently-encountered grandparents predicted more positive attitudes towards older people outside the family, although this effect hinged on grandchildren being conscious of age differences and perceiving their grandparents as representative of older persons in general. These findings are intriguing. On the one hand, it is when age is salient during GP-GC conversations that younger family members project experiences with grandparents onto older adults more broadly (Harwood et al., 2005). On the other hand, age salience is typically heightened in the GP-GC relationship by communication behaviors that are seen as problematic and that predict reduced closeness (Harwood et al., 2006).

Notably, in Harwood et al.'s (2005) work, only two grandparent communication behaviors made age *less* salient for grandchildren—telling stories and demonstrating wisdom/giving advice. Strikingly, these same behaviors predicted increased closeness in the relationship. That expressions of wisdom and storytelling are well-received by grandchildren is unsurprising, for research shows that family story-telling enhances family functioning and strengthens familial identity, as well as providing opportunities for sense-making and value transference (Kellas, 2005). Several studies suggest that—via the inculcation of particular values—the impact of storytelling within IGFRs extends beyond the family itself. It is particularly noteworthy, perhaps, that intergenerational storytelling contributes to the gender socialization of younger family members, thereby shaping their values as they enter the workplace and engage in relationships outside of the family. In Taylor, Fisackerly, Mauren, and Taylor (2013) study of young adults, for instance, researchers asked students to write a paper about a meaningful family story. For most participants, grandparents were the source of the stories relayed, which varied along gendered lines: The stories most often recalled by women emphasized relational themes, and were, most often, described as having taught recipients to be appreciative and loving. Conversely, male participants most typically recalled stories addressing the overcoming of hardship (or involving humorous anecdotes), which led them to develop a strong work ethic, show respect for others, and display strength or courage.

Interestingly, Taylor et al.'s findings echo earlier research showing that grandmothers and grandfathers take a gendered approach to telling "meaningful" stories. In Nussbaum and Bettini's (1994) study, for example, grandmothers' stories focused overwhelmingly on family history. Conversely, a majority of grandfathers took the opportunity to provide moral instruction or to discuss the preciousness of life. A recent investigation (Odenweller, Brann, Rittenour, & Myers, 2018) of memorable messages received by sons about "being a man" found that similar themes were emphasized (e.g., work ethic, strength, being a good provider), which suggests that grandparents' and parents' narratives influence gender socialization and the adoption of particular values and priorities that affect younger family members as they navigate what it means to be a man or a woman. With men often being encouraged to "find a good job to provide for their future families, and women often encouraged to find men who would provide for them and their children" (Taylor et al., 2013, p. 385), recent and current cohorts of grandchildren may often encounter family stories that reify traditional notions of gender.

Implications for Scholars and Practitioners

As we conclude this chapter, we hope to explain why we are optimistic regarding the ability of families to manage the inter-age element of their relationship. One encouraging area of research stresses that members of different ages can transcend divergent group identities by recognizing a shared superordinate group status. Inspired by the common ingroup identity model (Gaertner & Dovidio, 2000), Soliz's work (2007; Soliz & Harwood, 2006) identifies specific grandparent communication behaviors (e.g., providing social support, mutual openness, avoiding nonaccommodation) that promote in grandchildren a shared sense of family identity that overshadows age-based intergroup elements of their relationship.

A second cause for optimism derives from research showing that by responding with assertiveness, humor, and appreciation, older adults have agency to challenge ageist assumptions of incompetence and limit their internalization of negative stereotypes of aging (Harwood, Giles, Fox, Ryan, & Williams, 1993; Ryan, Anas, & Friedman, 2006). Likewise, researchers also stress that younger adults can communicate with older kin in ways that facilitate the development and maintenance of positive age identities by adapting their communication to the individualized needs and preferences of older interactants (rather than to a generic stereotype of older persons) (Ryan, Meredith, MacLean, & Orange, 1995).

Ryan et al. (1995) propose that intergenerational conversations can become venues for the empowerment of older persons and the promotion of health and vitality. This suggestion is neither utopian nor unrealistic. Currently, communication training targeted at families tends to focus on communication *down* the generational line. For example, it is easy to find workshops that help parents talk to their children about online safety, sexual health, and so on. It is considerably harder to find workshops focused on improving communication towards *older* family members. Some training programs that help younger interactants recognize when they are engaging in problematic communication with older adults *do* exist, albeit in professional contexts. Nonetheless, they are effective at reducing the use of overaccommodative behaviors such as terms of endearment, collective pronouns, simplified/shortened speech, and helping participants communicate with older persons in ways that are judged to be less controlling and more respectful (Williams, Kemper, & Hummert, 2003). Scholars and practitioners should consider how such programs might be adapted for family settings.

Finally, IGFRs may also be strengthened by increased use of digital communication, for communication technology (CT) has important implications for associational and functional aspects of intergenerational solidarity (Peng et al., 2019). Indeed, because young adults often help older family members get the most out of new technologies (Child, Duck, Andrews, Butauski, & Petronio, 2015; Taipale, 2019), Strom and Strom (2015) suggest "adolescents [have] opportunities to assume a leadership role in improving intergenerational communication" (p. 50).

Research on computer-mediated IGFRs suggests that the use of CT needs to be handled carefully. Taipale (2019) observes, for instance, that some family members feel excluded from (or opt-out of) group-based communication tools (e.g., WhatsApp), and that people may perceive family members' online presence and postings as embarrassing or offensive. Moreover, generational differences in norms of face-to-face communication carry over into the digital space, suggesting that younger and older family members must learn to accommodate one another's preferences and standards for online discourse, both with respect to style and content. Taipale (2019) notes that among a Finnish sample, "younger family members were more accustomed to open and straightforward online communication…[while]…older ones called for thoughtfulness and linguistic correctness" (p. 108).

Scholarship grounded in communication privacy management theory (e.g., Child et al., 2015; Child & Westermann, 2013) suggests that although concerns about maintaining digital privacy boundary between oneself and one's older family members may not be widespread, young adults are more prone to adjust privacy settings (e.g., regarding what is visible to older relatives with whom they are Facebook friends) when trust is lower in the relationship. To the extent that younger relatives (e.g., grandchildren) feel that older relatives have inaccurate perceptions of who they are, or feel constrained from revealing who they *really* are to older relatives, they may experience "identity gaps," which are predictive of decreased relational closeness (Pusateri, Roaché, & Kam, 2016). An interesting possibility is that communication technology may affect families differently depending on pre-existing levels of intimacy and openness: Open, intimate families for whom digital channels offer additional opportunities to interact may benefit from technology, whereas families whose constituent members are less trusting, share less consensus in their beliefs, and feel unable to "be themselves," may experience new relational challenges as they adopt new technologies.

Conclusion

Family members are often able to spend several decades journeying through the lifespan together. Although they may encounter challenges with respect to finding common ground and mitigating communicative implications of age stereotypes, such challenges are surmountable. By cultivating a shared sense of family identity, managing ageist assumptions, finding ways to communicatively empower one another, and tapping into the benefits of digital technologies, contemporary families can transcend the barriers to intimacy that divergent age identities may erect.

Note

1. That is, simultaneous aliveness, *not* coresidence.

References

Aquilino, W. S. (1997). From adolescent to young adult: A prospective study of parent-child relations during the transition to adulthood. *Journal of Marriage and Family, 59*, 670–686. doi:10.2307/353953

Bengtson, V. L., & Kuypers, J. A. (1971). Generational difference and the developmental stake. *International Journal of Aging and Human Development, 2*, 249–260. doi:10.2190/AG.2.4.b

Birditt, K. S., Fingerman, K. L., Lefkowitz, E. S., & Kamp Dush, C. M. (2008). Parents perceived as peers: Filial maturity in adulthood. *Journal of Adult Development, 15*, 1–12. doi:10.1007/s10804-007-9019-2

Burke, J. L. (1982). Young children's attitudes and perceptions of older adults. *International Journal of Aging and Human Development, 14*, 205–222. doi:10.2190/4J7N-RG79-HJQR-FLDN

Carstensen, L. L. (1992). Social and emotional patterns in adulthood: Support for socioemotional selectivity theory. *Psychology and Aging, 7*, 331–338. doi:10.1037/0882-7974.7.3.331

Carstensen, L. L. (2009). *A long bright future: An action plan for a lifetime of happiness, health, and financial security*. New York, NY: Random House.

Child, J. T., Duck, A. R., Andrews, L. A., Butauski, M., & Petronio, S. (2015). Young adults' management of privacy on Facebook with multiple generations of family members. *Journal of Family Communication, 15*, 349–367. doi:10.1080/15267431.2015.1076425

Child, J. T., & Westermann, D. A. (2013). Let's be Facebook friends: Exploring parental Facebook friend requests from a communication privacy management (CPM) perspective. *Journal of Family Communication, 13*, 46–59. doi:10.1080/15267431.2012.742089

Coudin, G., & Alexopoulos, T. (2010). 'Help me! I'm old!' How negative aging stereotypes create dependency among older adults. *Aging & Mental Health*, *14*, 516–523. doi:10.1080/13607861003713182

Coupland, J., Coupland, N., Giles, H., & Henwood, K. (1991). Formulating age: Dimensions of age identity in elderly talk. *Discourse Processes*, *14*, 87–106. doi:10.1080/01638539109544776

De Goede, I. H. A., Branje, S. J. T., & Meeus, W. H. J. (2009). Developmental changes in adolescents' perceptions of relationships with their parents. *Journal of Youth and Adolescence*, *38*, 75–88. doi:10.1007/s10964-008-9286-7

Dykstra, P. A., & Komter, A. E. (2012). Generational interdependencies in families: The MULTILINKS research programme. *Demographic Research*, *27*, 487–506.

Eibach, R. P., Mock, S. E., & Courtney, E. A. (2010). Having a "senior moment": Induced aging phenomenology, subjective age, and susceptibility to ageist stereotypes. *Journal of Experimental Social Psychology*, *46*, 643–649. doi:10.1016/j.jesp.2010.03.002

Ellis, S. R., & Morrison, T. G. (2005). Stereotypes of ageing: Messages promoted by age-specific paper birthday cards available in Canada. *International Journal of Aging and Human Development*, *61*, 57–73. doi:10.2190/ULUU-UN83-8W18-EP70

Fingerman, K. L. (2003). *Mothers and their adult daughters: Mixed emotions, enduring bonds*. New York, NY: Prometheus Books.

Fingerman, K. L., & Baker, B. (2006). Socioemotional aspects of aging. In J. Wilmouth & K. Ferraro (Eds.), *Gerontology: Perspectives and issues* (3rd ed., pp. 183–202). New York, NY: Springer.

Fingerman, K. L., Miller, L., & Charles, S. (2008). Saving the best for last: How adults treat social partners of different ages. *Psychology and Aging*, *23*, 399–409. doi:10.1037/0882-7974.23.2.399

Gaertner, S. L., & Dovidio, J. F. (2000). *Reducing intergroup bias: The common ingroup identity model*. New York, NY: Psychology Press.

Gasiorek, J., Fowler, C. A., & Giles, H. (2016). Communication and successful aging. In J. F. Nussbaum (Ed.), *Communication across the lifespan* (pp. 35–50). New York: Peter Lang.

Giles, H. (Ed.). (2012). *The handbook of intergroup communication*. New York, NY: Routledge.

Giles, H. (Ed.). (2016). *Communication accommodation theory: Negotiating personal relationships and social identities across contexts*. Cambridge, UK: Cambridge University Press.

Giles, H., & Gasiorek, J. (2011). Intergenerational communication practices. In K. W. Schaie & S. Willis (Eds.), *Handbook of the psychology of aging* (7th ed., pp. 231–245). New York: Elsevier.

Grünheid, E., & Scharein, M. G. (2011). On developments in the mean joint lifetimes of three- and four-generation families in Western and Eastern Germany: A model calculation. *Comparative Population Studies*, *36*, 41–76. doi:10.4232/10.CPoS-2011-01en

Hagestad, G. (1988). Demographic change and the life course: Some emerging trends in the family realm. *Family Relations*, *37*, 405–410. doi:10.2307/584111

Hagestad, G. O., & Uhlenberg, P. (2007). The impact of demographic changes on relations between age groups and generations: A comparative perspective. In K. W. Schaie & P. Uhlenberg (Eds.), *Social structures: Demographic changes and the well-being of older persons.* New York, NY: Springer.

Harwood, J. (2007). *Understanding communication and aging: Developing knowledge and awareness.* Thousand Oaks, CA: Sage.

Harwood, J. (2008). Age identity and communication. In W. Donsbach (Ed.), *The international encyclopedia of communication.* doi:10.1002/9781405186407.wbieca034

Harwood, J., & Anderson, K. (2002). The presence and portrayal of social groups on prime-time television. *Communication Reports*, *15*, 81–97. doi:10.1080/08934210209367756

Harwood, J., Giles, H., Fox, S., Ryan, E. B., & Williams, A. (1993). Patronizing young and elderly adults: Response strategies in a community setting. *Journal of Applied Communication Research*, *21*. doi:10.1080/00909889309365368

Harwood, J., Hewstone, M., Paolini, S., & Voci, A. (2005). Grandparent-grandchild contact and attitudes toward older adults: Moderator and mediator effects. *Personality and Social Psychology Bulletin*, *31*, 393–406. doi:10.1177/0146167204271577

Harwood, J., Raman, P., & Hewstone, M. (2006). The family and communication dynamics of group salience. *Journal of Family Communication*, *6*, 181–200. doi:10.1207/s15327698jfc0603_2

Herlofson, K., & Hagestad, G. O. (2011). Challenges in moving from macro to micro: Population and family structure in ageing societies. *Demographic Research*, *25*, 337–370. doi:10.4054/DemRes.2011.25.10

Holladay, S. J. (2002). "Have fun while you can," "You're only as old as you feel," and "Don't ever get old!": An examination of memorable messages about aging. *Journal of Communication*, *52*, 681–697. doi:10.1111/j.1460-2466.2002.tb02568.x

Kaufman, G., & Elder, G. H., Jr. (2002). Revisiting age identity: A research note. *Journal of Aging Studies*, *16*, 169–176. doi:10.1016/S0890-4065(02)00042-7

Kellas, J. K. (2005). Family ties: Communicating identity through jointly told family stories. *Communication Monographs*, *72*, 365–389. doi:10.1080/03637750500322453

La Tourette, T. R., & Meeks, S. (2000). Perceptions of patronizing speech by older women in nursing homes and in the community: Impact of cognitive ability and place of residence. *Journal of Language and Social Psychology*, *19*, 463–473. doi:10.1177/0261927X00019004004

Levy, B. R. (2009). Stereotype embodiment: A psychosocial approach to aging. *Current Directions in Psychological Science*, *18*, 332–336. doi:10.1111/j.1467-8721.2009.01662.x

Lloyd, K., Devine, P., & Carney, G. M. (2018). Imagining their future selves: Children's attitudes to older people and their expectations of life at age 70. *Children & Society*, *32*, 444–456. doi:10.1111/chso.12289

Logan, J. R., Ward, R., & Spitze, G. (1992). As old as you feel: Age identity in middle and later life. *Social Forces*, *71*, 451–467, doi:10.2307/2580019

Lundholm, E., & Malmberg, G. (2009). Between elderly parents and grandchildren: Geographic proximity and trends in four-generation families. *Population Ageing*, *2*, 121–137. doi:10.1007/s12062-010-9022-4

Margolis, R. (2016). The changing demography of grandparenthood. *Journal of Marriage and family*, *78*, 610–622. doi:10.1111/jomf.12286

Margolis, R., & Wright, L. (2017). Older adults with three generations of kin: Prevalence, correlates, and transfers. *Journals of Gerontology: Social Sciences*, *72*, 1067–1072. doi:10.1093/geronb/gbv158

Martens, A., Goldenberg, J. L., & Greenberg, J. (2005). A terror management perspective on ageism. *Journal of Social Issues*, *61*, 223–239. doi:10.1111/j.1540-4560.2005.00403.x

Matthews, S. H., & Sun, R. (2006). Incidence of four-generation family lineages: Is timing of fertility or mortality a better explanation? *Journal of Gerontology: Social Sciences*, *61B*, S99–S106. doi:10.1093/geronb/61.2.S99

Mendonça, J., Marques, S., & Abrams, D. (2018). Children's attitudes toward older people: Current and future directions. In L. Ayalon & C. Tesch-Römer (Eds.), *Contemporary perspectives on ageism* (pp. 517–548). doi:10.1007/978-3-319-73820-8_30

Nussbaum, J. F., & Bettini, L. M. (1994). Shared stories of the grandparent-grandchild relationship. *International Journal of Aging and Human Development*, *39*, 67–80. doi:10.2190/7WPK-LM6C-QCA4-GQ4R

Nussbaum, J. F., Pitts, M. J., Huber, F. N., Raup Krieger, J. L., & Ohs, J. E. (2005). Ageism and ageist language across the lifespan: Intimate relationships and non-intimate interactions. *Journal of Social Issues*, *61*, 287–305. doi:10.1111/j.1540-4560.2005.00406.x

O'Connor, B. P., & Rigby, H. (1996). Perceptions of baby talk, frequency of receiving baby talk, and self-esteem among community and nursing home residents. *Psychology and Aging*, *11*, 147–154. doi:10.1037/0882-7974.11.1.147

Odenweller, K. G., Brann, M., Rittenour, C. E., & Myers, S. A. (2018). Intergenerational transmission of traditional and contemporary gender ideologies via father-son memorable messages. *Communication Research Reports*, *35*, 232–244. doi:10.1080/08824096.2018.1442823

Page, S., Olivas, R., Driver, J., & Driver, R. (1981). Children's attitudes toward the elderly and aging. *Educational Gerontology*, *7*, 43–47. doi:10.1080/0360127810070105

Pecchioni, L. L., & Croghan, J. M. (2002). Young adults' stereotypes of older adults with their grandparents as the targets. *Journal of Communication*, *52*, 715–730. doi:10.1111/j.1460-2466.2002.tb02570.x

Peng, S., Silverstein, M., Suitor, J. J., Gilligan, M., Hwang, W., Nam, S., & Routh, B. (2019). Use of communication technology to maintain intergenerational contact: toward an understanding of 'digital solidarity. In B. B. Neves & C. Casimiro (Eds.), *Connecting families? Information & communication technologies, generations, and the life course* (pp. 159–180). Bristol, UK: Policy Press.

Pusateri, K. B., Roaché, D. J., & Kam, J. A. (2016). Grandparents' and young adult grandchildren's identity gaps and perceived caregiving intentions: An actor-partner interdependence model. *Journal of Social and Personal Relationships, 32,* 191–216. doi:10.1177/0265407514568750

Rodin, J., & Langer, E. (1980). Aging labels: The decline of control and the fall of self-esteem. *Journal of Social Issues, 36,* 12–29. doi:10.1111/j.1540-4560.1980.tb02019.x

Ryan, E. B., Anas, A. P., & Friedman, D. B. (2006). Evaluations of older adult assertiveness in problematic clinical encounters. *Journal of Language and Social Psychology, 25,* 129–145. doi:10.1177/0261927X06286350

Ryan, E. B., Bourhis, R. Y., & Knops, U. (1991). Evaluative perceptions of patronizing speech addressed to elders. *Psychology and Aging, 6,* 442–450. doi:10.1037/0882-7974.6.3.442

Ryan, E. B., Giles, H., Bartolucci, G., & Henwood, K. (1986). Psycholinguistic and social psychological components of communication by and with the elderly. *Language & Communication, 6,* 1–24. doi:10.1016/0271-5309(86)90002-9

Ryan, E. B., Kwong See, S., Meneer, W. B., & Trovato, D. (1992). Age-based perceptions of language performance among younger and older adults. *Communication Research, 19,* 423–443. doi:10.1177/009365092019004002

Ryan, E. B., Meredith, S. D., MacLean, M. J., & Orange, J. B. (1995). Changing the way we talk with elders: Promoting health using the communication enhancement model. *International Journal of Aging and Human Development, 41,* 89–107. doi:10.2190/FP05-FM8V-0Y9F-53FX

Ryff, C. D. (1991). Possible selves in adulthood and old age: A tale of shifting horizons. *Psychology and Aging, 6,* 286–295. doi:10.1037/0882-7974.6.2.286

Seefeldt, C., Jantz, R. K., Galper, A., & Serock, K. (1977). Using pictures to explore children's attitudes toward the elderly. *Gerontologist, 17,* 506–512. doi:10.1093/geront/17.6.506 17.6.506

Silverstein, M., & Long, J. D. (1998). Trajectories of grandparents' perceived solidarity with adult grandchildren: A growth curve analysis over 23 years. *Journal of Marriage and Family, 60,* 912–923. doi:10.2307/353634

Smith, J,. & Freund, A. M. (2002). The dynamics of possible selves in old age. *Journals of Gerontology: Psychological Sciences, 57,* P492–P500. doi:10.1093/geronb/57.6.P492

Soliz, J. (2007). Communicative predictors of a shared family identity: Comparison of grandchildren's perceptions of family-of-origin grandparents and stepgrandparents. *Journal of Family Communication, 7,* 177–194. doi:10.1080/15267430701221636

Soliz, J., & Harwood, J. (2006). Shared family identity, age salience, and intergroup contact: Investigation of the grandparent-grandchild relationship. *Communication Monographs, 73,* 87–107. doi:10.1080/03637750500534388

Soliz, J., & Rittenour, C. E. (2012). Family as an intergroup arena. In H. Giles (Ed.), *The handbook of intergroup communication* (pp. 331–343). New York, NY: Routledge. doi:10.4324/9780203148624

Strom, R. D., & Strom, P. S. (2015). Assessment of intergenerational communication and relationships. *Educational Gerontology*, *41*, 41–52. doi:10.1080/03601277.2014.912454

Taipale, S. (2019). *Intergenerational connections in digital families*. Springer. doi:10.1007/978-3-030-11947-8

Taylor, A. C., Fisackerly, B. L., Mauren, E. R., & Taylor, K. D. (2013). "Grandma, tell me another story": Family narratives and their impact on young adult development. *Marriage & Family Review*, *49*(5), 367–390. doi:10.1080/01494929.2012.762450

Taylor, B. C. (1992). Elderly identity in conversation: Producing frailty. *Communication Research*, *19*, 493–515. doi:10.1177/009365092019004006

Uhlenberg, P. (1993). Demographic change and kin relationships in later life. *Annual review of gerontology and geriatrics*, *13*, 219–238. doi:10.1891/argg.13.1

Uhlenberg, P. (1996). Mortality decline in the twentieth century and supply of kin over the life course. *Gerontologist*, *36*, 681–685. doi:10.1093/geront/36.5.681

van Gaalen, R., & Deerenberg, I. (2014). More old-age pensioners, but the number who are living together with their adult children remains stable. Retrieved from https://www.cbs.nl/en-gb/news/2014/27/more-old-age-pensioners-but-the-number-who-are-living-together-with-their-adult-children-remains-stable. Centraal Bureau voor de Statistiek.

Williams, K., Kemper, S., & Hummert, M. L. (2003). Improving nursing home communication: An intervention to reduce elderspeak. *Gerontologist*, *43*, 242–247. doi:10.1093/geront/43.2.242

Williams, A., Ota, H., Giles, H., Pierson, H. D., Gallois, C., Ng, S.-H., … Harwood, J. (1997). Young people's beliefs about intergenerational communication: An initial cross-cultural comparison. *Communication Research*, *24*, 370–393. doi:10.1177/009365097024004003

2. *Negotiating and Communicating about Identity Within Multi-Ethnic/ Multi-Racial Families*

Tina M. Harris, Farrah Youn-Heil and Hue T. Duong

The U. S. has historically been a country consumed with race and perpetuating a racial hierarchy fueling a false binary regarding the perception of superiority of whites and inferiority of all other racial/ethnic groups. This binary is fueled by racist ideologies entrenched in everyday interactions across diverse relational contexts. One such context is the family. Many life lessons are learned through familial relationships, and such is the case when it comes to race, racism, and racial identities (Odenweller & Harris, 2018). The family is the first interpersonal network with whom we come into contact. They are also the individuals from whom we learn our lessons about who we are as individuals, a family unit, and a society. These lessons are oftentimes inherently complex, and they become even more so when racial, ethnic, and cultural differences exist within the family (Rockquemore, Brunsma, & Delgado, 2009). Much like interracial, multiracial, interethnic, and multiethnic individuals, families comprised of individuals from diverse racial and ethnic backgrounds also learn and are taught life lessons designed to foster fulfilling individual, familial, and/or communal identities. Indeed, these relationships are similar to same-race relationships in that they experience tensions; however, little is known about the communicative processes involved in how these families engage in communication during one's identity development (Manning, 2006). Thus, it is the goal of this chapter to provide an overview of current literature on family communication as it occurs within the multiracial/multiethnic (MR/ME) family.

Scholars who do research on racial identity development from various disciplines are in agreement that identity politics in the U. S. became even more salient when the government released the 2000 Census (Rockquemore et al., 2009; Samuels, 2009; Schlabach, 2013) and with the election and re-election of President Barack Hussein Obama (Logan, 2014). The 2000 Census "caused a national crisis in racial meanings" (Samuels, 2009, p. 93) with the inclusion of a multiracial category designed to account for individuals who do not identify as monoracial or belonging solely to one race or ethnicity. While this potentially gave agency to racially diverse individuals, it also held significance on a societal level regarding the importance of race and ethnicity as a cultural marker. The value of both was compounded nearly a decade later by twice-elected President Barack Obama (Logan, 2014). This historic moment introduced new race politics and involved the articulation of "a set of racialized expectations of nonwhites in exchange for white acceptance and incorporation" (Logan, 2014, p. 125), which introduced to many an alternative ideology to colorblindness. Logan explains that this is a "class-specific discourse of race" pitting the "black poor against the black upwardly mobile," while also separating "good blacks 'like Obama'" from seemingly "more problematic black others" (p. 125). These racial discourses occurring on a national platform have undoubtedly impacted race relations and fueled racial identity politics in very pointed and powerful ways. By extension, they have certainly informed the ways in which people racially identify, thus politicizing racial identities for people from the margins.

This post-racial era in the U. S. (DePouw, 2018) has set the stage for scholars and lay people (i.e., families, children, teachers, counselors) alike to gain a better understanding of racial identity politics and how to best deal with them in everyday life. According to Rockquemore et al. (2009) and Lorenzo-Blanco, Banes, and Delva (2013), mixed race and mixed ethnicity (MR/ME) people are in a precarious and unique position in that they potentially face unique identity issues that are markedly different from those of monoracial individuals. They are sometimes forced to deal with identity politics from parents, extended family, and strangers as well as society at large (Nishi, 2018). While scholars across disciplines have done research on racial identity development for MR/ME people, the research is "deeply fragmented and inconsistent" due to "a lack of connection between theory and empirical work in the area, and the seemingly insurmountable challenge of removing disciplinary blinders" (Rockquemore et al., 2009, p. 14). Thus, there is a serious need for research on the racial identity development process for MR/ME people. Findings from such efforts will serve to educate people about this process, empower MR/ME in their journey toward self-discovery, and equip scholars and practitioners with the knowledge necessary for providing proper information about and resources for promoting understanding of and sensitivity towards MR/ME individuals amongst family, friends, classmates, teachers, administrators, and society as a whole.

Indeed, there is a growing body of research on racial identity development, and what is pointedly missing is the role that communication plays in that process (Soliz, Thorson, & Rittenour, 2009). Important contributions have been made regarding understanding of how family members, classmates, and society members (Odenweller & Harris, 2018) directly impact MR/ME individuals and their identity journeys. These findings have also revealed the deep-rooted racist and prejudiced attitudes people have towards people of color and those hailing from diverse racial and ethnic backgrounds. In this chapter, the goal is to provide an overview of the research on family communication and identity negotiation for MR/ME individuals, highlighting specific themes in the literature, while paying particular attention to family communication and attitudes outside of the family and the implications these findings have for scholars and practitioners.

Internal Stressors and Racial Categorization

Rockquemore (1999) and Rockquemore et al. (2009) are regularly cited as scholars leading the charge to better understand racial identity development of MR/ME individuals. Rockquemore, along with other colleagues, has extended the early work of Phinney (1990), essentially setting the golden standard by which to measure the ways in which MR/ME self-identify. She identified four identity options that MR/ME individuals choose to use a scholarly approach to gather information on the experiences of bi- and multiracial related to how they choose to racially identify: (1) singular identity, (2) border identity, (3) protean identity, and (4) transcendent identity. The singular identity option refers to those who choose a monoracial identity or to identify solely with one race (i.e., Black, White, Hispanic). The border identity option is for those who prefer to self-identify as only biracial. The protean identity option involves recognition of a fluid identity and a preference to shift between racial identities according to social context. The transcendent identity option refers to a positionality that extends beyond race. Rather than recognize their racial identities, these individuals believe their identity " 'transcends' racial categorization altogether" and they can "be simply 'human' " (Lou, Lalonde, & Wilson, 2011, p. 83; see Rockquemore & Arend, 2002). MR/ME individuals have choices in how they choose to racially categorize themselves, and research has revealed that they oftentimes are forced to deal with stressors independently from their parents and siblings. We will discuss later the impact family and non-family members have on the racial identity development process for MR/ME people.

Internal stressors are commonly identified by researchers as effecting how MR/ME individuals self-identify (Samuels, 2009; Schlabach, 2013). Internal stressors can be understood as stressful events related to identity management that create an internal struggle and/or prompt the search for an appropriate label or racial category. In her study on transracial adoptions, Samuels found that MR/ME individuals sometimes have a need for and then seek identity affirmation from others. Participants were individuals who were either Black and White or multiracial (Black, White, and other) and adopted by White parents. They reported the need for "biological mirrors" or family members who bore some resemblance to them. Because their parents were of a different race/ethnicity, the MR/ME child's sense of connection and belonging was missing, which oftentimes lead to "racial resemblance talk" (p. 80). There was a desire to share physical markers with their families, and because their racial/ethnic differences were apparent, MR/ME children were oftentimes struggling with how this marked them as an outsider, being that they were the only person who was unlike the other family members.

Samuels (2009) also highlights how another internal stressor MR/ME children face occurs because "transracial adoptive families and multiracial individuals contradict biological and monocentric race and kinship norms" (p. 83), which means these families go against the norm because the family and the MR/ME adoptee do not share a "single racial identity and heritage" (p. 82). It stands to reason that these different types of stress will have a direct impact on the well-being of the adoptee (Hoffman & Peña, 2013). Schlabach's (2013) work on the well-being of MR/ME adolescents from a nationally representative sample offers insight into the impact of these stressors on their sense of self. She found that some families chose to prioritize and placed greater value on "family-based social capital," or "parental involvement, parent-child relationship quality, and family structure" (p. 155). The result was less connection with one's racial/ethnic identity. The findings also revealed a gender bias whereby White mothers were perceived as being less supportive than mothers from other races/ethnicities and fathers in general. Schlabach (2013) explains that White mothers are:

> more likely to come from households with lower family income, but that they will also experience higher levels of stigma, have more issues with their family of origin, and that their lack of previous experiences with racism will not allow them to help their child navigate racism. (p. 158)

She further notes that MR/ME children with White mothers will have worse wellbeing than those with mothers from other races/ethnicities or children who were monoracial. This was found to be the case especially for those children with Native American fathers and White mothers. The children with White mothers reported seeking social support from their fathers (Schlabach, 2013), which can be assumed to cause tensions and stress within the relationship with each parent and for the child who is also dealing with the frustration of having no support system in place.

Racial categorization is another facet of racial identity development scholars have explored in their efforts to best understand how families communicate about this process (Butler-Sweet, 2011; Lou et al., 2011; Rockquemore, 1999). Racial categorization is a clear theme in the literature and refers to the racial label that is either chosen by an MR/ME individual or assigned to them by others. For example, a woman who is Native American and White chooses to identify as biracial, but extended family members and strangers categorize her race as Native American since they believe her phenotypic features (i.e., skin color, hair, nose) represent her Native American ethnicity. Regardless of the source, racial categorization can be a difficult process for MR/ME individuals, as they are possibly dealing with internal as well as external pressure to identify a certain way. The one-drop rule practiced in the U. S. classified, per se, bi- and multiracial individuals as Black (Butler-Sweet, 2011) because it was deemed inferior to White.

As previously noted, Rockquemore and Brunsma (2009) identified four different identities or racial categories that aptly describe the labels MR/ME individuals typically choose in order to define themselves. These categories reflect a decision-making process for people that is most likely prompted by an interaction, event, or moment of self-reflection that leads the MR/ME individual on a journey towards self-discovery and understanding. While the literature addresses the process, very little attention is given to the actual communication and interpersonal interactions that MR/ME individuals experience and are deemed pivotal to their decision-making. Lou et al. (2011) explain that there is a serious need for research on how "biracial people view their social identities as compatible or oppositional to one another" (p. 80). The "how" in this process speaks to the specific experiences leading them to reconcile the tension(s) surrounding their racial/ethnic identity; however, what is undergirding this inquiry is the role that the actual verbal and nonverbal messages received from orientational others (i.e., family, friends, siblings) and generalized others (i.e., co-workers, strangers, associates) play in prompting identity exploration. Research findings demonstrate that interactions are a vital part of this process, but scholars are failing to illuminate how communication is at the center of this phenomenon. In other words, MR/ME individuals are having conversations with others and/or receiving nonverbal messages (i.e., disapproving looks, being ignored) that undoubtedly impact how they self-identify.

According to Lou et al. (2011), MR/ME individuals commonly are in the precarious position of having to deal with social identities that are not always "compatible." They tested Rockquemore's (2002) identity model in order to demonstrate the need for a multi-dimensional framework to examine ME as a process. Their findings indicate that communication is, in fact, a critical part of racial identity development for MR/ME individuals and what we are referring to as "external racial appraisals" from orientational and generalized others. Lou et al. (2011) explain that MR/ME individuals receive messages as validating or invalidating their chosen racial categorization. They specifically refer to the "validated border" and "invalidated border" labels as examples of how affirming or disconfirming messages from others are communicated and effect how they define themselves. MR/ME individuals are engaging in interpersonal exchanges that, to varying degrees, cause them to think critically about their decision to identify a certain way. As Butler-Sweet (2011) notes, many MR/ME individuals are subjected to the judgement of others who are unsettled about the MR/ME individual's perceived "racial ambiguity," which oftentimes leads to the MR/ME person being racially misclassified. In short, this cognitive dissonance, or receipt of seemingly contradictory messages, speaks to the prejudices and stereotypes they hold about racial/ethnic group membership as well as their obsession with racial categorization, the latter of which is the result of pervasive social ideologies regarding race and racial hierarchies. Similarly, racial misclassification (Butler-Sweet, 2011) is reflective of stereotypical thinking and (sub)conscious efforts to impose identity politics onto MR/ME people. Both behaviors are examples of verbal and nonverbal messages MR/ME individuals receive that undoubtedly impact how they self-identify as raced beings. As with other MR/ME identity research, the current study and many others fail to label these experiences as communication-centered phenomena.

This is also evidenced in research on MR/ME individuals who have at least one parent that is an immigrant (Waring & Purkayasha, 2017). Most other studies focus on domestic experiences of MR/ME people whose connections are primarily with parents—biological and adoptive—who are U. S. citizens. Waring and Purkayasha introduce an increasingly important issue regarding identity for MR/ME individuals by gathering data from people who have at least one immigrant parent. They recognized an aspect of racial identity development that was largely being ignored by scholars and broadened the scope of the scholarship by offering insight into the unique experiences of "biracial Americans with immigrant ties" in order to make sense of the complex issue of race relative to "racial superiority and inferiority, racial relations, and racial stereotypes" (p. 615). Moreover, they were interested in the role of family socialization in this identity development process as well. Using the qualitative approach of in-depth, semi-structured interviews, the researchers solicited responses from biracial Americans with one Black parent and one White parent, and at least one of the parents is an immigrant. They note that 11 nationalities were represented. Their findings reveal that these MR/ME individuals voice[d] clear understandings of the existent racial hierarchy in the U. S. and its impact on interracial interactions and society as a whole. The major findings were that, for these individuals, it was important to place significance on their ethnic heritage, as that "allows them to avoid [the] social consequences of being (half) white or (half) black" (Waring & Purkayastha, 2017, p. 614). As they note, the reported experiences with racial socialization in general and in relation to family relationships indicate there is indeed a "slipperiness of race" for biracial (BI) Americans. They also offer firsthand evidence that biracial individuals (and their families) have "difficulty discussing race," "struggle to articulate the meaning of race," and "assert specific racial/ethnic identities to circumvent stereotypical connotations of whiteness and blackness" (p. 614).

By including the experiences of an underresearched microculture within the MR/ME community, Waring and Prukayastha (2017) enrich this area of scholarship by demonstrating that people who are not monoracial and those who are monoracial receive and respond to messages from orientational others, generalized others, and society in markedly different ways. More importantly, BI/MR/ME face more stringent racial identity politics that oftentimes result in them disavowing any connection to a non-White ethnicity, thus either consciously or subconsciously engaging in what we are calling racial distancing (see also Rockquemore & Arend, 2002). We are defining it as the use of verbal and/or nonverbal strategies to avoid affiliation or identification with a race/ethnicity in one's lineage considered to be inferior according to a societal racial hierarchy. Thus, Waring and Prukayastha (2017) offer even more data supporting existing literature arguing that racial identity development for BI/MR/ME individuals is very complex and is subjected to racial socialization processes that problematize identities that are not monoracial.

Parenting Styles and Racial Identity Development

Another area of research on family communication and racial identity development centers around parenting styles among/within interracial couples and MR families (Lorenzo-Blanco et al., 2013; Soliz et al., 2009). Due to space limitations, we highlight two specific articles that we believe offer a nuanced glimpse into the communication that occurs between family members that either intentionally or unintentionally impact how MR/ME may choose to identify. The studies use diverse methodologies, which further demonstrates the richness that lies within the different relational contexts of focus in the area of racial identity development for people from historically marginalized groups.

Lorenzo-Blanco et al. (2013) provide evidence that parenting styles are another factor that might impact how MR/ME negotiate their identity development process. Although they did not explicitly refer to communication as we define it in the discipline, it is clear that the exchange of verbal messages between relational partners—in this case, parents and/or children—is perceived as a critical part of this process for the parents, and subsequently MR/ME children. They specifically wanted to understand how the parents decide how to best parent their children, so they gathered data from monoracial families (i. e., African American, Hispanic, and white) and interracial families. Lorenzo-Blanco et al. (2013) found that interracial parents experience a negotiation stage when it comes to parenting. This involves a modification of their respective styles in direct response to stereotypes ascribed to their MR/ME children and an effort to shield them from such treatment. The findings also showed that MR/ME children did not feel supported by their parents, felt less cohesion with their mothers, and felt less satisfied with their parent-child relationships. Lorenzo-Blanco et al. (2013) attributed these disconnects to gendered parenting expectations and stereotypes that "may lead to higher standards for their mothers" (p. 134). In comparison, MR/ME children felt independent or believed they had freedom, much like their White peers, but they attended more family events (at least twice a month) as did African American and Hispanic peers. These differences might be attributed to cultural differences that are informing the ideals of individualism and collectivism typically associated with White culture, per se, and communities of color respectively. A final finding was that interracial parents exerted less control over their children than African American and Hispanic monoracial children, which Lorenzo-Blanco et al. (2013) attribute to cultural differences as well.

Soliz et al. (2009) use a communication-centric approach to understand the interpersonal dynamics of families dealing with this phenomenon. Unlike other scholars, they use theories such as the Communication Accommodation Theory to identify specific communication behaviors that are used within MR/ME families. Supportive communication, self-disclosure, and identity accommodation were of particular interest, which is important given that a different set of communication rules, norms, and behaviors is even more likely when individuals from different racial/ethnic backgrounds are in a committed relationship. The partners are bringing their personal histories and identities into the relationship, and when children enter the picture, they (ideally) have explicit conversations about how to manage their new identity. In the case of interracial couples and their multiracial families, communication becomes even more vital since they must now negotiate how to parent the child(ren) using a tool set that addresses MR/ME identity and how to best deal with racism, prejudice, and stereotyping.

The findings from their study revealed a direct correlation between supportive communication, self-disclosure, and identity accommodation and relational satisfaction (Soliz et al., 2009). It may be assumed that members of these multiracial families were satisfied with their relationships because emotional intimacy (i.e., closeness) was something everyone worked towards and contributed to. MR/ME families were found to have an ingroup identity as a family due to supportive communication and self-disclosure (Soliz et al., 2009) and "lower levels of perceived group differences" due to supportive communication (p. 829). These findings suggest that families do communicate and have connections with each other, but that does not necessarily mean they will have pointed and productive conversations about race and racial identities (Soliz et al., 2009). Nevertheless, this work sets the foundation for others to design studies where MR/ME families explicitly identify how they cope with external stressors (i.e., prejudice, stereotyping) and make decisions about the racial identity development process for the family, the parents, and the child(ren).

Beyond the Family: Family Communication and Society

As the literature has demonstrated thus far, MR/ME families and individuals have unique challenges when it comes to racial identity development of all its members. Much like monoracial families, there are relational dialectics and tensions that define the members and impact how they communicate with each other (Rogan, Piacentini, & Hopkinson, 2018). What makes the MR/ME family different is that it is dealing with the additional pressure of not conforming to societal norms of homogeneity, and if they choose to have children, then they possibly are faced with whether or not and how they will help the child(ren) decide how they will racially identify. This process also involves identifying ways to cope with racism, prejudice, and stereotyping, but the literature on the racial identity development process does not account for that. More specifically, it does not address how these individuals or families deal with these stressors in general or when they are coming from trusted and beloved family members and friends.

Samuels (2009) refers to this phenomenon as intrafamilial racism. Her interviews with MR/ME families and children revealed that many parents either ignore or minimize racist behavior from others, which she refers to as "discordant parent-child experiences" (p. 87). This approach was definitely enacted by many participants in response to racially prejudiced extended family members and ongoing intrafamilial racism. These negative attitudes were towards the marriage/relationship or the MR/ME children, and instead of dealing directly with the offending party, parents were more inclined to use a negative management strategy (Samuels, 2009). This is a troubling pattern because it fails to resolve the issues of racism and prejudice for the family. Additionally, the MR/ME child(ren) is failed, so to speak, because they are not equipped with the necessary skills for coping with the negative behaviors of extended family members or society at all. The parents choosing to ignore or minimize the racism their child(ren) will face are contributing to the MR/ME's difficulty managing their identity development and making them underprepared for dealing with the systemic racism that they will inevitably face as a member of a minority group.

According to Waring and Purkayasha (2017), MR/ME children subjected to racism and prejudice on a societal level are very likely to internalize those negative messages, thus negatively impacting their racial identity development process. The same can be said for similar messages received from family members, but the impact might be more profound because of an expectation or assumption of relational intimacy and commitment. The overall wellbeing of the child(ren) and family is at risk (Schlabach, 2013) because the race issues are not being addressed. As Schlabach (2013) notes, MR/ME individuals are already dealing with typical family issues, and when coupled with interracial conflict within the family, societal racial miscategorization, and societal discomfort with racial ambiguity (Butler-Sweet, 2011), this causes MR/ME individuals additional stress and can potentially thwart the racial identity development process; therefore, it is important to consider how family therapy can possibly help interracial couples and MR/ME individuals when they are subjected to these and other stressors (Baptiste, 1984).

The research has shown that the family is an excellent context for understanding how racial identities are formed. This area of research is even more important given the prediction of the U. S. demographics changing such that people of Hispanic descent will be the majority group. There will continue to be increased racial tensions in society related to this shift in the racial landscape of the country, as evidenced by the rise in hate crimes and number of murders of people of color because of police brutality. Not only will interracial partners be subjected to racism, prejudice, and discrimination, but so will their offspring, thus making it imperative that all members of society become educated about the fact that race is a social construct. As such, there will hopefully be a rethinking and challenging of the importance of not imposing racial categories and a racial hierarchy onto MR/ME individuals who do not conform to societal expectations of what it means to racially identify in a certain way.

Implications for Scholars and Practitioners

Understanding how families communicate has significance for both research and real-world contexts. As this chapter has demonstrated, negotiating and communicating about identity within MR/ME families is a phenomenon that is very unique to families where members come from diverse racial/ethnic backgrounds (Romero, Gonzalez, & Smith, 2015). While other families socialize their members (i.e., children) to understand their monoracial or cultural identities (Crawford & Alaggia, 2008), MR/ME families have a unique task of teasing out how to best assist members in understanding who they are as part of a family that does not conform to societal norms of homogeneity. This process becomes even more complex when we consider the future of the U. S. when it comes to racial groups. It is predicted that people of Hispanic descent will be the majority group by the year 2050. This means that there will be increased interracial/interethnic interactions leading to a rise in interracial/interethnic relationships and MR/ME individuals, thus warranting the need for more research on communication within this relational context. The findings from this research can ultimately lead to the development of models, theories, and counseling practices that facilitate family communication and identity negotiation in very productive and insightful ways.

In order to understand what that might look like, we pose the following questions. How can MR/ME families best help members develop a positive racial identity? What can parents do to embolden their children to have a healthy attitude towards race/ethnicity? What strategies can MR/ME children use to develop a healthy racial identity in the absence of a either a supportive or encouraging family environment? Moreover, each of these questions directs our attention to the role that communication (i.e., message exchange) plays in racial identify development for MR/ME individuals. The families are most likely engaging in communication with each other that has different levels of relational intimacy; however, what is not understood is the exact verbal and nonverbal messages they receive from family members—both immediate and extended—that either positively or negatively influence how they perceive themselves. Do the parents purposely avoid talking about racial/ethnic identities? If so, why? How might their connection to their own/individual racial identities effect how they guide their children through the racial identity development process? It would also be important to know if, when, and how often they have in-depth conversations about how they define their interracial relationship, and how they plan (or not) to educate their child(ren) about their racial/ethnic heritages and the options they have for identifying however they choose.

Relatedly, research on this process for MR/ME individuals should involve in-depth interviews with the parent(s) and child together to discuss their relationships and identify specific messages communicated between family members that impacted how they all dealt with race (see Romero, Gonzalez, & Smith, 2015). Additionally, narratives might be shared that offer insight into how the family's communication has impacted the parent/child relation into adulthood. While there is the potential for recall to be inaccurate, the experience of group/family interview may encourage the family to reach a turning point in their relationship where they commit to and discuss how to have more healthy communication about all of their identities. These conversations might also include time devoted to identifying strategies for confronting intrafamilial racism (Nadal, Sriken, Davidoff, Wong, & McLean, 2013). As adults, the MR/ME children can use their experiences to offer advice on either how well their parents did in assisting with their racial identity development or what their parents should/could have done differently so they could be a well-adjusted MR/ME person. The interviews could potentially lead to scholars developing communication models illustrating best practices for nurturing a positive racial identity for parents, children, and the family, providing resources designed to further educate all parties on this process. The models could then be used to launch a series of longitudinal studies testing the effectiveness of the strategies and equip interracial families and MR/ME children with the requisite communication skills, knowledge, and resources for the development of positive interracial, monoracial, and MR/ME identities within the context of family.

It is abundantly clear that racial identity development is a much-needed area of research, and with the racial landscape predictably making a marked shift, there is an even greater need to explore how families communicate about the racial identity development process(es) with which they have direct experience. Much of the research has involved persuasive arguments for such an area of scholarly research. Scholars have stressed how racial identity politics have become increasingly salient due to the 2000 Census (Samuels, 2009; Schlabach, 2013), the election of President Barack Obama (Logan, 2014), and transracial adoption (Anderson, Rueter, & Lee, 2015; Butler-Sweet, 2011). Thus, it is imperative that communication scholars assume a more active role in positioning the discipline as an important lens through which to better and more accurately understand the identity development process.

References

Anderson, K., Rueter, M., & Lee, R. (2015). Discussions about racial and ethnic differences in internationally adoptive families: Links with family engagement, warmth, and control. *Journal of Family Communication, 15*, 289–308.

Baptiste, D. A. (1984). Marital and family therapy with racially/culturally intermarried stepfamilies: Issues and guidelines. *Family Relations, 33*(3), 373.

Butler-Sweet, C. (2011). 'Race isn't what defines me': Exploring identity choices in transracial, biracial, and monoracial families. *Social Identities, 17*(6), 747–769.

Crawford, S. E., & Alaggia, R. (2008). The best of both worlds? Family influences on mixed race youth identity development. *Qualitative Social Work, 7*(1), 81–98.

DePouw, C. (2018). Intersectionality and critical race parenting. *International Journal of Qualitative Studies in Education, 31*(1), 55–69.

Hoffman, J., & Peña, E. V. (2013). Too Korean to be white and too white to be Korean: Ethnic identity development among transracial Korean American adoptees. *Journal of Student Affairs Research and Practice, 50*(2), 152–170.

Logan, E. (2014). Barack Obama, the new politics of race, and classed constructions of racial Blackness. *The Sociological Quarterly, 55*(4), 653–682.

Lorenzo-Blanco, E. I., Bares, C. B., & Delva,J. (2013). Parenting, family processes, relationships, and parental support in multiracial and multiethnic families: An exploratory study of youth perceptions. *Family Relations, 62*(1), 125–139.

Lou, E., Lalonde, R. N., & Wilson, C. (2011). Examining a multidimensional framework of racial identity across different biracial groups. *Asian American Journal of Psychology, 2*(2), 79.

Manning, L. D. (2006). "Presenting opportunities:" Communicatively constructing a shared family identity. *International & Intercultural Communication Annual, 29*, 43–67.

Nadal, K. L., Sriken, J., Davidoff, K. C., Wong, Y., & McLean, K. (2013). Microaggressions within families: Experiences of multiracial people. *Family Relations, 62*(1), 190–201.

Nishi, N. W. (2018). "You need to do love": Autoethnographic mother-writing in applying ParentCrit. *International Journal of Qualitative Studies in Education, 31*(1), 3–24.

Odenweller, K., & Harris, T. M. (2018). Intergroup socialization: The influence of parents' family communication patterns on adult children's racial prejudice and tolerance. *Communication Quarterly, 66*(5), 501–521.

Phinney, J. S. (1990). Ethnic identity in adolescents and adults: Review of research. *Psychological Bulletin, 108*, 499–514.

Rockquemore, K. A. (1999). Between black and white: Exploring the "biracial" experience. *Race and Society*, *1*, 197–212.

Rockquemore, K. A., & Arend, P. (2002). Opting for White: Choice, fluidity and racial identity construction in post civil-rights America. *Race and Society*, *5*, 49–64.

Rockquemore, K. A., Brunsma, D. L., & Delgado, D. J. (2009). Racing to theory or retheorizing race? Understanding the struggle to build a multiracial identity theory. *Journal of Social Issues*, *65*(1), 13–34.

Rogan, D., Piacentini, M., & Hopkinson, G., (2018). Intercultural household food tensions: A relational dialectics analysis, *European Journal of Marketing*, *52*(12), 2289–2311.

Romero, A. J., Gonzalez, H., & Smith, B. A. (2015). Qualitative exploration of adolescent discrimination: Experiences and responses of Mexican-American parents and teens. *Journal of Child and Family Studies*, *24*(6), 1531–1543.

Samuels, G. M. (2009). "Being raised by white people": Navigating racial difference among adopted multiracial adults. *Journal of Marriage and Family*, *71*(1), 80–94.

Schlabach, S. (2013). The importance of family, race, and gender for multiracial adolescent well-being. *Family Relations*, *62*(1), 154–174.

Soliz, J., Thorson, A., & Rittenour, C. (2009). Communicative correlates of satisfaction, family identity, and group salience in multiracial/ethnic families. *Journal of Marriage and Family*, *71*(4), 819.

Waring, C. D., & Purkayastha, B. (2017). I'm a different kind of biracial': How black/white biracial Americans with immigrant parents negotiate race. *Social Identities*, *23*(5), 614–630.

3. *Navigating Interfaith Family Communication: Research Trends and Applied Implications*

STELLA TING-TOOMEY AND LAURA V. MARTINEZ

The religious marital landscape of the United States is rapidly changing. Interfaith marriages (i.e., marriages in which partners are affiliated with different religious belief systems), while once historically considered unorthodox, are now becoming more acceptable. A Pew Research Center Religious Landscape study (Murphy, 2015) indicates that while same-faith marriages are still the majority in the U.S. society, interfaith marital relationships are becoming more common, especially among young adults. The same Religious Landscape study reports that since 2010, almost 40% of U.S. Americans are married to someone with a different religious affiliation. Those numbers only increase concerning unmarried cohabiting couples, with 49% of these reporting an interfaith relationship.

Indeed, there is tremendous variability between religious groups to account for when considering the growing trend and acceptance of interfaith unions. The concept of religious homogamy (i.e., sharing the same religious denomination and same religiousness and practices) versus religious heterogamy (i.e., religious dissimilarity and different religious beliefs and practices) may help to understand the types and degrees of challenges that face an interfaith intimate couple. For example, according to Kim and Swan (2019), while religious homogamy contributes to relationship adjustment and satisfaction, religious heterogamy contributes to marital conflicts and spill over to a child well-being and stability. However, parents' active engagement with the child can act as a moderating variable between religious heterogamy and child well-being. The wider the religious heterogamous gap between the intimate partners, the more effort and skills it takes for partners to build a strong foundation in their relationship and family system.

The increase of interfaith marriages and cohabitation unions in both the U.S. and globally has contributed to increases of children raised in an interfaith upbringing, with one in five adults in the United States being raised in an interfaith family (Pew Research Center, 2016). Thus, "interfaith families" include family members holding "different religious identities across broad religious groups (e.g., Christian, Jewish, Muslim) [and also] different denominations within a broader faith (e.g., Lutheran and Catholic), or based on divergent religious philosophies (e.g., fundamentalist vs. progressive Protestant) and/or salience (i.e., degree of importance of religious identity)" (Soliz & Colaner, 2014, p. 402).

To provide a broad review synthesizing the various research trends in interfaith relationships and families as well as addressing applied implications, this chapter is organized in three sections: (a) A synthetic literature review of studies on interfaith unions and interfaith family interaction, noting some viable research trends; (b) an interface section connecting constructive interfaith family practices with the larger sociocultural-religious community; and (c) an implication section for family communication scholars and practitioners with proposed directions for future research and applied work.

Interfaith Coupledom and Family Interaction: Research Trends

Interfaith relationships have been on a steady rise in the United States since the 1960s through the current decade. Interfaith marriage was once considered a taboo topic but now in an upward acceleration pace. Concurrently, the increase of interfaith relationships has resulted in an increase of interfaith families and produced families in which the children have differing religious views and affiliations than those of their parents (Pew Research Center, 2016). Some of the children or teenagers, while they subscribe to some different elements of their respective parental religious belief, may also sprinkle their own individuated stamp of, for example, "new age" practice (Soliz & Colaner, 2014). Furthermore, the trend on family and social network's negative reactions concerning the interfaith union continues to rise and create further turbulence in the couplehood relationship and the interfaith family socialization process (Bystydzienski, 2011). Thus, it is necessary to understand the interpersonal dynamics of the interfaith family structure: from identity negotiation between partners to interfaith parent-child interaction in the non-traditional family structure.

Interfaith Couplehood Relationships

Research trends on interfaith families and relationships have looked at the importance of religion when choosing a marital partner, and the pressures and reactions of the partners' social networks (Bystydzienski, 2011). In forming a family connective system, researchers have also examined the topics of how the couple negotiates the celebration of religious holidays and rituals and the placement of religious artifacts in the home, among other factors (Hoffman-Hussain, 2015). They also studied the various communication strategies that couples used to navigate the potential turbulent water of "religious talks" and other communication dynamics (e.g., Martinez, Ting-Toomey, & Dorjee, 2016). Furthermore, from the family communication lens, researchers have focused their effort on addressing the challenges and rewards of a multi-ethnic-racial identity relationship (e.g., Soliz, Cronan, Bergquist, Nuru, & Rittenour, 2017) which can have potential implications for interfaith parent-child households.

Classic research on interfaith marriage focused on the negative aspects of the interfaith intimate relationship development. Research studies (e.g., Hughes & Dickson, 2005; Myers, 2006) indicated that interfaith marriages experience higher dissolution rates and higher levels of dissatisfaction than same-faith marriages. Some of the reasons given for those statistics are that partners' contradicting belief systems will cause heightened conflict and turmoil, failed attempts to convert the other, and an inability to support the religious aspect of each partner's identity (e.g., Colaner, 2009). In addition, other factors include: reduced interaction from having two distinct sets of religious social network, disagreement over celebrating distinct religious holidays, and differences over children's upbringing, among others. Overall, the broader research trend on interfaith marriages has focused on the negative aspects and significant challenges of these relationships. Additionally, the majority of studies on this population are from a quantitative methodological angle, minus a few exceptions.

To illustrate, guided by Identity Management Theory (Imahori & Cupach, 2005), Martinez et al. (2016) interviewed 16 married individuals concerning their interfaith marital highs and lows. The thematic analysis findings highlight the development of the interfaith relational identity via the co-creation of a superordinate spiritual and value system, an implementation of relational boundaries to prioritize the relational identity, and the identification of key milestone decisions (i.e., wedding plans and children socialization coordination). Overall, interfaith partners indicated the two fundamental stages of life when they needed to seriously sort out their religious differences head on: planning the wedding and raising children. According to the interview data, almost all couples have to face the challenging issue of religious upbringing of their children and what, if any, religious education they would receive. Interfaith partners identified this stage of raising children as the one in which their religious differences were most prominently factored. Couples also had the added pressure from their family and social networks in terms of how to raise their children properly.

Perhaps one of the most interesting trends in investigating interfaith unions is conversation surrounding major family development trajectory. For example, Martinez, Ting-Toomey, and Dorjee (2018) uncovered various conversational events that stirred turbulence in the couplehood communication: wedding planning, birth of child religious ritual, religious event celebration rituals, coming of age ritual, and end of life expectation and burial ritual. Intriguingly, when discussing end of life arrangements, interviewees revealed their strong intergroup religious identity preference as an important factor in mulling over a conjoint solution. Due to the fact that certain religions had strict guidelines for interment, cremation, and funeral services, relational partners would need to bring up the topic to find out the wishes of the spouse upon or prior to health deterioration and death.

Captivatingly, another notable research trend in the couplehood interaction concerns the placement of religious artifacts in interfaith homes. While the negotiation of religious and relational identities often occurs in conversation and specific actions (e.g., socializing with members of each other's religious organizations), the placement of artifacts in the home introduces an interesting palpable angle to this interfaith dynamic (e.g., Hoffman-Hussain, 2015). Research indicates that there are two key areas of negotiation of placement of religious artifacts: regular day-to-day placement of artifacts in the home (e.g., a version of The Last Supper) and temporary artifacts that come about during religious holidays (e.g., the Christmas tree, the Menorah). Given that religious belongingness is expressed via the display of artifacts, the materiality of these artifacts and their placement in the home incorporate the intersection of identity and group membership and religious and relational identification all in one. Gleaning from Martinez et al.'s (2016) study, many interviewees highlighted conflicts arising from differing views on *what* religious artifacts will be present, *where* these should be displayed, and the *size* of the artifacts. The embodied act of displaying religious icons demonstrates the materiality of this intergroup dynamic, illustrating how artifact placement both communicates religious identification and causes further communication turmoil.

Beyond internal challenges in the interfaith couplehood construction, one of the key external challenges that interfaith marriages face is external attitudes from partners' social networks. For example, a classic study (Hughes & Dickson, 2006) found that it is the *extrinsic* religious identity orientation (such as extended family or social network disapproval) that creates the marital conflict negotiation of demand-withdrawal rigid pattern more so than the *intrinsic* religious identity orientation (such as identifying devoutly to the religious principles and doctrines). Ultimately, the rigid marital communication pattern leads to low marital satisfaction and dealing with social network stressors in a negative manner. Alternatively, individuals with *intrinsic* religious identity orientation actually practice more constructive communication skills with each other such as attentive listening and productive self-disclosure. They also stand shoulder-to-shoulder together in dealing with outside attitudes about and criticism of their relationship bond. Unsurprisingly, as the interfaith dating relationship becomes more serious, the amount of opposition that couples may experience from close others may increase in intensity (Heard Sahl & Batson, 2011). A possible explanation for this is that an individual's family may perceive a new interfaith relationship as just a fling and expect it to organically die out. However, once relational partners become more committed, extended family members often start to reveal their true sentiments of disapproval and exclusion.

Interfaith Parent-Child Relationships

In the context of interfaith family socialization, parents easily slip back into their own childhood memories and use their own family models in deciding how to discipline, guide, and raise their children in developing their moral compass. Some of these interfaith parents may hold conflicting values and attitudes in teaching their children "moral" from "immoral" principles, or "proper" from "improper" ways of relating with their grandparents, parents, siblings, and extended family members. How parents talk to each other about their children's religious upbringing—especially when both partners deem their religious identity to be a salient aspect of their everyday identity—is one of the key research trends in interfaith family interaction. There appears to be a boomerang effect in terms of how productively (or unproductively) a couple can handle conversional topics on religious upbringing of their children, thereby fostering the relational and individual well-being of their children (Kim & Swan, 2019).

Furthermore, Colaner, Soliz, and Nelson (2014), using communication accommodation theory (CAT), examined the communication management processes between interfaith parents and children (i.e., parent-child relationships in which the parent and children identify with differing religious sets of beliefs). The researchers found that religious difference was indeed correlated with reduced parent-children satisfaction and reduced shared family identity. However, when parents engaged in accommodative communication such as supportive messages in respecting the adolescents' right to choose their religious beliefs and also displaying respect to listen to their religious opinions, these parent-children relationships experienced increased relational satisfaction. They also found that inappropriate self-disclosure, over-emphasizing divergent values, and pushing parents' unwanted advice to their adolescent kids had an adverse effect on the shared family identity unit. Thus, it may not necessarily be the religious differences themselves that cause the relational turmoil but, rather, the ways these differences or conflicts are communicatively managed and constructively handled.

Overall, research on the children of interfaith marriages has all been fairly recent, considering that scholars primarily looked at the relationships of the parents. We suggest that the research findings on mixed-heritage adolescents and adults (see, for example, Soliz et al., 2017; Toomey, Dorjee, & Ting-Toomey, 2013) can help to enhance and inform our understanding of the socialization of dual-faith children. To illustrate, some of the identity struggles of these multiethnic heritage individuals include the constant situational shifting of identities, communal reaction concerns, the problematic bracketing of which members are considered as ingroup or outgroup, and the perpetual longing for inclusion. Toomey et al. (2013) uncovered that some bicultural identity individuals are resourceful enough to use a double-swing "infinity loop identity" lens to view their own identity as situationally dynamic and adaptive. More research studies, however, are needed to explore holistically and developmentally the family system communication features that contribute to adolescents who have developed a secure versus vulnerable dual-faith identity.

Beyond the Interfaith Family: Connecting with the Larger Sociocultural Community

Although the majority of past research does indicate that the interfaith relationship is much more challenging to handle than the within-faith intimate relationship, this does not mean that interfaith relationships are doomed to failure. One can argue that interfaith or intercultural relationships provide rich insights into managing value differences at the core sociocultural membership contact level. Soliz et al. (2017), in researching adults with mixed heritage, noted that rather than viewing the perceived benefits and challenges of multiethnic/multiracial family in binary "either-or" terms, the mixed-heritage individuals actually often assess their identity "mixing" as "a constellation of experiences" of their dynamic, multiplex selves. Perhaps we can cross-transfer the constructive communication strategies used in raising secure dual-faith/bicultural children to the larger sociocultural community of practice.

We focus on three topics in this section: questions to consider in raising dual-faith identity children, developing a conjoint family spiritual vision, and drawing lessons from the dual-religious family socialization experience and applying them to the larger multi-religious community

Raising Dual-Faith Identity Children

In any intimate relationship, the topic of raising children "properly" is a major family concern. Adding religious and cultural factors to this mix, both parents and children have multiple issues with which to deal and pre-plan. In contemplating an interfaith union, the following reflective questions may help to guide the parents or committed couples: Does one parent identify with her or his religious faith with a greater intensity than the other? Does one or both parents subscribe strongly to significant religious rites of passage and rituals (e.g., birth, adolescence/coming of age, marriage, sickness/healing, death, ceremonial events)? Does one parent uphold the daily religious rituals, dietary practice, and praying practice more so than the other? Do parents openly discuss or reach a mutually satisfactory religious education plan for raising their kids prior to their marriage or prior to the arrival of their first child? Do they assess the benefits and challenges of the multiple religious options (such as socialization preference of dual-faith Catholic-Jewish upbringing, Catholic primarily, Jewish primarily, deemphasizing both religious affiliations, or create a "third spiritual" outlook) facing their children?

What degree of involvement do members of the immediate and extended families play in the child's life? What is the cultural and religious composition of the environment, neighborhoods, and schools? Do they have a trusted spiritual counselor in proximity who can guide them with wise balance in their development of the dual-religious socialization process of their children? Do they have the communication suppleness and adequate dual-religious knowledge themselves to deal with the ups and downs of raising dual-faith bicultural children?

Interfaith couples may have the unique opportunity to experience growth in their communication interactions stemming from mutual learning and the curious interfaith questions that their children pose. Even more importantly, the dynamic of the interfaith parent-child relationship further raises the stakes in developing competent interfaith communication practices on both the couplehood level and the parent-child engagement level (Bhatoo & Bhowon, 2018; Ting-Toomey, 2009). The aforementioned inquiry observations rely on research input from across the interdisciplinary research fields such as psychology, sociology, theology, family development and counseling, interfaith education, and human communication studies, among others (e.g., see Gonzalez & Harris, 2013; Gordon & Arenstein, 2017; Karis & Killian, 2009; Ting-Toomey, 2014; Van Niekerk & Verkuyten, 2018).

Interfaith children, bicultural/mixed-heritage children, and trans-adopted children often face more identity-curious questions and identity complexity reflections during various stages of their life-cycle development. Decisions about which religious or cultural group to identify with or not, which label they themselves prefer, which set of grandparents to which they are drawn closer, what peer groups with which they feel comfortable, and which close friends they have in terms of a stronger sense of connection, and the context that triggers an identity are often part of the bi-religious identity struggles among children and adolescents.

Children or teenagers at different developmental stages may experience the emotional highs and lows related to their sense of sociocultural membership self, their relational role self, and their individuated personal self. Ultimately, they may opt for totally different identity forms—depending on their peer group's attitudes, their parents' socialization efforts, their own self-identity explorations, and the larger society's support or rejection of such an identity discovery and search journey.

Developing a Conjoint Family Spiritual Vision via Creative Communication Skills

Cohen (2019), in his autobiographical tale about his 37 years of interfaith Jewish-Christian marriage, summarizes the following key communication visions as paramount to a satisfying interfaith union: (1) concentrate on what you can learn from each other and do good with each other rather than compete over which possesses the greatest truth; (2) have a willingness to listen to each other without feeling compelled to defend your own religious loyalty; and (3) practice dialogue and collaboration without the need for conversion.

Soliz and Colaner (2014) and Reiter and Gee (2008) considered open communication about religion and religious difference is a key feature to promote harmony in interfaith coupledom. Open communication includes the use of explicit support messages to support a partner's religious faith. It also means an active involvement and engagement in the partner's religious activities if at all possible. It also connotes taking an active, committed interest in the partner's religious identity development and spiritual growth.

Martinez et al. (2018) reinforced the importance of the following two communication strategies in forging interfaith couple's connection and mutual valuation: *parallel integrative strategy* and *creative compromise*. A *parallel integrative strategy* involves adopting different elements from both religions to create a "double holiday celebration" or integrating the broad spirit of celebration without honing in on either one of the religious traditions. However, some interfaith couples had a difficult time reconciling certain elements of their spouse's religious traditions. They proceeded to engage in *creative compromise*, defined as incorporating elements of both religions but intentionally removing the religious-sensitive aspects that cause discomfort. For example, Julianne (Female, Jewish-Christian) told her partner that she felt "uncomfortable" having a traditional Christmas tree in the house, "I said--put up any colors you want, just don't make it red and green. So he put up white lights everywhere. I was happy.... I just said --*Don't make it look too Christian.*"

It seems that in a constructive interfaith family communication process, relational partners need to exercise exceptionally elastic and creative communication skills to negotiate their polarized traditions. They also need to do plentiful creative reframing—whether to layer some mixing of both religious traditions or discard some of the religious symbolic facets altogether—to create some operational common ground and also pass on some of these "third culture" (Casmir, 1997) traditions and visions to their children or grandchildren.

Constructive Interfaith Family Communication: Application to the Community Level

We recommend the application of the Appreciative Inquiry (AI) philosophy and its 5-D cycle model (Cooperrider & Whitney, 2005; Watkins, Mohr, & Kelly, 2011) as a connective bridge in the dual-religious family socialization process and in lessons that can be applied to the external multi-religious community. The 5-D cycle model, for example, in the context of the family topic of "raising a secure dual-faith child," can include the following schema: (a) *Define*: each partner can define the meaning she or he has concerning the term "a secure dual-faith child"; (b) *Discovery*: each partner identifies distinctive rewarding (and challenging) family situations and religious community prescriptions in guiding their child to develop dual-faith practices; (c) *Dream*: the couple articulates their individual and conjoint faith-based visions and particular scenarios when they would be in agreement (or disagreement) of how to socialize their kid; (d) *Design*: the couple sets parameters, timeline, criteria rules, and short-term and long-term goals to assess their family religious education program; and (e) *Destiny (or Delivery)*: both partners think and share intentionally what processes and activities in which they can engage their kids for reaching the Design goals and also in alignment with their underlying conjoint beliefs and visions.

Community members can use some of the 5-D cycle model steps to engage in constructive dialogue with religious-diverse others. The 5-D cycle of Define, Discovery, Dream, Design, and Destiny can help different religious groups from the grass-root "living room chat" level to the wider community level to learn about each other's religious beliefs, traditions, and practices. Community members can learn to define and discover together what it means to develop a harmonious, multi-religious community. They can collectively discover deeper faith-based similarities and distinctive differences of each religious denomination. They can learn to dream together, or for example, learn to design a multi-religious community-based center together. They can also learn to design particular distinctive sacred spaces for praying, common spaces for their kids to play and eat and get to know each other, or hold informal sessions of learning about each other sacred texts and parables. They can also hold joyous faith-based festivals together—in a shared sense of interdependent, communal destiny and connective humanity.

To engage in a meaning-centered dialogue approach in implementing the Appreciative Inquiry 5-D steps, Broome (2013) develops his framework of "a culture of peace via dialogue" features: (a) Promoting constructive and sustained intergroup contact; (b) reducing deep-seated intergroup hostility via the constant practice of emotional resonance and forgiveness; (c) nurturing respect for the *Other* via deep listening; (d) developing a narrative of hope and peace via an acute awareness of our humanistic interconnectedness; and (e) establishing a basis for intergroup cooperation via incremental time, patience, good-faith hard work, respect, and trust.

More specifically, in the interfaith education program arena, Gordon and Arenstein (2017) develop a comprehensive model of an 8-course educational curriculum and content activities on the motif of raising harmonious dual-faith children. While the model is targeted to educating families with Jewish and Christian heritages in the U.S., the educational leaders Shiela Gordon and Benjamin Arenstein believe their model has cross application to other bi-religious families and also on a global level. They advocated for the importance of intercultural and interreligious communication competencies as important family and personal life skills.

Implications for Family Communication Scholars and Practitioners

Interfaith Family Communication: Future Directions for Theorizing and Researching

Multifaceted identity negotiation is the cornerstone of understanding interfaith marriage and family communication. The way in which both partners learn to manage their religious and individual identity differences shapes the culture of the relationship and, subsequently, the relationship with their children. Through the ebbs and flows of the developmental trajectory of the relational identity, the committed partners involved in the interfaith marriage become skilled negotiators when juggling their multiple identity facets. On the theoretical level, we believe three theories have potential to increase our depth of understanding of interfaith family communication: integrative identity negotiation theory (Ting-Toomey, 2005; Ting-Toomey & Dorjee, 2019), communication theory of identity (Hecht Warren, Jung, & Krieger, 2005; Phillips, Ledbetter, Soliz, & Bergquist, 2018), and CAT (Giles, 2008; Harwood, Soliz, & Lin, 2006). All three theories emphasize the critical role of paying attention to sociocultural membership identity in developing quality intergroup-interpersonal relationships.

Briefly stated, drawing from social identity theory (Tajfel & Turner, 1979) and social identity complexity theory (e.g., Brewer, 1991, 2010), the newly-revised integrative identity negotiation theory (IINT: Ting-Toomey & Dorjee, 2019) emphasizes the importance of taking all three identity types into account in any intergroup-interpersonal encountering arena. We believe IINT has high explanatory value in explaining and understanding interfaith family communication due to its emphasis on the tripartite components of sociocultural membership identity (e.g., with spiritual/religious identity as part of this component), sociorelational role identity (e.g., with marital couplehood role and family parenting role included), and personal identity attributes (e.g., the dual-faith child will cultivate her or his unique personalities, desires, and personalized spiritual dream plan). The IINT dialectic notions can also reflect the struggling sense of interfaith partner's motivational orientation in passing down their religious heritage of continuity and historical maintenance. Lastly, the IINT also has built-in assumptions on the "how" of competent identity negotiation and the "outcome" of satisfactory identity negotiation in developing quality intergroup-interpersonal bonding issues.

Complementing IINT is the Communication Theory of Identity (CTI: Hecht et al., 2005; Phillips et al., 2018) in understanding the role of sociocultural membership in intergroup-interpersonal encounters. We believe the key motif of "perceived identity gaps" in the CTI can contribute significantly to researchers' understanding of how the interfaith couple's interaction and family interaction can play out productively or unproductively. "Identity gaps" refer to the perceived dissonance or incongruity that an individual perceives on the interface between the personal, relational, communal, and enactment identity layers. In the developmental journey of socialization their kids to be dual-faith subscribers, the more gaps the children perceive in their parents' religious affiliations (or in the couple's relationship negotiation), the more likely the children would experience identity contradictions and stressors. The more complementary facets they experience in their everyday spiritual lives, the more likely they learn to appreciate the vibrancy of dual or multiple-faith blessings and illuminations.

The third theory we believe has strong explanatory and heuristic value in explaining the communication process in interfaith family is Communication Accommodation Theory (CAT: Gallois, Ogay, & Giles, 2005; Giles, 2008; Soliz, Thornton, & Rittenour, 2009). CAT emphasizes the importance of examining perceived intergroup and interpersonal factors that shape the accommodation or non-accommodation behaviors in an interactive situation. Pitts and Harwood (2015) actually define communication accommodation competence as "knowing when and how to accommodate and showing the willingness to do so to accomplish interaction goals" (p. 92). In the context of interfaith family communication, where sociocultural membership and relational role identity take such central focus, parental partners communicating with each other about sociocultural-religious issues inside and outside the household will require flexible accommodation competence. Additionally, how they motivate their dual-faith children to be open to the common ground and distinctive facets of their respective religious doctrines will also depend heavily on their artful convergence and divergence identity navigational skills.

In terms of topical research areas in interfaith family communication, we believe the following five suggested topics may help to move interfaith family research to a more fertile ground of understanding. First, more research attention is needed to explore social identity intersection and complexity of how interfaith partners bring their ethnic/racial identity background and overlay this co-culture identity with their religious identity. Second, more research attention is needed to include marginalized identity voices (e.g., LGBTQ) with interfaith coupledom and the receptivity of the extended family and the larger religious community. Third, more studies are needed to identify the particular verbal and nonverbal transformational strategies that can create the most optimally nurturing environment for the dual-faith children to feel safe and included. Fourth, more longitudinal research is needed to track the ebbs and flows of how committed interfaith partners socialize their kids to whole-heartedly embrace their dual faiths or create a "third culture" spiritual outlook in carving their own paths. Fifth, most of the research studies reported in this chapter are based on a U.S.-centric view of interfaith pairings or interfaith family communication. We need to work on more collaborative research efforts internationally to gain a global lens on how various interfaith couples struggle, navigate, strive, or even thrive in their own cultural turfs despite harsh marginalization or exclusion from their immediate families or larger surrounding community. Connecting the macro-, exo-, meso-, and micro-level of analysis (e.g., from the social ecological model, Ting-Toomey & Oetzel, 2013) on interfaith family bonding issues may yield a richly-textured and multi-layered picture of the complex identity negotiation puzzles in the interfaith family unit.

Interfaith Family: Some Directions and Guidelines for Practitioners and Families

Interfaith family comes in different sizes, shapes, and standpoints. Intergroup-interpersonal researchers need to pair productively with family therapists, school counselors, or social workers to elicit their metaphors and narratives of what they think are the knowledge gaps in the interfaith family research arena. If indeed interfaith family workshops or educational programs are being conducted in a community, we need more longitudinal data in terms of pre-test and post-test of assessing the rate of success of these workshops. Intergroup contact in more personalized relationship contexts can build relationship rapport and trust (Pettigrew, 1998). If we can bring in different types of interfaith couples and also other marginalized identity couples face-to-face with each other and let them tell their stories, we may learn that each family has its own distinctive struggles yet share some similar and profound gut-wrenching aches and pain. We may also learn some resilient and triumphant lessons from others that can apply to our own family situations. Resourceful children would strive to integrate or maintain in parallel some of the different facets of their parents' religious traditions and rituals. Some practical guidelines are provided here to facilitate a stronger dialogue between parents/practitioners and children regarding cultural and religious identity socialization issues in the household. First, take time and make a commitment to work out a family identity process as early in your couplehood relationship as possible; understand deeply the important aspects of your own and your partner's cultural-ethnic and religious identity and salient beliefs. Second, make time to listen to your children's identity stories and experiences; their ambivalence is oftentimes part of a normal, developmental process. Learn not to judge or be hurt by their truthful revelations and disclosures. Third, try to provide your children with plenty of cultural and religious enrichment opportunities that celebrate the diversity of both of your religious traditions; offer them positive experiences to appreciate and synthesize the differences or keep both traditions in parallel with each other with clear explanations of their religious importance to your kids. Fourth, realize that each child is a unique person on her or his own—each child's reaction may be quite different from her or his sibling interpretation or meaning construction process about her or his faith-based pathway and affiliation.

Fifth, be truthful in dealing with religious prejudice and biased issues in the larger society and also extended family reactions. Sixth, parents should model constructive, assertive behaviors in confronting prejudice and religious hate issues within and beyond the family system. Seventh, pay attention to other salient intersecting identities (e.g., gender ideology, political activism identity, ability/disability identity, racial/ethnic identity, interlacing with religious identity) that may be creating additional anguish or shame in your children, as these may contradict the often-preached religious doctrines at home. Eighth, nurture a secure sense of sociocultural membership identity, superordinate spiritual identity, and secure personal self-esteem and self-worth in your children regardless of how they wish to identify themselves religiously. Ninth, divide some balanced attention and time to your partner in conjunction with being overly worried about how to socialize your children religiously. Finally, recognize that your children will grow up and choose their own path; keep the dialogue open and let your young children or teenagers know that you will always be there for them.

Creating a secure and safe home environment, listening to their stories with patience and mindfulness, and finding meaningful ways to relate to who they are and how they are becoming are some very basic means that parents can use to signal their heartfelt caring and attuning presence in their children's spiritual lives. The spiritual doctrines that cross all religious faiths such as prayers, compassion, forgiveness, and reconciliation can also bind fragile and sensitive hearts together. In the end, making that special spiritual connection with your relational partner and child on a soulful relatedness level may help you to enter a sense of grace and balance within yourself, in your family system, and in connection with the larger community in which you call "home."

References

Bhatoo, S., & Bhowon, U. (2018). Voices of young women in interfaith marriages: Experiences and challenges. *Asian Journal of Social Science, 46*, 281–303.

Brewer, M. B. (1991). The social self: On being the same and different at the same time. *Personality and Social Psychology Bulletin, 17*, 475–442. doi:10.1177/0146167291175001

Brewer, M. B. (2010). Social identity complexity and acceptance of diversity. In R. J. Crisp (Ed.), *Social issues and interventions: The psychology of social and cultural diversity* (pp. 11–33). West Sussex, UK: Wiley-Blackwell.

Bystydzienski, J. M. (2011). *Intercultural couples: Crossing boundaries, negotiating difference.* New York: New York University Press.

Casmir, F. (1997). *Ethics in intercultural and international communication.* Mahwah, NJ: Lawrence Erlbaum.

Cohen, C. L. (2019). A tale of interfaith marriage. *Missiology: An International Review, 47*, 37–44. doi:10.1177/0091829618814830

Colaner, C. W. (2009). Exploring the communication of Evangelical families: The impact of Evangelical gender role identity on family communication patterns. *Communication Studies, 60*, 97–113.

Colaner, C. W., Soliz, J., & Nelson, L. R. (2014). Communicatively managing religious identity difference in parent-child relationships: The role of accommodative and non-accommodative communication. *Journal of Family Communication, 14*, 310–327.

Cooperrider, D. L., & Whitney, D. (2005). *Appreciative inquiry: A positive revolution in change.* San Francisco, CA: Berrett-Koehler.

Gallois, C., Ogay, T., & Giles, H. (2005). Communication accommodation theory: A look back and a look ahead. In W. B. Gudykunst (Ed.), *Theorizing about intercultural communication* (pp. 121–148). Thousand Oaks, CA: Sage.

Giles, H. (2008). Communication accommodation theory. In L. A. Baxter & D. O. Braithwaite (Eds.), *Engaging in interpersonal communication: Multiple perspectives* (pp. 161–173). Thousand Oaks, CA: Sage.

Gonzalez, A., & Harris, T. (Eds.). (2013). *Mediating cultures: Parent communication in intercultural contexts.* New York: Routledge.

Gordon, S. C., & Arenstein, B. (2017). Interfaith education: A new model for today's interfaith families. *International Review of Education, 63*, 169–195. doi:10.1007/s11159-017-9629-2

Harwood, J., Soliz, J. E., & Lin, M. C. (2006). Communication accommodation theory: An intergroup approach to family relationships. In D. Braithwaite & L. Baxter (Eds.), *Engaging theories in family communication: Multiple perspectives* (pp. 19–34). Thousand Oaks, CA: Sage.

Heard Sahl, A., & Batson, C. D. (2011). Race and religion in the Bible belt: Parental attitudes toward interfaith relationships. *Sociological Spectrum, 31*, 444–465.

Hecht, M. L., Warren, J. R., Jung, E., & Krieger, J. L. (2005). A communication theory of identity: Development, theoretical perspective, and future directions. In W. B. Gudykunst (Ed.), *Theorizing about intercultural communication* (pp. 257–278). Thousand Oaks, CA: Sage.

Hoffman-Hussain, C. (2015). Interfaith home decorating: An exploration of religiosity and home artifacts within British interfaith hybrid coupledom. In T.W. Jones & L. Matthews-Jones (Eds.), *Material religion in modern Britain* (pp. 147–163). London, UK: Palgrave Macmillan.

Hughes, P. C., & Dickson, F. C. (2005). Communication, marital satisfaction, and religious orientation in interfaith marriages. *Journal of Family Communication, 5*, 25–41.

Hughes, P. C., & Dickson, F. C. (2006). Relational dynamics of interfaith marriages. In L. H. Turner & R. West (Eds.), *The family communication sourcebook* (pp. 373–388). Thousand Oaks, CA: Sage.

Imahori, T. T., & Cupach, W. R. (2005). Identity management theory. In W. B. Gudykunst (Ed.), *Theorizing about intercultural communication* (pp. 195–210). Thousand Oaks, CA: Sage.

Karis, T. A., & Killian, K. D. (Eds.). (2009). *Intercultural couples.* New York: Routledge.

Kim, Y.-I., & Swan, I. (2019). Religious heterogamy, marital quality, and paternal engagement. *Religions, 10*, 1–11.

Martinez, L., Ting-Toomey, S., & Dorjee, T. (2016). Identity management and relational culture in interfaith marital communication in a United States context: A qualitative study. *Journal of Intercultural Communication Research, 45*, 503–525.

Martinez, L., Ting-Toomey, S., & Dorjee, T. (2018, May). *Negotiating religious and relational identity in interfaith marital communication: An interpretive study.* International Communication Association conference, Prague, Czech Republic.

Murphy, C. (2015). Interfaith marriage is common in U.S., particularly among the recently wed. *Pew Research Center- Fact-tank.* Retrieved from https://www.pewresearch.org/fact-tank/2015/06/02/interfaith-marriage/

Myers, S. (2006). Religious homogamy and marital quality: Historical and generational pattern. *Journal of Marriage and the Family, 68*, 292–304.

Pettigrew, T. F. (1998). Intergroup contact theory. *Annual Review of Psychology, 49*, 65–85.

Pew Research Center. (2016). One-in-five U.S. adults were raised in interfaith homes. Retrieved from https://www.pewforum.org/2016/10/26/one-in-five-u-s-adults-were-raised-in-interfaith-homes/

Phillips, K. E., Ledbetter, A. M., Soliz, J. E., & Bergquist, G. (2018). Investigating the interplay between identity gaps and communication patterns in predicting relational intentions in families in the United States. *Journal of Communication, 68*, 590–611.

Pitts, M. J., & Harwood, J. T. (2015). Communication accommodation competence: The nature and nurture of accommodative resources across the lifespan. *Language and Communication, 41*, 89–99.

Reiter, M. J., & Gee, C. B. (2008). Open communication and partner support in intercultural and interfaith romantic relationships: A relational maintenance approach. *Journal of Social and Personal Relationships, 25*, 539–599. doi:10.1177/0265407508090872

Soliz, J. E., & Colaner, C. W. (2014). Familial solidarity and religious identity: Communication and interfaith families. In L. H. Turner (Ed.), *The Sage handbook of family communication* (pp. 401–416). Thousand Oaks, CA: Sage.

Soliz, J., Cronan, S., Bergquist, G., Nuru, A. K., & Rittenour, C. E. (2017). Perceived benefits and challenges of a multiethnic-racial identity: Insight from adults with mixed heritage. *Identity: An International Journal of Theory and Research*, *17*, 267–281. doi:10.1080/15283488.2017.1379907

Soliz, J., Thornton, A., & Rittenour, C. E. (2009). Communicative correlates of satisfaction, family, identity, and group salience in multiracial/ethnic families. *Journal of Marriage and the Family*, *71*, 819–832.

Tajfel, H., & Turner, J. C. (1979). An integrative theory of intergroup conflict. In W. G. Austin & S. Worchel (Eds.), *The social psychology of intergroup relations* (pp. 33–47). Monterey, CA: Brooks/Cole.

Ting-Toomey, S. (2005). Identity negotiation theory: Crossing cultural boundaries. In W. B. Gudykunst (Ed.), *Theorizing about intercultural communication* (pp. 211–233). Thousand Oaks, CA: Sage.

Ting-Toomey, S. (2009). A mindful approach to managing conflicts in intercultural-intimate couples. In T. A. Karis & K. Killian (Eds.), *Intercultural couples: Exploring diversity in intimate relationships* (pp. 31–49). New York: Routledge/Taylor & Francis Group.

Ting-Toomey, S. (2014). Managing identity issues in intercultural conflict communication: Developing a multicultural identity attunement lens. In V. Benet-Martinez & Y.-Y. Hong (Eds.), *Oxford handbook of multicultural identity* (pp. 485–506). New York: Oxford University Press.

Ting-Toomey, S., & Dorjee, T. (2019). *Communicating across cultures, second edition.* New York: The Guilford Press.

Ting-Toomey, S., & Oetzel, J. G. (2013). Culture-based situational conflict model: An update and expansion. In J. G. Oetzel & S. Ting-Toomey (Eds.), *The Sage handbook of conflict communication* (2nd ed., pp. 763–789). Thousand Oaks, CA: Sage.

Toomey, A., Dorjee, T., & Ting-Toomey, S. (2013). Bicultural identity negotiation, conflicts, and intergroup communication strategies. *Journal of Intercultural Communication Research*, *42*, 112–134.

Van Niekerk, J., & Verkuyten, M. (2018). Interfaith marriage attitudes in Muslim majority countries: A multilevel approach. *The International Journal of Psychology of Religion*, *28*, 257–270.

Watkins, M. J., Mohr, B., & Kelly, R. (2011). *Appreciative inquiry: Change at the speed of imagination, second edition.* San Francisco: Wiley.

4. *Communication and Political Difference in the Family*

Benjamin R. Warner and Jihye Park

Ruth Dorancy changed her wedding plans after the 2016 U.S. presidential election. She moved the location from the United States (where she lives) to Italy so that her relatives would be unable to attend. In explaining her decision to the *New York Times*, she said of her family, "I just don't want them around me on the most important day of my life" (Tavernise & Seelye, 2016, para. 7). Dorancy knew that some of her family had voted for Donald Trump, a decision she described as "a rejection of everyone who looks like me" (Tavernise & Seelye, 2016, para. 6). Dorancy's story is but one example of an apparent trend in which strife resulting from the 2016 election reduced the time families spent together. For example, using anonymized data from over 10 million smart phones and precinct-level information about vote-share in the 2016 election, Chen and Rohla (2018) estimated that political disagreement cut Thanksgiving dinners by almost an hour in the weeks following the 2016 election. They estimated that the partisan fallout of the election resulted in a loss of almost 74 million hours of time with the family.

Political disagreement not only reduces the time family spends with one another, it also diminishes people's desire to discuss politics. Pew Research Center found that 65% of U.S. adults reported that most of their family members agreed with them about politics compared to 33% who indicated that only a few or none of their family shared their views (Oliphant, 2018). Among those who mostly agree with their family, 82% said it was okay to have family discussions about politics. For those who mostly disagreed with their family, a paltry 28% felt it was appropriate to talk about politics.

Political disagreement can thus reduce family communication and connectedness. However, the trend in the U.S. is toward more homogenous political attitudes within family units—an outcome that suggests families are more likely to exacerbate rather than ameliorate growing political polarization (Iyengar, Konitzer, & Kent, 2018). In the chapter that follows we will briefly review what is known about political polarization with a special emphasis on how it relates to the family. As part of this review, we will present research that documents the role of the family in the formation of partisan identities. We will also consider whether there is any evidence that the U.S. case is unique compared to families in other countries. Following this review, we will present findings from original data to further explore the influence of political disagreement in the family on political polarization. Having reviewed the political dynamic in the family, we will discuss some of the broader implications of this research before concluding with a consideration of implications for scholars and practitioners.

Political Polarization and the Family

A Brief Review of Research on Political Polarization

The extent to which people in the U.S. are polarized has been the source of considerable debate among political scientists (see, e.g., Abramowitz, 2010; Fiorina, Abrams, & Pope, 2011). Much of this debate has focused on disagreements over whether the typical voter has extreme attitudes on divisive political issues such as abortion or gun control. However, few people are actually ideological—meaning that most people's political attitudes and behaviors are not constrained by a set of policy preferences united around a coherent political philosophy (Converse, 1964; Kinder & Kalmoe, 2017). Instead, the reverse may be true, people seem to adopt political attitudes consistent with their partisan identification (Achen & Bartles, 2016). In this sense, partisanship can be thought of as a social identity (Greene, 1999) not unlike other important social categories such as race or nationality.

Drawing on the insight that partisanship is a social identity, Iyengar, Sood, and Lelkes (2012) argued that polarization is better understood as a growing divide between how partisans feel about members of their own party versus how they feel about members of the other political party. They called this growing animosity toward the political outgroup *affective polarization*, and found that, over the past half-dozen decades, evaluations of the outparty have become colder on a 0–100 feeling thermometer, outparty trait attributions have become more negative, and a there is greater desire for social distance with the outparty including an aversion to cross-partisan marriage. On these metrics partisans in the U.S. have grown increasingly hostile to members of the political outgroup even as ingroup favorability has remained stable.

Given increasing polarization in the U.S., it is worth briefly reviewing evidence about the causes and—to the extent there are any—remedies. For their part, Iyengar et al. (2012) present some evidence that campaign activity (especially negative advertising) is partially to blame. Much of the academic literature has focused on the polarizing effects of an increasingly partisan media environment (Jamieson & Cappella, 2008; Levendusky, 2013; Stroud, 2011). For example, Stroud (2010) leveraged nationally representative panel data to demonstrate that those who consumed more partisan media provided more polarized feeling thermometer evaluations of John Kerry and George W. Bush (the two candidates for U.S. president in 2004). This effect was later replicated with samples of both U.S. and Israeli voters using both self-reported and observational data (Garrett et al., 2014). Partisan media can also polarize evaluations of down-ballot candidates who are not the source of media coverage (Warner, 2018) as well as attitudes on salient issues in the U.S. (Levendusky, 2013; Warner, 2010) and Europe (Wojcieszak, Azrout, & de Vreese, 2017). There is even evidence that partisan media fosters greater belief in conspiracy theories (Warner & Neville-Shepard, 2014). Non-partisan news media also contribute to polarization by emphasizing conflict frames (Han & Federico, 2017)—as does the emergence of social media (Settle, 2018). Though initial evidence suggested that viewers of televised presidential campaign debates also became more polarized (Cho & Ha, 2012; Warner & McKinney, 2013), the most comprehensive evidence suggests inconclusive results—with some debates resulting in greater polarization and other debates reducing polarization (Warner, McKinney, Bramlett, Jennings, & Funk, 2019). Finally, as will be discussed in more detail below, partisan sorting in romantic relationships contributes to greater polarization (Iyengar et al., 2018).

Though there is ample research on the causes of affective polarization, little is known about possible remedies. Levendusky (2018) found that asking people to write about their national identities (i.e., about being American) subordinated partisanship and elevated a common ingroup identity (shared citizenship). This strategy effectively reduced affective polarization, though in another study Wojcieszak and Garrett (2018) found that the same national identity prompts increased hostility toward immigrants. In our own work on affective polarization, we have found that intergroup contact, even indirect forms of contact such as imagined interactions or observed interactions, can reduce affective polarization (Warner, Horstman, & Kearney, 2019; Warner & Villamil, 2017; Wojcieszak & Warner, 2019).

One might hope that political diversity in the family could serve as a source of positive intergroup interactions. After all, families can be an important site of intergroup interactions (Soliz & Harwood, 2006). Unfortunately, as we demonstrate below, the family is an unlikely remedy for political polarization for a few reasons. First, political disagreement within the core family unit is uncommon. Second, to the extent that there is difference in the family, it is likely to only depolarize those partisans who need it least. The already polarized seem either immune to the depolarizing potential of their relatives or may respond by becoming even more polarized.

Political Homogeneity in the Family

Political socialization is a broad category of research that examines the formation of all facets of political identities. Though it is not a central focus of this chapter, there is a considerable amount of research exploring why some adolescents become politically knowledgeable and active when others do not. There are four crucial factors in determining whether adolescents will become active and knowledgeable participants in politics: the communication patterns in the family, exposure to civics education at school, the decision to opt into news about politics and current events, and the attitudes and behaviors of peer groups (Shah, McLeod, & Lee, 2009). Families that are high in both socio and concept orientations are more likely to socialize their children into high levels of political participation, though the effect appears to be mediated by subsequent expressive activities adopted by the child at school and among their peers (Shah et al., 2009).

Though schools, peers, and the media are thought to potentially overwhelm the family with regard to the formation of political engagement, families are still considered the primary source of partisan identities (Niemi, Ross, & Alexander, 1978)—a correspondence explained by the family transmission model (Jennings, Kent, & Niemi, 1974; Jennings, Stoker, & Bowers, 2009). Following social learning theory, the family transmission model argues that children receive cues from parents about which sorts of political attitudes to adopt. Early tests of this model underwhelmed contemporary scholars because issue-attitude correspondence was low (Jennings et al., 1974; Niemi et al., 1978). However, as articulated above, issue-attitudes do not dictate political behavior—partisan alignments do (Kinder & Kalmoe, 2017). Partisanship is consistently the strongest form of political correspondence between parent and child (Niemi et al., 1978; Jennings et al., 1974) and is strongest in families who frequently discuss politics—especially if the parents share the same political views and therefore send consistent partisan cues to their children (Jennings et al., 2009).

The strong correspondence in partisanship between parent and child has been demonstrated in a variety of international contexts. Jennings (2009) summarized cross-national comparisons primarily examining Europe. Because most non-U.S. democracies have a multi-party system, it was initially unclear whether the family transmission model would translate globally. Nevertheless, the research summarized by Jennings (2009) generally found that a core left-right orientation transferred from parents to children. Rico and Jennings (2016) extended the contexts to which the family transmission model has been applied by testing intergenerational correspondence in a sample from Catalonia, Spain. They selected Catalonia as an especially challenging cross-cultural test because, in Catalonia, the left-right orientation is cleaved by a center-periphery orientation rooted in a highly salient regional identity. Rico and Jennings (2016) found moderate transmission of a parent's left-right orientation on their children and a strong transmission of regional identity (i.e., the more salient Catalonian center-periphery orientation).

If proponents of the family transmission model have begun expanding the cultural contexts in which the model has been tested, their approach to communication is still developing. Transmission of partisanship from parents to children is known to be enhanced by communication when political beliefs are salient and when the parents are highly political. Communication scholars have expanded the role of communication in family transmission in two crucial respects. First, family communication patterns are important to the transmission of political attitudes from parents to children, as is evident in Ledbetter's (2015) finding that both socio and concept orientation were related to a more conservative ideology. Communication scholars have also recovered the agency of children in the socialization process. When children initiate conversation about politics (typically as a result of civics curriculum at school), parents often become more politically engaged to rebalance the family hierarchy (McDevitt, 2005; McDevitt & Chaffee, 2002). This increases intergenerational correspondence because children can influence the partisanship of their parents (Shulman & DeAndrea, 2014). Specifically, Shulman and DeAndrea (2014) found that roughly two-thirds of children perceived that they shared the same political views as their parents but, among the one-third who said that their parents disagreed with them about politics, most reported mutual influence between parent and child on their attitudes such that they persuaded one-another to change their political views.

Political Homogeneity among Spouses

The research on intergenerational transmission of political orientation from parent to child consistently finds that this transmission is strongest when both parents share the same political orientation because parental disagreement reduces political conversation in the home and, when politics is discussed, parents send inconsistent partisan cues (Jennings et al., 2009). Shared partisanship between parents is becoming increasingly common. Alford, Hatemi, Hibbing, Martin, and Eaves (2011) analyzed survey responses from over 5,000 couples to compare political similarity within marriage to other physical and social characteristics. They found that only five of the seventeen traits included in their study were indicative of strong spousal correspondence; political partisanship, aggregated political issue attitudes, church attendance, frequency of alcohol consumption, and educational attainment.

Though there are many possible explanations for the strong political correspondence between spouses, the strongest explanation is that people use political agreement as a decision-making criterion when initiating romantic relationships. Huber and Malhorta (2017) experimentally manipulated online dating profiles to demonstrate that people were more likely to express interest in initiating contact with and responding to messages from profiles that were politically similar. They followed up this experiment with an analysis of the behavior of more than 250,000 people in an online dating community, where they observed that people were more likely to send and respond to messages if they had initial political similarity. Their data therefore substantially strengthen the view that political correspondence among married couples is a result of active selection rather than rival explanations such as context (i.e., social and geographic political segregation) or persuasion (i.e., spouses becoming more politically similar over time).

The correspondence between spouses on politics is not only high, it is growing. Iyengar et al. (2018) compared spousal political correspondence from 1965 to 2015 and found that it increased by more than 8% such that, in 2015, 81.5% of married couples shared the same partisan identification. They also found that spousal correspondence on feeling thermometer scores increased dramatically from 1965, when the correlation between spouses was .39, to 2015, when a spousal correlation of .77 was observed. Both Alford et al. (2011) and Iyengar et al. (2018) tested whether the correlation grew over the duration of a marriage to rule out persuasion as an explanation for spousal correspondence. Both found that political attitudes did not converge over the length of a marriage. To rule out contextual explanations (i.e., geographic and social sorting), Iyengar et al. (2018) compared people who live in zip-codes characterized by extreme political homogeneity to those who live in politically diverse zip-codes and found that, though geographic homogeneity was associated with higher levels of spousal political correspondence, 80% of spouses who lived in the most politically diverse zip-codes shared the same partisan affiliation. Finally, Iyengar et al. (2018) compared political correspondence to religious and educational correspondence to rule out incidental sorting and found, consistent with the previous studies (Alford et al. 2011; Huber & Malhorta, 2017) that a preference for partisan similarity was the best explanation for high rates of political correspondence between spouses.

Because children are more likely to adopt the political beliefs of their parents if their parents share the same views, Iyengar et al. (2018) posited that the transmission of partisanship from parents to children should also have increased over the past fifty years. This is in fact what they found: the level of intergenerational correspondence increased since 1965, with shared partisan identification from parent to child increasing by 6% points up to 74.2% and the intergenerational correlation on the feeling thermometer scores going from .20 in 1965 to .64 in 2015. Furthermore, the transmission of parental political attitudes for parents who have the same political views was almost 86% compared to 39% for parents who had divergent partisan identifications. In short, the increasing extent to which people select romantic mates on the basis of political identities should also result in stronger intergenerational transmission of partisanship from parents to their children.

Politics and Polarization in the Family

Though the most common family circumstance is political agreement, one crucial objective of this chapter is to consider the implications of political disagreement in the family. This is in part motivated by the hope that the family context can create the opportunity for positive intergroup interactions—perhaps a left-leaning father and right-leaning daughter can be the source of intergroup empathy and understanding.

To explore the nature of political disagreement in families, we conducted an original survey using Qualtrics online panels. Participants were contacted from December 5–14 of 2016. They had been previously interviewed two times prior to the 2016 presidential election. The initial sample was quota-stratified to match recent U.S. Census data on age, gender, and race/ethnicity. In total, 804 people participated in the December survey (down from 2014 in the first wave and 998 in the second wave). The average respondent age was 51 (SD = 15.6), a majority were male (n = 439, 55%) and white/Caucasian (n = 584, 73%, compared to 12% African American, 9% Latinx, and 5% Asian). An overwhelming majority of our respondents (n = 685, 85%) indicated that they were sure they had voted in the 2016 election, a number much higher than the actual 61% voter participation rate observed in 2016 but in line with the well-documented propensity for people to lie when asked if they voted. Of those who said they were sure the voted, a plurality (n = 338, 49%) said they voted for Clinton compared to Trump (n = 307, 45%). Every respondent was asked, "If you had to pick, which candidate would you prefer had won the election?" More said Clinton (n = 422, 52%) than Trump (n = 382, 48%).

Near the end of the survey, we introduced the idea of family disagreement about politics. Because we were contacting people in early December, we used the tradition of family gathering during the holidays to approach the subject. We asked respondents to read the following prompt:

> Finally, we'd like to ask you some questions about your family. Many people view the holidays as an opportunity to catch up with their families. However, after a contentious election, sometimes tense conversations come up when families disagree about politics. Perhaps you experience things like this in your family. We want to ask you some questions about your family and how the election might or might not come up.

We then asked them to "think of a member of your family who has political views that are the most different from your own. Think of someone you might be most likely to argue with about the election." A majority of respondents (n = 473, 59%) indicated that they were most likely to argue about the election with an extended relative such as a grandparent, niece/nephew, uncle/aunt, or cousin. However, many (n = 328, 41%) indicated that they would be most likely to argue with a close relative such as a parent (n = 122, 15%), child (n = 68, 8%), or sibling (n = 138, 17%). The low absolute percentage of respondents who report a parent or child as the most likely source of political conflict corresponds with the research reviewed above regarding the high intergenerational transmission of political attitudes.

Our interest here is in exploring the consequences of having a close member of one's family as a source of political disagreement and/or conflict. Based on work that has applied intergroup contact theory to political polarization (Warner & Villamil, 2017; Wojcieszak & Warner, 2019), we suspect that people who have a close relative with whom they disagree will also have more favorable attitudes towards supporters of the other political party. However, it is likely that this effect will be conditioned by prior attitudes (Lodge & Taber, 2013) such that those who have highly polarized attitudes about the 2016 election will be more resistant to the depolarizing influence of intergroup contact. In other words, the presence of a close relative who supports the other party should result in more favorable attitudes toward cross-partisan supporters, but more so for people who do not harbor strong feelings of animosity toward the partisan outgroup.

To evaluate people's attitudes toward supporters of the political outgroup we asked them to rate three groups on the standard 0–100 feeling thermometer: (a) [Trump/Clinton] supporters; (b) people who attended [Trump/Clinton] rallies; and (c) people who voted for [Trump/Clinton].

Table 4.1: Effects of Family Disagreement on Feeling Thermometer Evaluations of Supporters of the Political Outgroup

	B	*SE B*	*p*
Intercept	35.502	2.407	<.0001
Parent	13.480	4.575	.0033
Sibling	2.042	4.685	.6631
Child	15.220	7.577	.0449
Polarization	-0.204	0.034	<.0001
Parent*Polarization	-0.199	0.069	.0041
Sibling*Polarization	0.004	0.070	.9498
Child*Polarization	-0.217	0.108	.0459

People were only asked about the outgroup such that those who indicated that they wanted Clinton to win the election were asked to evaluate Trump supporters and vice versa (α = .96, *M* = 23.8, *SD* = 24.07). Following prior research (Stroud, 2010), affective polarization was measured by computing the absolute value of the difference between feeling thermometer evaluations of Donald Trump and Hillary Clinton (*M* = 61.34, *SD* = 31.21).

We then assessed the implications of having parent, child, or sibling as the primary source of disagreement within the family. We estimated a linear model that included dummy variables for having a parent, child, or sibling most likely to disagree as predictors of feeling toward supporters of the outgroup candidate. We included affective polarization as a covariate and added interaction terms for affective polarization and each category of family member. The results (reported in Table 4.1 and depicted in Figure 4.1) illustrate that disagreeing with a parent was associated with more positive feelings toward supporters of the outgroup candidate.

The distribution of affective polarization is included in the bottom of Figure 4.1. As can be seen, most people were highly affectively polarized. The modal score was a maximum possible value of 100, 99 was the second most common score, and 15% (*n* = 122) of the sample had a polarization score between 98 and 100. For these people, disagreeing with a parent seemed to actually reduce feelings toward the political outgroup, though the effect was not statistically distinguishable from zero. People who named a parent as a primary source of political disagreement and had an affective polarization score of 100 were estimated to rate supporters of the outparty a *seven* on the 101-point feeling thermometer scale. This compares to an estimated score of 15.5 for those who had a polarization score of 100 but reported an extended relative as their primary source of disagreement.

The third most common value for affective polarization was zero and about 20% ($n = 157$) of respondents had an affective polarization score below thirty. This was roughly the range at which disagreeing with a parent could be expected to reduce affective polarization. The estimated feeling thermometer evaluation for supporters of the outgroup among those with a polarization score of zero and for whom a parent is the most commons source of political disagreement is 48.89—compared to an evaluation of 35.5 for those with a polarization score of zero and an extended relative as the most common source of disagreement.

In other words, disagreeing with a parent about politics was associated with warmer feelings toward the political outgroup, but only for those who did not express polarized evaluations of the presidential candidates. Among those who were already polarized, disagreement with a parent did not reduce (and may have increased) hostility toward the outgroup.

As can be seen in Table 4.1 and Figure 4.2, having a child as the primary source of political disagreement appeared to exert a similar influence but with

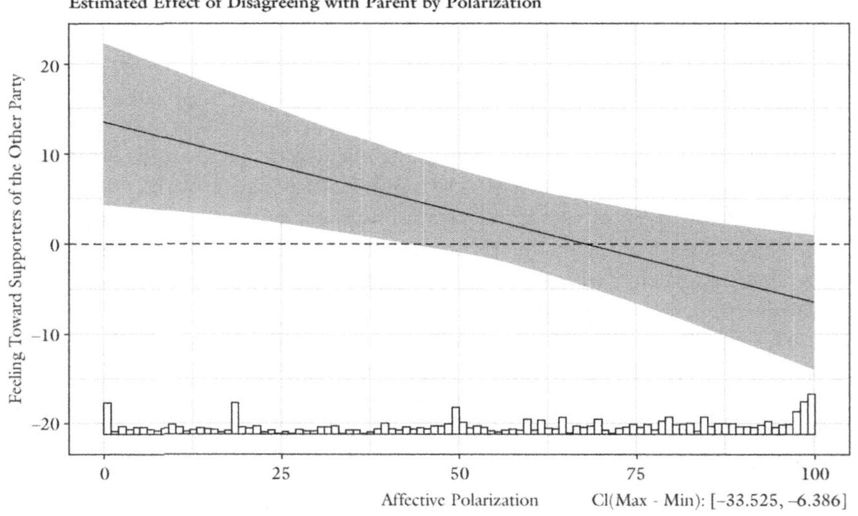

Figure 4.1: Effect of Disagreeing with Parent Conditioned by Polarization

Note: The line represents the estimated effect of having a parent as the primary source of political disagreement in the family on feelings toward supporters of the outgroup at varying levels of affective polarization. The observed distribution of affective polarization is displayed along the x-axis. The shaded area around the line represents the 95% confidence interval of the effect.

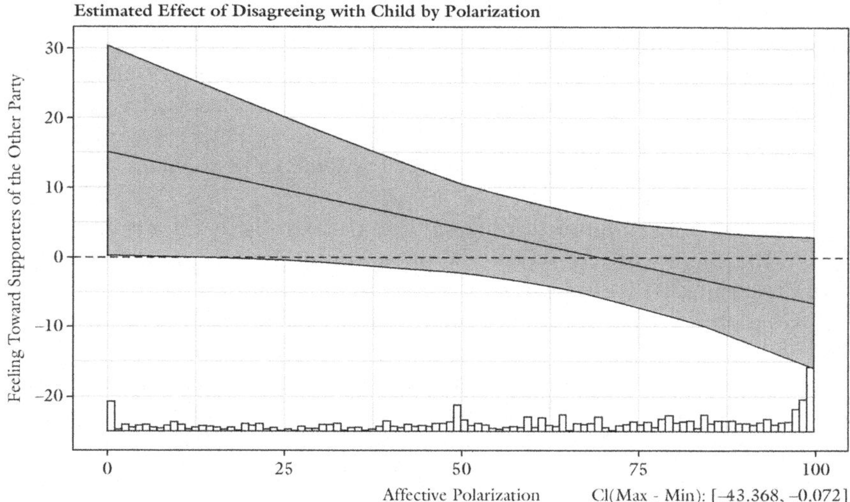

Figure 4.2: Effect of Disagreeing with Child Conditioned by Polarization

Note: The line represents the estimated effect of having a child as the primary source of political disagreement in the family on feelings toward supporters of the outgroup at varying levels of affective polarization. The observed distribution of affective polarization is displayed along the x-axis. The shaded area around the line represents the 95% confidence interval of the effect.

considerably less statistical confidence. This was likely due to the lower statistical power resulting from a smaller number of people who reported their child as the primary source of political disagreement (n = 68 compared to n = 122 for parents). Conversely, there was no effect, conditional or otherwise, of having a sibling as the primary source of political disagreement.

All of this suggests that having a parent (and probably child) as a source of political disagreement can result in more favorable attitudes toward supporters of the political outgroup. This is consistent with intergroup contact theory. However, this effect was conditioned by people's prior levels of polarization. Those who had extreme attitudes about Clinton and Trump were either immune to the depolarizing effects of intergroup contact through the family or may have even become more polarized as a result of this disagreement.

Beyond the Family: Family Communication and Society

The information presented above paints a picture of families as key sites of political identity formation. Thus, there is a high correspondence in political beliefs between parents and children particularly when parents share the same political preferences. Furthermore, it is quite common for parents to share political views—increasingly so—as people use partisanship as a selection criterion when choosing with whom to marry and start a family. Iyengar et al. (2018) project that this will generate even more political polarization as families become echo-chambers that reinforce the same set of attitudes and beliefs across generations.

The increasing alignment of family and partisanship is yet another example of the alignment of political identities with other important social identities (Mason, 2018). Indeed, families are an important social identity (Soliz & Rittenour, 2012). As more social identities align with political views, the stakes of intergroup competition will only increase. Political disagreement crosses familial, religious, socio-economic, and cultural fault lines. The social consequences are potentially dramatic. Increased affective polarization reduces incentive for legislative compromise and can therefore undermine effective democratic governance (Wolf, Strachan, & Shea, 2012). Affective polarization has also been linked to acceptance of political violence (Warner & Villamil, 2017), a troubling attitude that signifies decay in our democratic culture and could presage actual political violence (Kalmoe, 2014).

Though political agreement is the most likely structure of attitudes in families, some do disagree (Oliphant, 2018). In our survey data, almost a quarter of respondents cited either a parent or child as the person they would be most likely to disagree with about politics. This suggests that at least some family contexts could reduce affective polarization. Unfortunately, our data suggest that the only people for whom disagreeing with a parent or child was associated with warmer evaluations of the outgroup were those who were already the least polarized. In fact, our data suggests that the most polarized individuals—those for whom positive intergroup contact would be the most essential—are either completely unaffected by the cross-party contact with a member of their close family or, worse, become more polarized as a result.

Implications for Scholars and Practitioners

To summarize the above, families impart political attitudes on their children in a way that is more likely to enhance the trend toward greater political polarization than it is to ameliorate this trend. One might be tempted to search for solutions to change this reality. Perhaps strategies could be devised to encourage cross-partisan marriage or to incentivize children to challenge their parents' beliefs. We are skeptical of such solutions. Political beliefs often stem from core values and important identity categories. Parents may want their children to share their core family values. Furthermore, people may be entirely justified in considering political compatibility when entering a romantic relationship. Perhaps, however, it is possible for families that do disagree about politics to have healthier templates for this disagreement. Our data suggest that political disagreement may be a source of tension for highly polarized families, and Chen & Rohla's (2018) Thanksgiving study demonstrates that this tension is already cutting short time spent with families. The problem in polarized families may not be that there is contact with a parent or child who disagrees but rather that this contact is negative. Allport (1954) identified a variety of conditions that enhance the effectiveness of intergroup contact. Family communication scholars and practitioners should expand upon this area of research to identify healthy forms of familial disagreement that can foster empathy and understanding rather than conflict and division.

Beyond this, there is still tremendous space for research in the area of family communication about politics. Very few studies have considered the role of family communication patterns in the transfer of political identities (though see Ledbetter, 2015; Shulman & DeAndrea, 2014). With recent advances in the theoretical conceptualization of the socio-orientation (Horstman et al., 2018), there is even more space to explore how the style of family communication influences the formation of political attitudes and values. Furthermore, little is known about how disagreement in the family affects the relationships between those who disagree. Families who disagree about religion must communicate about these disagreements in accommodative ways or they risk undermining the familial bond (Colaner, Soliz, & Nelson, 2014). Political disagreement may pose similar threats to relational satisfaction within families.

Conclusion

As we hope is clear, there is tremendous space for further research both on the causes and consequences of political heterogeneity within the family context. There is also a need for more work on political disagreement in families to help practitioners navigate these flashpoints for disagreement. When there is disagreement—particularly with regard to extended family members with whom disagreement is more common and avoidance is often relatively simple—maintaining healthy relationships may require research about how to productively manage these disagreements. As illustrated by Ruth Dorancy's story from the introduction (Tavernise & Seelye, 2016), the stakes of political disagreement rise as identities coalesce around partisanship. A family member's decision to support one candidate over another can feel like a betrayal or rejection of someone's core identity. Strategies that help families transcend these difficult conflicts are becoming more important even as nuclear families are becoming more politically homogenous.

Though families are a potential site of political disagreement, attitude congruence is the most likely outcome in the nuclear family. Parents transmit political orientations to children through active communication. When parents share the same political alignment, they send a consistent stream of partisan cues to their children that their children are likely to adopt later in life. Furthermore, people are increasingly using political agreement as a decision-making criterion when selecting marital partners. This increases the rate of spousal correspondence; it also increases the probability that children will adopt their parents' political identities. However, political disagreement can be present in families, particularly among extended family members. This disagreement has the potential to reduce polarization but does not seem to affect those who are already highly polarized. Instead, political disagreement appears to make families avoid discussing politics or, that failing, avoid one another altogether. It is our hope that future research can provide a framework to help families navigate these differences in ways that both preserve relationships and help promote more normatively desirable political attitudes and behaviors.

References

Abramowitz, A. (2010). *The disappearing center: Engaged citizens, polarization, and American democracy*. New Haven, CN: Yale University Press.

Achen, C. H., & Bartles, L. M. (2016). *Democracy for realists: Why elections do not produce responsive government*. Princeton, NJ: Princeton University Press.

Alford, J. R., Hatemi, P. K., Hibbing, J. R., Martin, N. G., & Eaves, L. J. (2011). The politics of mate choice. *The Journal of Politics*, *73*, 362–379. doi:10.1017/s0022381611000016

Allport, G. W. (1954). *The nature of prejudice*. Cambridge, MA: Perseus Books.

Chen, M. K., & Rohla, R. (2018). The effects of partisanship and political advertising on close family ties. *Science*, *360*, 1020–1024. doi:10.1126/science.aaq1433

Cho, J., & Ha, Y. (2012). On the communicative underpinnings of campaign effects: Presidential debates, citizen communication, and polarization in evaluations of candidates. *Political Communication*, *29*, 184–204. doi:10.1080/10584609.2012.671233

Colaner, C. W., Soliz, J., & Nelson, L. R. (2014). Communicatively managing religious identity difference in parent-child relationships: The role of accommodative and non-accommodative communication. *Journal of Family Communication*, *14*, 310–327. doi:10.1080/15267431.2014.945700

Converse, P. (1964, 2004). The nature of belief systems in mass publics. *Critical Review, 18*, 1–74. doi:10.1080/08913810608443650

Fiorina, M., Abrams, S., & Pope, J. (2011). *Culture war: The myth of a polarized America.* Boston, MA: Longman.

Garrett, K. R., Dvir Gvirsman, S., Johnson, B. K., Tsfati, Y., Neo, R., & Dal, A. (2014). Implications of pro- and counterattitudinal information exposure for affective polarization. *Human Communication Research, 40*, 309–332. doi:10.1111/hcre.12028

Greene, S. (1999). Understanding party identification: A social identity approach. *Political Psychology, 20*, 393–403. doi:10.1111/0162-895X.00150

Han, J., & Federico, C. M. (2017). Conflict-framed news, self-categorization, and partisan polarization. *Mass Communication and Society, 20*, 455–480. doi:10.1080/15205436.2017.1292530

Horstman, H. K., Schrodt, P., Warner, B., Koerner, A., Maliski, R., Hays, A., & Colaner, C. W. (2018). Expanding the conceptual and empirical boundaries of family communication patterns: The development and validation of an Expanded Conformity Orientation Scale. *Communication Monographs, 85*, 157–180. doi:10.1080/03637751.2018.1428354

Huber, G. A., & Malhotra, N. (2017). Political homophily in social relationships: Evidence from online dating behavior. *The Journal of Politics, 79*, 269–283. doi:10.1086/687533

Iyengar, S., Konitzer, T., & Tedin, K. (2018). The home as a political fortress: Family agreement in an era of polarization. *The Journal of Politics, 80*, 1326–1338. doi:10.1086/698929

Iyengar, S., Sood, G., & Lelkes, Y. (2012). Affect, not ideology: A social identity perspective on polarization. *Public Opinion Quarterly, 76*, 405–431. doi:10.1093/poq/nfs038

Iyengar, S., & Westwood, S. J. (2014). Fear and loathing across party lines: New evidence on group polarization. *American Journal of Political Science, 59*, 690–707.

Jamieson, K. H., & Cappella, J. N. (2008). *Echo Chamber: Rush Limbaugh and the conservative media establishment.* New York: Oxford University Press.

Jennings, M. K. (2009). Political socialization. In R. J. Dalton & H. Klingemann (Eds.), *Oxford handbook of political psychology* (pp. 29–44). Oxford, UK: Oxford University Press.

Jennings, M. K., & Niemi, R. G. (1974). *Political character of adolescence: The influence of families and schools.* Princeton, NJ: Princeton University Press.

Jennings, M. K., Stoker, L., & Bowers, J. (2009). Politics across generations: Family transmission reexamined. *The Journal of Politics, 71*, 782–799. doi:10.1017/S0022381609090719

Kalmoe, N. (2014). Fueling the fire: Violent metaphors, trait aggression, and support for political violence. *Political Communication, 31*, 545–563. doi:10.1080/10584609.2013.852642

Kinder, D. R., & Kalmoe, N. P. (2017). *Neither liberal nor conservative: Ideological innocence in the American public.* Chicago, IL: The University of Chicago Press.

Ledbetter, A. M. (2015). Political philosophy as a (partial) mediator of the association between family communication patterns and perception of candidate credibility in the 2012 U.S. presidential election. *Journal of Family Communication, 15,* 214–231. doi :10.1080/15267431.2015.1043432

Levendusky, M. (2013). *How partisan media polarize America.* Chicago, IL: The University of Chicago Press.

Levendusky, M. (2018). Americans, not partisans: Can priming American national identity reduce affective polarization? *Journal of Politics, 80,* 59–70. doi:10.1086/693987

Lodge, M. & Taber, C. S. (2013). The rationalizing voter. New York, NY: Cambridge.

Mason, L. (2018). *Uncivil agreement: How politics became our identity.* Chicago, IL: University of Chicago Press.

McDevitt, M. (2005). The partisan child: Developmental provocation as a model of political socialization. *International Journal of Public Opinion Research, 18,* 67–88. doi:10.1093/ijpor/edh079

McDevitt, M., & Chaffee, S. (2002). From top-down to trickle-up influence: Revisiting assumptions about the family in political socialization. *Political Communication, 19,* 281–301. doi:10.1080/01957470290055501

Niemi, R. G., Danforth Ross, R., & Alexander, J. (1978). The similarity of political values of parents and college-age youths. *Public Opinion Quarterly, 42,* 503–520. doi:10.1086/268476

Oliphant, J. B. (2018, Novemeber 20). Most say their family is ok with discussing politics—but it helps if they family agrees. *Pew Research Center.* Accessed online: pewresearch.org/fact-tank/2018/11/20/most-say-their-family-is-ok-with-discussing-politics-but-it-helps-if-the-family-agrees/

Rico, G., & Jennings, M. K. (2016). The formation of the left-right identification: Pathways and correlations of parental influence. *Political Psychology, 37,* 237–252. doi:10.1111/pops.12243

Settle, J. E. (2018). *Frenemies: How social media polarizes America.* Cambridge, UK: Cambridge University Press.

Shah, D. V., McLeod, J. M., & Lee, N. J. (2009). Communication competence as a foundation for civic competence: Processes of socialization into citizenship. *Political Communication, 26,* 102–117. doi:10.1080/10584600802710384

Soliz, J., & Harwood, J. (2006). Shared family identity, age salience, and intergroup contact: Investigation of the grandparent–grandchild relationship. *Communication Monographs, 73,* 87–107. doi:10.1080/03637750500534388

Soliz, J., & Rittenour, C. E. (2012). Family as an intergroup area. In H. Giles (Ed.), *The handbook of intergroup communication* (pp. 331–334). New York: Routledge.

Shulman, H. C., & DeAndrea, D. C. (2014). Predicting success: Revisiting assumptions about family political socialization. *Communication Monographs, 81*, 386–406.

Stroud, N. J. (2010). Polarization and partisan selective exposure. *Journal of Communication, 60*, 556–576. doi:10.1111/j.1460-2466.2010.01497.x

Stroud, N. J. (2011). *Niche news: The politics of news choice.* New York: Oxford University.

Tavernise, S., & Seelye, K. Q. (2016, November 15). Political divide splits relationships—And Thanksgiving, too. *New York Times.* Accessed online: nytimes.com/2016/11/16/us/ political-divide-splits-relationships-and-thanksgiving-too.html

Warner, B. R. (2010). Segmenting the electorate: The effects of exposure to political extremism online. *Communication Studies, 61*, 430–444. doi:10.1080/10510974.2010.497069

Warner, B. R. (2018). Modeling partisan media effects in the 2014 U.S. midterm elections. *Journalism & Mass Communication Quarterly, 95*, 647–699. doi:10.1177/1077699017712991

Warner, B. R., & Colaner, C. W. (2016). Talking politics at the dinner table: The effects of family communication styles on young citizens' normative political attitudes. In M. S. McKinney, E. Thorson, & D. Shah (Eds.), *Political Socialization of Young Citizens* (pp. 195–211). New York: Peter Lang.

Warner, B. R., Horstman, H., & Kearney, C. C. (2019, May). Testing a narrative writing intervention to reduce affective political polarization, paper presented to the International Communication Association Annual Conference, Washington, DC.

Warner, B. R., & McKinney, M. S. (2013). To unite and divide: The polarizing effect of presidential debates. *Communication Studies, 64*, 508–527. doi:10.1080/10510974.2013.832341

Warner, B. R., McKinney, M. S., Bramlett, J., Jennings, F. J., & Funk, M. (2019). Reconsidering partisanship as a constraint on the persuasive effects of debates. *Communication Monographs, 87*. doi:10.1080/03637751.2019.1641731

Warner, B. R., & Neville-Shepard, R. (2014). Echoes of a conspiracy: Birthers, Truthers, and the cultivation of extremism. *Communication Quarterly, 62*, 1–17. doi:10.1080/01463373.2013.822407

Warner, B. R., & Villamil, A. (2017). A test of imagined contact as a means to improve cross-partisan feelings and reduce attribution of malevolence and acceptance of political violence. *Communication Monographs, 84*, 447–465. doi:10.1080/03637751.2017.1336779

Wojcieszak, M. E., Azrout, R., & de Vreese, C. (2017). Waving the red cloth: Media coverage of contentious issues triggers polarization. *Public Opinion Quarterly, 82*, 87–109. doi:10.1093/poq/nfx040

Wojcieszak, M. E., & Garrett, R. K. (2018). Social identity, selective exposure, and affective polarization: How priming national identity shapes attitudes toward immigrants via news selection. *Human Communication Research, 13*, 5–27. doi:10.1093/hcr/hqx010

Wojcieszak, M. E., & Warner, B. R. (2019, May). Can intergroup contact reduce affective polarization among Democrats and Republicans? Systematic test of four different forms of intergroup contact, paper presented to the International Communication Association Annual Conference, Washington, DC.

Wolf, M. R., Strachan, J. C., & Shea, D. M. (2012). Incivility and standing firm: A second layer of partisan division. *PS: Political Science & Politics, 45*, 428–434. doi:10.1017/S1049096512000509

5. *Queering Family Communication*

Jimmie Manning

Queer families, simply put, are families where one more of the family members are queer *or* where something about the structure/nature/being/doing of the family is inherently queer. As bloggers K&W explain,

> A queer family could certainly be a family with or without kids. Queer families can have two moms or two dads. They can have one mom and one dad. They have one parent. They can have more than two parents. They can also include one or more people who identify as trans* or genderqueer. They can include bisexual, omnisexual, pansexual, polysexual, asexual, or queer people. Queer families have kids by marriage, kids from previous relationships and/or pregnancies. They can add kids through foster care, adoption, surrogacy, sperm donors (both on and off the books), and good old-fashioned P-I-V intercourse. They can include beloved furbabies (our pet children). They can include supportive queer family relationships that came about out of kinship or necessity in place of or in addition to our legal/bio families. (2013, 6)

It is difficult to ascertain how many queer families exist, especially because in many parts of the world there are severe social and legal penalties for expressing queer identity and/or engaging in acts that are deemed queer. Although queer marriage is now legal in over 30 countries (Masci, Sciupac, & Lipka, 2019), homosexuality is illegal in many nation-states around the world, with 13 United Nations member states still enforcing the death penalty for queer sexual acts (Simmons, 2017). As these facts suggest, rights and acceptance for queer families vary world-wide.

Because queer families are often stigmatized, many queer family communication studies have examined topics related to difficulties, struggles, and hardships. Still, it is important to consider that for many families "queer" is but one marker that might be placed upon them; that not all queer people are victims; and that, in many ways, queer families have some advantages others do not. Differences between queer and non-queer families, while important, should not be overemphasized, as they usually only involve family structure and/or awareness of queer identities and issues (Tasker, 2005). Queer and heterosexual families share more similarities than differences.

With that backdrop set, this essay offers a review of queer family communication scholarship. Although the catch-all term *queer* is used to characterize this work, it is important to note that most studies do not study queer families broadly; but, instead, examine particular types of queer families (e.g., lesbian mothers, queer children, etc.). This review primarily focuses on interpersonal and relational communication literatures. Other studies have examined public discourses about family, such as social movements or media representations, but due to space limitations that work cannot be covered here. Following the literature review, future research considerations are offered, with a particular focus on the value of queer-theoretical approaches. Throughout the essay, practical applications of queer family communication studies are also considered.

Reviewing Queer Family Communication Research

As Suter (2015) observed, studies of queer family communication mostly germinated in the late 2000s and came into full focus in the 2010s. That observation is reflected in this review, where the research can be broken into four primary areas: queer partnerships, queer parenting, coming out, and trans families.

Queer Partnerships

The modern roots of queer family communication can be traced back to two primary research lines: Pamela J. Lannutti's work regarding same-sex partnerships and Elizabeth A. Suter and colleagues' work about symbolic rituals for queer partners. Lannutti's earlier work, much of which was completed in the United States before same-sex/same-gender marriage was legalized, does not explicitly label queer partnerships as family. It does, however, raise many important questions that are salient to understanding queer families. As one example, her examinations of same-sex marriage indicate that couples believed marriage would allow them to feel as if their relationships were "more real" (Lannutti, 2007, p. 135) and that, even if they decided not to get married, same-sex relationships in general would be considered more legitimate (Lannutti, 2014).

Around the same time, Suter's work explored more of the symbolic and meaning-making aspects of queer partnerships, often establishing them as families with rituals and relational meaning systems. For example, in one study she and her colleagues learned that 85% of queer couples indicated that rings served as a nonverbal way to communicate their commitment, with 90% reporting the same about their home (Suter & Daas, 2007). The work also established that many unmarried queer couples still celebrated anniversaries, with less of a reliance on wedding dates and more of a focus on important events or moments that are considered the symbolic beginning of their partnered relationship (Suter, Daas, & Bergen, 2008).

As same-sex/same-gender marriage rights gained traction in the U.S., such research evolved to include a deeper focus on family aspects of such relationships. Suter's work began to take on issues related to queer parenting; whereas Lannutti's work focused on queer partner issues, often examining how queer partners in the U.S. navigated relationships in a post-queer marriage world. For example, in one study she examined how married queer people dealt with privacy, examining issues such as wanting to maintain privacy during an adoption process or how ready families were to hear about the queer aspects of couple relationships (Lannutti, 2013).

More recently, studies of queer marriage have expanded beyond the U.S. For example, Bie and Tang (2016) explain the challenges gay men face when it comes to marriage and family. As they indicate, Chinese men are under more scrutiny and pressure to marry and create a family than men in other cultures. Such pressure leads to their negotiating with lesbian women to create *xinghun*, a marriage where "a gay man marries a lesbian so that they will appear to be a normal married couple" (Bie & Tang, 2016, p. 353). In this marriage arrangement, each member of the couple clearly understands that their obligation is to attend family events and keep up the appearance of marriage for the sake of the family. Because China is becoming more friendly toward same-sex relationships, this pressure continues to lessen, albeit slowly, with more queer individuals avoiding marriage altogether (Bie & Tang, 2016).

Queer Parenting

Early queer family communication studies also focused on queer parents, especially studies of lesbian motherhood. The results of these studies established a deep sense how family was constituted via communication. For example, one study found that sharing a last name, similar to how it works in heteronormative families, increases a sense of family belonging (Suter, Daas, & Bergen, 2008). That same study also established how everyday family activities, from taking a walk to attending church together, formed family rituals that created a sense of familial wholeness (Suter et al., 2008). In another study, with especially practical implications, participants indicated that a child who has the same last name as a parent's can help to prevent confusion about the parent-child relationship in emergencies (Bergen, Suter, & Dass, 2006). Additionally, documents indicating power of attorney, explicit wills, formalized parental agreements, and other paper trails have the potential to both create a sense of family and protect parental rights (Bergen et al., 2006).

Other research about meaning-making in queer-parent families has examined how parents explain aspects of their family queerness to their children. In one such study, Suter and colleagues interviewed co-mothers about their family-of-origin stories. That study revealed that many family-of-origin stories involved "normalizing" aspects of establishing family in two-mother households (Suter, Koenig Kellas, Webb, & Allen, 2016, p. 310). Specifically, participants talked about the use of normalizing conversations to explain topics such as sperm donors and invitro fertilization; as well as taking normalizing actions such as exposing their children to other two-mom families so they could see such a family structure as normal (Suter et al., 2016).

Research often indicates that the need to explain queer family is also the result of messages family members, especially children, receive from outsiders. For example, Breshears (2010) found that lesbian mothers reported their children received negative messages from schoolmates regarding having two moms. In another study, lesbian mothers reported that the parents of other children would not allow their kids to play together; and that others also questioned how a family could function or exist without a male role model (Koenig Kellas & Suter, 2012). In response, the mothers talked with their children, reaffirming family status and emphasizing love's role in creating family.

Sometimes parents also have to talk to children about messages received from *within* the larger family unit that challenge legitimacy. Research shows other family members, particularly grandparents, sometimes expressed their disapproval of same-sex relationships (Breshears, 2010). In response, mothers defended their family status and stressed that although their families were different from most, they were not lesser or wrong. Interestingly, in a study of gay fathers Baker (2019) discovered that competing discourses about traditional and non-traditional families could actually strengthen notions that families can be queer, similar to a finding about lesbian motherhood from Suter and colleagues (2015).

Finally, it is important to consider that the children of queer parents have to come out as queer family members. Children often do so in an affirming environment, when the disclosure is somewhat relevant, and when the risk-reward ratio is favorable (Breshears & DiVerniero, 2015). In talking about these experiences, children tended to marginalize negative discourses and favor the positive. Specifically, children emphasized that opposing views were ignorant, many religious-oriented arguments were flawed, and others had no right to judge their family and their family's love. Children also noted that in such discussions they were open to hearing and considering the views of others and that they respected peoples' rights to have different opinions (Breshears & Braithwaite, 2014).

Coming Out in Families

In addition to studies about coming out as a queer family, other work has examined coming out as gay, lesbian, or bisexual *within* a family (Manning, 2014). Until the early 2010s, most empirical research avoided examining communicative aspects of coming out (Manning, 2015a). That is, researchers were mostly focusing on psychological aspects of coming out, such as self-acceptance or discovery of same-sex/same-gender attraction (Manning, 2015c). Manning (2016) argued that such an approach was insufficient, as often the communicative aspects of coming out were assumed in psychological and sociological work, especially in terms of the context and structures of such interactions. His constitutive model of coming out (Manning, 2016; see Figure 5.1) foregrounds communicative practices in an interplay of cognitive/intrapersonal, relational/interpersonal, and cultural levels of meaning-making.

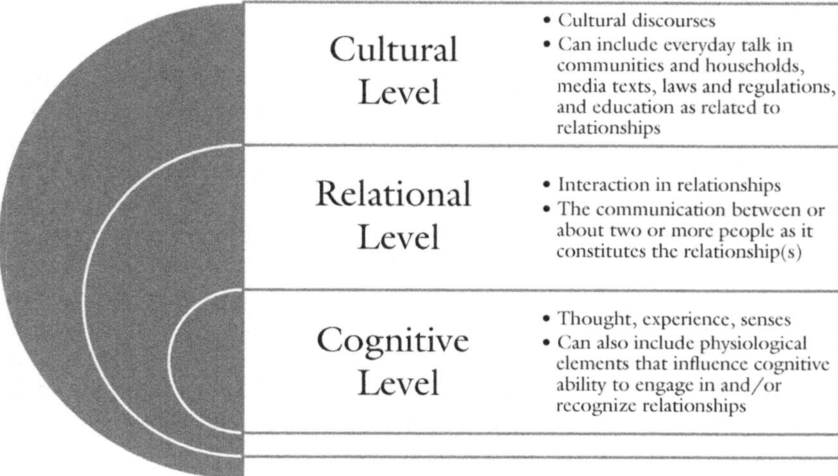

Cultural Level
• Cultural discourses
• Can include everyday talk in communities and households, media texts, laws and regulations, and education as related to relationships
Relational Level
• Interaction in relationships
• The communication between or about two or more people as it constitutes the relationship(s)
Cognitive Level
• Thought, experience, senses
• Can also include physiological elements that influence cognitive ability to engage in and/or recognize relationships

Figure 5.1: Constitutive Model of Coming Out (Adapted from Manning, 2016)

At the cultural level, notions of how a particular culture accepts and/or understands queerness is considered. As one example, in Adams's (2011) study of the closet, he argues that culturally-constructed rules place an unfair onus on queer people in terms of when to come out. If someone comes out too soon, then they are at risk of making the recipient feel uncomfortable; yet, if they wait too long to come out then they might be blamed for hiding their identity (Adams, 2011). Johnson (2008) offers additional cultural-level insights about coming out and families, with his primary focus being on black queerness in the Southern U.S. As he notes, when cultures and cultural groups are especially homophobic, sometimes families serve as a mechanism for coming out. Specifically, it is not uncommon for a queer family member to tell a family member who they know will likely tell others and lessen the often-awkward and consistently ongoing labor of coming out.

Offering a perspective that is not centered in Western-individualistic values, Bie and Tang (2016) note that whereas U.S. and European coming out narratives are often centered on the individual, gay men in China and Singapore often related their sexual identities to cultural expectations regarding family. They do note, however, that this strong cultural expectation of continuing the family via heterosexual marriage is what paradoxically leads to many Chinese men coming out. When they enter their 20s or 30s, they often break, as they feel they cannot take the ongoing pressure to maintain a heterosexual appearance. Their work also echoed an earlier study, this one involving participants from numerous national/cultural backgrounds that indicated people felt dishonest and deceitful by not coming out (Manning, 2015a).

In a separate study, Manning (2015b) notes several positive characteristics of coming-out conversations that can be beneficial when a family member comes out: making affirming direct relational statements; nonverbal immediacy; appropriate joking and laughter; and keeping communication channels open after the conversation (Manning, 2015b). That same study also found several negative behaviors to avoid, both for the person coming out (indirectly approaching the topic, lack of preparation, and nervous nonverbal behaviors) and for the person who was receiving the disclosure (denying the person's sexuality, talking about religion, inappropriate questions or comments, shaming statements, and aggression). In a different study examining the characteristics of coming-out conversations, DiVerniero and Breshears (2017) noted that children reported offering support and asking questions/seeking information when parents came out to them.

More recently, Li and Samp (2019) have started a new line of theoretical research that establishes communicative aspects of coming out at the cognitive level. Their theory is labeled coming-out message production (COMP) and indicates that disclosure-related goals drive coming-out disclosures. Five goal types influence an individual's coming out: concerns for the self (self-oriented), concerns about the receiver (disclosure target-oriented), relationship management (non-romantic relational and romantic relational), and resource goals (task). Their research suggests that as these disclosure goals are more salient, individuals will disclose more in pursuit of these goals. The development of this theory offers the potential for enhanced understandings of how personal needs relate to coming out in relationships.

Trans Families

A particularly understudied area of queer family communication is research about trans families. Although sexual identity and gender identity are often categorized together, research indicates that there are often notable differences between sexuality (e.g., gay, lesbian, or bisexual identity) and gender (e.g., trans identity) when it comes to social understandings (Institute, 2011). These differences certainly extend to family communication research. Historically, research about trans identities has focused on individuals and their psychological experiences, but recently research exploring the relationships trans people have with their family, friends, and significant others has expanded (Norwood, 2015). For trans people, family support can be especially crucial as they navigate deep cultural prejudice and misunderstanding about trans identity and seek to navigate specialized health care needs (Manning & Thompson, 2016). Initial research about trans families has focused less on trans people and more on how families work to understand, support, and come to terms with having a trans family member.

This work has been led by Kristen Norwood, who notes that the stress families face related to trans identity disclosures and transitions can be significant (Norwood, 2015). Part of the ability to provide support to a trans family member means accepting trans identity, and as Norwood's (2012) research indicates, a part of that is grieving the loss of identity. Specifically, family members feel a sense of ambiguous loss as they recognize that their relative—oftentimes a child—is not fully the person they understood them to be. This sense of loss is exacerbated by rigid, gendered understandings of identities. As Norwood (2013) explains,

> Transition as replacement means that family members talked of their trans-identified relative/partner as a different person because of transition. In communicating this, participants' talk was largely anchored by biological essentialism, in which sex/gender is natural, binary, and a fundamental component of personhood.

> When male and female are conceived of as opposite categories of personhood, transition from one to the other functions as a replacement of one *person* with another. In other words, someone who changes from male to female cannot be the same person, because men and women are fundamentally different. (p. 32, emphasis in original)

To be clear, Norwood is not arguing for gender essentialism, but rather points to how a family member's identity is so bound up in gender that a change in gender identity feels as if it is a change in the social self. Alternately, some family members reported that they were able to frame transition in a way that avoided such gendered confusion, both minimizing the grief they felt and allowing them to offer better support. These family members focused less on transition being a *change of the person*, and more on a change in the *outward identity of the person* (Norwood, 2013). Much more research, especially outside of the context of U.S. families, is needed in this area.

Beyond the Family: Family Communication and Society

As individual families become queerer, so, too, do all families. Queer families have undoubtedly changed ideas about what families look like, the forms and functions of family, how gender roles are enacted in families, and notions of practical aspects of family such as divisions of domestic labor. In cultures where queer families are becoming more visible, resistance to such familial changes are evident as critics decry the loss of 'traditional' family values (Foster, 2014). Yes, in examining the research about queer families, it is evident that they are more often than not re-centering heteronormative aspects of family—especially in families with children, where messages about queer families being the same as others are shared to create a sense of normalcy. Even in childfree families, heteronormative patterns persist such as the use of similar terms to note family relations (e.g., spouse, boyfriend/girlfriend, etc.; Heisterkamp, 2016) and a feeling from queer partners that they have to prove their sense of commitment in a way that positions them just as dedicated as a heterosexual couple (Foster, 2008).

Given the heteronormative assimilation of queer families, it is possible that the emergence of visibly queer families in such cultures speaks more to the fragile nature of heteronormativity and notions of "traditional family" than it does to any problem with queer families. Yet, at the same time, conservative resistance to queer families taking on heteronormative structures, roles, functions, or labels demonstrates exactly how non-assimilationist and also subversive it can be for queer families to take on these institutions that have been reserved for the heteronorm. Of course, such delineations between traditional/heteronormative and queer families cannot be simply made. Queerness informs heteronormativity just as heteronormativity informs queerness. The relationship is not linear, but rather involves twisting, murmurs, thrusts, and explosions of a wide array sexuality and gender characteristics as they morph in and out of a particular family and/or family context.

As Johnson (2001) noted when considering the lines between queer and straight,

> Still, one might wonder, what, if anything, could a poor, black, eighty-something, southern, homophobic woman teach her educated, middle-class, thirty-something, gay grandson about queer studies? Everything. Or almost everything. On the one hand, my grandmother uses "quare" to denote something or someone who is odd, irregular, or slightly off kilter—definitions in keeping with traditional understandings and uses of "queer." On the other hand, she also deploys "quare" to connote something excessive—something that might philosophically translate into an excess of discursive and epistemological meanings grounded in African American cultural rituals and lived experience. (p. 2)

Here, Johnson is pointing to the queerness/quareness that dominates not only bodies and identities, but the constitutive forces of everyday life. In that sense, families *all* certainly experience some queerness, even if it is not to the threshold of being called queer family.

To that end, those who worry about what queer families take away from society might consider instead what they offer. Research indicates that considering queer family communication offers connections to family interaction and patterns that are decidedly not queer. For example, research indicates that queer parents, similar to heterosexual single parents or a parent whose partner is disabled, might find it difficult to manage or secure work leave to care for a child. Dixon and Dougherty (2014) found that queer parents were paradoxically highlighted in the workplace as they sought to navigate policies that were written to support heteronormative families while simultaneously minimizing or ignoring the notion that queer people could have children (Dixon & Dougherty, 2014). As these findings indicate, workplace managers must develop policies that recognize family as fluid instead of fixed and that are adaptable to families, queer or otherwise, who might not fit the heteronorm.

Queering families also have many other positive attributes to offer to family structures as a whole. Queer families, especially lesbian women, are likely to maintain friendly relationships after breakup or divorce, often using the term *family* after a split even when children were not part of the relationship (Bacon, 2012). Numerous research studies show that even when one member of a married couple comes out as gay or lesbian, they might even stay together as a married family because the sense of commitment is so strong (Manning,

2008). Queer partnerships also often exhibit a strong sense of playfulness in everyday life, embracing ludic—and thus more pleasurable—qualities of relating (Heisterkamp, 2014). Studies of heterosexual families often show there is a questionable distribution of domestic labor (e.g., Riforgiate & Boren, 2015), but studies of queer families indicate a more-fair distribution (e.g., Barrett, 2015). Perhaps the most beneficial aspect of queer families that could be adopted by heteronormative families relates to partner jealousy, where research indicates queer families have less issues related to partners finding others as sexually desirable (Gabb, 2001).

Implications for Scholars and Practitioners

The research done to date about queer family communication has led to many practical considerations, many that have been highlighted throughout the chapter. Still, additional research about queer families is much needed. In the final section of this essay, suggestions for expanding queer family communication are offered. Both the theoretical and more practical aspects of such research are also explored.

Embracing Queer Theory in Family Communication Studies

First, given that gender and sexuality are inherent parts of all family communication, it is essential that family communication scholars—especially those who study queer families—embrace queer theory. Using a queer-theoretical approach does not simply mean involving queer participants (Lovaas, Elia, & Yep, 2006). Rather, it involves direct challenges to notions of heteronormativity that are often embedded in family communication research (Chevrette, 2013). In just about any culture, heterosexuality is both assumed until otherwise proven and compulsory in the sense that those who do not live up to heteronormative standards are subject to social resistance including discrimination and violence (Rich, 1980). Queer theory serves as a body of theories to critique, diminish, and de-stabilize heterosexuality—not via removing acts or performances that would be considered heterosexual, but instead seeking to remove the notion that particular sexualities and genders are read as being normal, abnormal, preferred, or pathological (Yep, 2003).

As this essay has demonstrated, so many aspects of queerness are related to family; and, indeed, many of the expectations for families are themselves constituted by heteronormative rules and assumptions. Yet it is evident that social scientific studies of families—or social scientific studies in general—have rarely involved the use of queer theory. Moore and Manning (2019) have noted this erasure, pointing to how reviews of family communication, including overviews of critical family communication or sexuality in families, have ignored both queer theory and the studies of families that use it. As Chevrette (2013) argues, incorporating queer theory will unpack heteronormative assumptions, especially as they relate to dyadic models of communication; challenge public/private bifurcations of families; complicate ideas of identity; and, potentially, emphasize intersectionality.

Importantly, queer theory is not limited to application to studies of queer families or individuals (Manning, 2015b). As one notable example, Manning (2015b) used queer theory in a qualitative study of purity pledge families. Specifically, he pointed out both how pledge families articulated what they saw as the abnormal and perverted nature of modern heterosexuality, thus creating pure (their) and impure (others') heterosexualities. Further, he pointed to how, paradoxically, the wearing of purity rings queered both the daughters and the families themselves, as their sexuality was marked as different from mainstream heterosexuality. This study not only pointed out the illusion of a unified heterosexuality, but examined how the pursuit of a pure heterosexuality in and of itself could be considered queer even if the families who were being interviewed would reject the notion that they had a queer identity.

In addition to considering queerness across all sexualities, family communication studies must also consider the complexities of how queerness intersects with other aspects of identity including race, ability, and/or nationality. To that end, intersectionality—a theoretical framework that calls for researchers to consider how multiple social identities and social locations overlap and/or conflict in and across specific contexts—is needed in family communication studies (Few-Demo, Moore, & Abdi, 2017), especially to understand how queerness intersects with other marginalized identities. Although embracing intersectionality offers the rich opportunity to consider how systems of privilege and oppression operate (Crenshaw, 1990), it also allows for rich, complex, and fully-realized theory building that evades the Whiteness that often dominates interpersonal and family communication studies (Moore & Manning, 2019). Those seeking to learn more about intersectionality in family communication studies should read Few-Demo et al.'s (2017) overview; and those seeking a review of queer methods and methodologies can consult Manning's (2017) review.

Expanding Methodological Approaches

This review of queer family communication studies also makes it evident that queer family communication studies is dominated by interpretive qualitative interview studies that primarily rely on one participant to serve as an informant of family life. Although such studies are valuable, embracing a richer methodological palette will expand understandings of queer family communication. Given past critiques regarding relying on one or two family members to try and understand an entire family, the increased use of dyadic and/or multiadic interviewing (Manning & Kunkel, 2015) could be beneficial. Such approaches will allow the different viewpoints of family members to be shared as well as offer a sense of how perspectives differ across a singular family unit. Additionally, it appears queer family communication studies is one of the rare areas of interpersonal or family communication studies where it can be argued that more quantitative research is needed. For an excellent example of how quantitative work can benefit queer family communication understandings, see Soliz, Ribarsky, Harrigan, and Tye-Williams's (2010) study where structural equation modeling is used to create a complex examination of how a queer family member is both an ingroup member (as a family member) and an outgroup member (as queer) and how that relates to family communication.

Finally, those designing studies should also consider heteronormative assumptions as they relate to theory. What would happen if classic interpersonal or family communication theories were reworked to include queer bodies and identities? In a study that did just that (Manning, 2019), social penetration theory (Altman & Taylor, 1973) was used in an empirical examination of how sexuality functions as information (e.g., Is it surface-level, peripheral-level, or intermediate-level?). In addition to contradicting the notion that sexuality was always private (e.g., some queer people reported that their bodies and actions would make sexuality always already surface-level information), the study also established that when a person came out as lesbian, gay, or bisexual, it belied the onion metaphor of social penetration theory in that family members responded that they felt as if they were re-learning who their relative was after the disclosure of queer identity (Manning, 2019). Simply put, social penetration theory functions differently for queer people and those relating with them. Future studies should examine other interpersonal and/or family communication theories in a similar fashion.

Practical Implications for Queer Families

Finally, despite many of the positive aspects of queer families articulated in the research reviewed in this essay, it is also apparent that more research that will lead to practical findings that can help queer families—especially those in communities, cultures, and nations where queer intolerance, discrimination, and/or violence persist—navigate their social worlds in safe, comfortable, and beneficial ways. As the review in this essay illustrates, queerness—whether it be expression of identity, acts marked as queer, or even queer marriage—might be rejected by individuals, families, communities, or governments, and recognizing the context of such interaction is important. To that end, research should especially consider those families who have the potential to be most injured by a lack of understanding about queerness.

Conclusion

In 1988, in one of the first scholarly works examining queer families, social work scholars Poverny and Finch (1988) made an impassioned call to their colleagues, noting,

> Social workers can help reformulate a more inclusive definition of the family. Toward this end, the National Association of Social Workers adopted, as part of its 1981 social policy statement on the family, the following definition: "a grouping that consists of two or more individuals who define themselves as a family and who, over time, assume those obligations to one an-other that are generally considered an essential component of family systems." This definition represents a step forward in the establishment of a new and more inclusive standard of family life. New mechanisms for population-and demographic-data collection that will accurately reflect the breadth and scope of family diversity are needed. In this way, social scientists and policy makers can better understand gay and lesbian relationships as well as other family forms and incorporate this understanding in their analyses and social policy development. (p. 120)

The optimism of their statement is crushing today, especially when considered globally. Over 30 years later, few advances have been made, in the grand scheme of things, when it comes to understanding queer families—particularly outside of nation-states where marriage equality and/or queer acceptance have been established. This essay should be able to cover many other topics related to queer families: raced and classed nuances; information seeking for queer people who want to become parents; work exploring trans worldviews; studies of bisexuality in families; or even a stronger sense of everyday roles and rituals in queer families, among many other topics. Unfortunately, such research largely does not yet exist. Although scholars have made considerable advances in exploring queer family communication—and that should be celebrated—there is much more to be done. Expanded and inclusive research that holds to the quality standards that have been established to this point will surely lead to theoretical growth and much-needed practical findings for queer families.

References

Adams, T. E. (2011). *Narrating the closet: An autoethnography of same-sex attraction.* New York, NY: Routledge.

Altman, I., & Taylor, D. A. (1973). *Social penetration: The development of interpersonal relationships.* New York, NY: Holt, Rinehart, & Winston.

Bacon, J. (2012). Until death do us part: Lesbian rhetorics of relational divorce. *Women's Studies in Communication, 35*(2), 158–177.

Baker, B. M. A. (2019). "We're just family, you know?" Exploring the discourses of family in gay parents' relational talk. *Journal of Family Communication, 19*(3), 213–227.

Barrett, C. (2015). Queering the home: The domestic labor of lesbian and gay couples in contemporary England. *Home Cultures, 12*(2), 193–211.

Bergen, K. M., Suter, E. A., & Daas, K. L. (2006). " About as solid as a fish net": Symbolic construction of a legitimate parental identity for nonbiological lesbian mothers. *The Journal of Family Communication, 6*(3), 201–220.

Bie, B., & Tang, L. (2016). Chinese gay men's coming out narratives: Connecting social relationship to co-cultural theory. *Journal of International and Intercultural Communication, 9*(4), 351–367.

Breshears, D. (2010). Coming out with our children: Turning points facilitating lesbian parent discourse with their children about family identity. *Communication Reports, 23*(2), 79–90.

Breshears, D., & Braithwaite, D. O. (2014). Discursive struggles animating individuals' talk about their parents' coming out as lesbian or gay. *Journal of Family Communication, 14*(3), 189–207.

Breshears, D., & DiVerniero, R. (2015). Communication privacy management among adult children with lesbian and gay parents. *Western Journal of Communication, 79*(5), 573–590.

Chevrette, R. (2013). Outing heteronormativity in interpersonal and family communication: Feminist applications of queer theory "beyond the sexy streets". *Communication Theory, 23*(2), 170–190.

Crenshaw, K. (1990). Mapping the margins: Intersectionality, identity politics, and violence against women of color. *Stanford Law Review, 43*, 1241.

DiVerniero, R., & Breshears, D. (2017). Verbal and emotional responses among children of lesbian and gay parents' coming out. *Qualitative Research Reports in Communication, 18*(1), 45–53.

Dixon, J., & Dougherty, D. S. (2014). A language convergence/meaning divergence analysis exploring how LGBTQ and single employees manage traditional family expectations in the workplace. *Journal of Applied Communication Research, 42*(1), 1–19.

Few-Demo, A. L., Moore, J., & Abdi, S. (2017). Intersectionality: (Re)considering family communication from within the margins. In D. O. Braithwaite, E. A. Suter, & K. Floyd (Eds.), *Engaging theories in family communication: Multiple perspectives* (2nd ed.; pp. 175–186). New York, NY: Routledge.

Foster, E. (2008). Commitment, communication, and contending with heteronormativity: An invitation to greater reflexivity in interpersonal research. *Southern Communication Journal, 73*(1), 84–101.

Foster, E. (2014). Communicating beyond the discipline: Autoethnography and the "N of 1." *Communication Studies, 65*(4), 446–450.

Gabb, J. (2001). Querying the discourses of love: An analysis of contemporary patterns of love and the stratification of intimacy within lesbian families. *European Journal of Women's Studies, 8*(3), 313–328.

Heisterkamp, B. L. (2014). Relationships in action: Categorization in gay and lesbian couples' talk. *International Journal of Linguistics, 2*(4), 9–23.

Heisterkamp, B. L. (2016). Challenging heteronormativity: Recontextualizing references to members of gay male and lesbian couples. *Journal of Language and Sexuality, 5*(1), 37–60.

Institute of Medicine. (2011). *The health of lesbian, gay, bisexual, and transgender people: Building a foundation for better understanding.* Washington, DC: National Academies.

Johnson, E. P. (2001). " Quare" studies, or (almost) everything I know about queer studies I learned from my grandmother. *Text and Performance Quarterly, 21*(1), 1–25.

Johnson, E. P. (2008). *Sweet tea: Black gay men of the South.* Chapel Hill, NC: University of North Carolina.

K&W. (2013). What is a queer family? *Queer Family Matters.* Retrieved from https://queerfamilymatters.com/2013/11/03/what-is-a-queer-family/

Koenig Kellas, J., & Suter, E. A. (2012). Accounting for lesbian-headed families: Lesbian mothers' responses to discursive challenges. *Communication Monographs, 79*(4), 475–498.

Lannutti, P. J. (2007). The influence of same-sex marriage on the understanding of same-sex relationships. *Journal of Homosexuality, 53*(3), 135–151.

Lannutti, P. J. (2013). Same-sex marriage and privacy management: Examining couples' communication with family members. *Journal of Family Communication, 13*(1), 60–75.

Lannutti, P. J. (2014). Families centered upon a same-sex relationship: Identity construction and maintenance in the context of legally recognized same-sex marriage. In L. A. Baxter (Ed.), *Remaking "family" communicatively* (pp. 51–68). New York, NY: Peter Lang.

Li, Y., & Samp, J. A. (2019). Predictors and outcomes of initial coming out messages: testing the theory of coming out message production. *Journal of Applied Communication Research, 47*(1), 69–89.

Lovaas, K. E., Elia, J. P., & Yep, G. A. (2006). Shifting ground (s) surveying the contested terrain of LGBT studies and queer theory. *Journal of Homosexuality, 52*(1–2), 1–18.

Manning, J. (2008). Gay/straight mixed-orientation marriages. In J. C. Hawley (Ed.), *LGBTQ America today* (pp. 726–728). New York: Greenwood.

Manning, J. (2014). Coming out conversations and gay/bisexual men's sexual health: A constitutive model study. In V. L. Harvey & T. H. Housel (Eds.), *Health care disparities and the LGBT population* (pp. 27–54). Lanham, MD: Lexington Books.

Manning, J. (2015a). Communicating sexual identities: A typology of coming out. *Sexuality & Culture, 19*(1), 122–138.

Manning, J. (2015b). Paradoxes of (im)purity: Affirming heteronormativity and queering heterosexuality in family discourses of purity pledges. *Women's Studies in Communication, 38*(1), 99–117.

Manning, J. (2015c). Positive and negative communicative behaviors in coming-out conversations. *Journal of Homosexuality, 62*(1), 67–97.

Manning, J. (2016). A constitutive model of coming out. In J. Manning & C. Noland (Eds.), *Contemporary studies of sexuality & communication: Theoretical and applied perspectives* (pp. 93–108). Dubuque, IA: Kendall Hunt.

Manning, J. (2017). Queer methods. In M. Allen (Ed.), *The SAGE encyclopedia of communication research methods* (pp. 1389–1396). Thousand Oaks, CA: Sage.

Manning, J. (2019). Thinking about interpersonal relationships and social penetration theory: Is it the same for lesbian, gay, or bisexual people? In C. J. Liberman, A. S. Rancer, & T. A. Avtgis (Eds.), *Casing communication theory* (pp. 293–303). Dubuque, IA: Kendall Hunt.

Manning, J., & Kunkel, A. (2015). Qualitative approaches to dyadic analyses in family communication research: An invited essay. *Journal of Family Communication, 15*, 185–192.

Manning, J., & Thompson, C. M. (2016). Transgender healthcare. In A. Goldberg (Ed.), *The SAGE encyclopedia of LGBTQ studies* (pp. 1221–1222). Thousand Oaks, CA: Sage.

Masci, D., Sciupac, E., & Lipka, M. (2019, May 17). Same-sex marriage around the world. *Pew Research Center Religion and Public Life.* Retrieved from https://www.pewforum.org/fact-sheet/gay-marriage-around-the-world/

Moore, J., & Manning, J. (2019). What counts as critical interpersonal and family communication research? A review of an emerging field of inquiry. *Annals of the International Communication Association, 43*(1), 40–57.

Norwood, K. (2012). Transitioning meanings? Family members' communicative struggles surrounding transgender identity. *Journal of Family Communication, 12*(1), 75–92.

Norwood, K. (2013). Grieving gender: Trans-identities, transition, and ambiguous loss. *Communication Monographs, 80*(1), 24–45.

Norwood, K. (2015). Communication in families with a transgender member. In C. R. Berger & M. E. Roloff (Eds.), *The international encyclopedia of interpersonal communication.* Retrieved from https://www.researchgate.net/publication/314701919_Communication_in_Families_with_a_Transgender_Member

Poverny, L. M., & Finch, W. A. (1988). Gay and lesbian domestic partnerships: Expanding the definition of family. *Social Casework: The Journal of Contemporary Social Work, 69*, 116–120.

Rich, A. (1980). Compulsory heterosexuality and lesbian existence. *Signs: Journal of Women in Culture and Society*, *5*(4), 631–660.

Riforgiate, S. E., & Boren, J. P. (2015). "I just can't clean the bathroom as well as you can!": Communicating domestic labor task equity-resistance and equity-restoring strategies among married individuals. *Journal of Family Communication*, *15*(4), 309–329.

Simmons, A. M. (2017). Seven striking statistics on the status of gay rights and homophobia across the globe. *Los Angeles Times*. Retrieved from https://www.latimes.com/world/la-fg-global-gays-rights-report-20170515-htmlstory.html

Soliz, J., Ribarsky, E., Harrigan, M. M., & Tye-Williams, S. (2010). Perceptions of communication with gay and lesbian family members: Predictors of relational satisfaction and implications for outgroup attitudes. *Communication Quarterly*, *58*(1), 77–95.

Suter, E. A. (2015). Communication in lesbian and gay families. In L. H. Turner & R. West (Eds.), *The SAGE handbook of family communication* (pp. 235–247). Thousand Oaks, CA: Sage.

Suter, E. A., & Daas, K. L. (2007). Negotiating heteronormativity dialectically: Lesbian couples' display of symbols in culture. *Western Journal of Communication*, *71*(3), 177–195.

Suter, E. A., Daas, K. L., & Bergen, K. M. (2008). Negotiating lesbian family identity via symbols and rituals. *Journal of Family Issues*, *29*(1), 26–47.

Suter, E. A., Koenig Kellas, J., Webb, S. K., & Allen, J. A. (2016). A tale of two mommies: (Re)storying family of origin narratives. *Journal of Family Communication*, *16*(4), 303–317.

Suter, E. A., Seurer, L. M., Webb, S., Grewe, B., & Koenig Kellas, J. (2015). Motherhood as contested ideological terrain: Essentialist and queer discourses of motherhood at play in female–female co-mothers' talk. *Communication Monographs*, *82*(4), 458–483.

Tasker, F. (2005). Lesbian mothers, gay fathers, and their children: A review. *Journal of Developmental & Behavioral Pediatrics*, *26*(3), 224–240.

Yep, G. A. (2003). The violence of heteronormativity in communication studies: Notes on injury, healing, and queer world-making. *Journal of Homosexuality*, *45*(2–4), 11–59.

6. *Social Class and Social Mobility: Considerations for Family Communication*

DEBBIE S. DOUGHERTY, MARCUS W. FERGUSON JR., AND NATILIE WILLIAMS

Social class is a human phenomenon that is both shaped by and uniquely shapes different cultures worldwide. Some cultures are explicitly structured by social class, whereas others, such as the United States, cling to the notion of a classless society (Dougherty, 2011). In this type of culture, social class is present in both material and discursive forms, shaping contemporary families in overt and covert ways.

Social class is a fundamentally misunderstood phenomenon among family scholars, with little systematic scholarly communication research. Yet in contemporary times, class distinctions in the United States are increasing in scope, with a widening gap between the rich and the poor (inequality.org, 2019). This gap is accompanied by political differences (Manza & Brooks, 2008), access to basic human resources such as food (Dougherty, Schraedley, Gist-Mackey, & Wickert, 2018), educational differences (Sheridan & McLaughlin, 2016), and access to work (Dougherty, Rick, & Moore, 2017). As a result, social class struggle very much shapes both the social and family landscape.

Contemporary families reflect social class differences. For example, social class is a major driver of family structure (Sawhill, 2013), with low income and less educated individuals less likely to marry and more likely to live in single parent households (Sawhill, 2013). Seven out of ten children living with a single mother live in poverty, compared to a little over three out of ten children living in other family structures (APA, n.d.; Shriberg, 2013). Social class is closely tied to race. Specifically, between 2014 and 2016, "the average household pretax income was $70,448. Pretax income varied by race and ethnicity, as the average was highest for Asians with $93,390 and lowest for Blacks or African Americans with $48,871" (U.S. Bureau of Labor Statistics, n.d.). In addition, family structure differed by race, with African American families more likely to have single mothers living with their own children than do families who identify with other races (U.S. Bureau of Labor Statistics, n.d.). The Brookings Institute reports, however, that the race-based gap in single mother households has narrowed, with an increasing number of white families also living in a single mother household (Sawhill, 2013). The gap dividing the social classes is larger than it has been historically, with the top 10% of earners averaging more than nine times as much income as the bottom 90% (inequality.org, 2019). Similar wealth and income gaps also exist at the global level, with an unprecedented growth in disparities between the wealthy and the poor.

Clearly, social class matters in terms of the shape and structure of contemporary families. However, social class is not always apparent. As Dougherty (2011) notes, social class is physically unmarked, but communicatively marked. As a result, it is possible to hide social class position by dressing differently or adorning oneself with aspirational material goods such as handbags and automobiles (Osteen, 2008). Yet despite the ability to obscure social class through the acquisition of material resources, social class differences continue to be a persistent problem. Obviously, something beyond simple resource allocation is happening here. Something bigger and more fundamental seems to be a central driver of social class.

What is social class and what is its relationship to communication and family? Most scholars define social class in simple terms. For example, there is a tendency to define social class as socio-economic status, which is primarily measured by a person's income. Other scholars define social class as cultural phenomenon in which class is best understood as habituated behavior enacted within a habitus (Bourdieu, 1984). Yet others define social class based on social structures, such as the economy. While none of these conceptualizations are exactly wrong, neither are they exactly right (Dougherty, 2011). Specifically, each conceptualization captures some of the dynamic of social class but misses the larger complexity. In a review of definitions of social class by communication scholars, Dougherty notes the extensive distinctions between the definitions. One commonality, she notes, is that scholars agree social class is embedded in social power. Beyond Dougherty's observation, it is also clear that scholars understand social class as a resource gap. People have access to different categories of resources, and those resources produce differing levels of precarity. Communication creates and sustains that gap such that social mobility is difficult to achieve. Social class then can be said to exist at the intersection of power, resource gaps, and communication. Dougherty suggests the web-of-power as a framework that can be used to better understand the relationship between communication and social class struggles. In the following section, the web-of-power is used to synthesize the literature.

Synthesis of Literature

Social class has an expansive existence in our society and its power is seemingly everywhere, interwoven into social life. The web-of-power provides one way to better understand the multi-faceted relationship between resource gaps, social class, and power. The relationship between resource gaps, social class, and power engage with all aspects of family life. The ways in which families communicate, socialize, and make decisions are entrenched in social class. Leaning on scholars such as Bourdieu (1984), Mumby (1998), and Ashcraft and Mumby (2004), Dougherty (2011), conceptualizes social class as an interwoven web-of-power which gives meaning to social class in contemporary western societies. It is important to understand that the web is not an end product, but is instead an ongoing process that is animated by social power and enacted in various ways. In addition, the web-of-power is incomplete, lacking the targeted focus on family, education, and the media. As a result, Dougherty encourages scholars to explore the ways in which the web-of-power is animated through communication, and through family communication in particular.

Dougherty (2011) explains, "When taken alone, each form of power can be resisted. When woven together, social class becomes a part of the social fabric of society" (p. 82). There are four strands in the web-of-power: Social class as a material/discursive dialectic, social class as simultaneously fluid and fixed, social class as a struggle over meaning, and social class as marked through communication.

Material/Discursive Dialectic

Although most scholars characterize social class as a resource gap separating different groups of people, this exclusively material focus is incomplete. While groups are separated by access to resources such as income and property ownership, these gaps are both created and made meaningful by the discourse that surrounds the material reality that shapes peoples' lives. For example, a blue-collar family in a rural community may be considered "normal" or well-off in a rural area. However, that same family may be deemed "lower class," in a more technology- or text work-focused area. Although, the families' resources and materials do not change, the discourse about the materials change. The primary means through which resources become meaningful is through the dialectic between materiality and discourse (Dougherty, 2011). Dialectics are unresolved tensions that result in situations caused by two contradictory or opposing forces (Putnam, 2004). In other words, social class is co-created by our simultaneous, tension-filled existence in both physical and socially constructed realities.

Social Class as Fluid and Fixed

Dougherty argues that social class is simultaneously fluid and fixed. Specifically, the people in a particular social class are generationally stable. This reality is so consistent that Conley (2008) suggests that people who are upwardly mobile should be regarded as extraordinary. Lubrano (2004) calls these people social class straddlers, noting the many unique challenges that these people face. For example, they often no longer communicatively fit into their family of origin, but also never fully communicatively socialize into their destination social class. This phenomenon occurs quite frequently with first generation college students, who function as familial first-time text workers (Wang, 2014). These individuals typically engage with a new or more privileged social class demographic than their family. With this change, there are internal and external pressures to adapt to the new social class while maintaining ties with the family of origin.

While social class is relatively fixed, it is also surprisingly fluid. How we talk about social class tends to change depending on who we are talking about. For example, most people in the United States identify themselves as middle class, regardless of their access to resources and the precarity of their finances. People do this by identifying people with fewer resources and people with greater resources. They then argue that their resources are in the middle (Dougherty, 2011; Lucas 2011a). Another strategy people use to place themselves in the middle is by defining middle class in a way that matches their own conditions. For example, Dougherty demonstrates how one family farmer in her study defined middle class as owning land. This farmer then explained how she owned land and was therefore middle class. This conclusion was made despite the reality that the land was double mortgaged and under constant threat of being repossessed. A second family farmer described middle class as having an advanced degree and speaking in a certain refined way. This farmer met those criteria and was therefore able to identify herself as middle class. A third farmer identified a middle class farmer as working a large acreage. This farmer worked a large acreage and was therefore able to define himself as middle class. Interestingly, these people were unlikely to view the other farmers as middle class because they did not meet their definition for what that status entails. These shifting definitions meant that social disparities went largely unchallenged in this farming community.

Social Class as Communicatively Marked

Social class is communicatively marked and physically unmarked (Dougherty, 2011). This strand in the web-of-power represents the reality that social class becomes apparent through discourse and is not necessarily apparent in the body. If people want to appear to belong to a particular social class, they might adorn their physical bodies with symbols from the destination social class through clothing, accessories, or other various behaviors (Dougherty, 2011). Parents may dress their children in expensive clothing, for example. Simply put, looking at one's physical body is a problematic way to understand a person's social class status or background.

It is more useful to consider the ways in which social class is communicatively marked. Differences in social class backgrounds emerge in both the mode and content of our communication (Dougherty, 2011). Various scholars note the ways social class differences correspond with communication differences (e.g. Dougherty, 2011; Lubrano, 2004; Lucas, 2011a, 2011b; Philipsen, 1976; Lareau, 2003). For example, individuals from differing social classes seem to use and value silence as a mode of communication differently (Dougherty, 2011; Lareau, 2003). Also, the flow of communication differs across social class lines, both within families (Lareau, 2003) and at work (Lubrano, 2004; Philipsen, 1976). Middle-class communication norms are privileged in America; when people fall outside those norms, they are often marked as socially awkward and communicatively incompetent. Family members are socialized into adopting communication norms, beliefs, and patterns (Odenweller & Harris, 2018). Unfortunately, families that do not teach or know the middle-class communication norms experience various negative connotations. Many times, these negative connotations correspond with stereotypes of various physically marked and marginalized social groups. People who are physically marked because of race, gender, age, or disability are also marked and marginalized in part due to their assumed lower social class status. In other words, in American culture, race serves as a "stand-in marker" of social class because racial minorities historically hold lower social statuses. In fact, unemployment-linked stigmas are based on social class, with racial assumptions closely tied to perceptions of class (Dougherty et al., 2017). As a result, race-based assumptions about social class add extra burdens to people of color who are seeking employment.

Social Class as Struggle

The final strand in the web recognizes the struggle that undergirds social class. This struggle can be recognized in both the struggle for upward mobility as well as the struggle for social equity. Because of the resource gap that divides social classes, and because that gap is widening, there is a corresponding widening of the power gap between lower and upper classes. Unions have historically provided one means through which working class people could pool their resources to create opportunities for upward mobility. However, as Cloud (2005) notes, unions cannot compete with the material resources available to the power brokers who own the organizations, especially when there is a ready supply of labor. Cloud demonstrates the ways in which one union used discourse to intercede in a labor dispute. Unfortunately, because of the resource disparity, the workers eventually lost both their bid for fair wages and their jobs. In contrast, Watt (2008) demonstrated how one organization was able to maintain public housing by avoiding class-specific language in favor of populist language such as "ordinary people." Discourse can be deployed to manage the resource gap, but its success is not guaranteed.

Not only is there a struggle for upward mobility, there is also a struggle to have the dignity of a particular social class position recognized. Because working class people do not have the same career trajectory as white collar workers, they adhere to what Lucas (2011b) calls "the working class promise," in which a person has dignity and the ability to take care of their family if they work hard enough. When that promise is broken through unemployment, working class people can feel betrayed (Dougherty et al., 2018).

Processes of Social Class

The web-of-power recognizes social class as an ongoing process rather than as an end state. As such, many of the characteristics that have been used to define social class—such as education, family structure, and labor would be better understood as outcomes of social class. To understand social class as a process, we next explore stigma and social class, financial precarity, social mobility, and the demographic gap as related to social class.

Stigma and Social Class. Goffman (1963) defines stigma as an "attribute that is deeply discrediting", reducing the stigma bearer "from a whole and usual person to a tainted, discounted one" (Goffman, 1963, p. 3). Communication scholars have conceptualized stigma into the following four components: labeling, stereotyping, separation (i.e., us vs. them), status loss, and discrimination (Link & Phelan, 2001). Power, a component not explicitly stated in the research, is foundational in the stigmatization process: "stigma is entirely dependent on social, economic, and political power—it takes power to stigmatize" (Link & Phelan, 2001, p. 375). Within the social sciences, researchers have identified three forms of stigma: moral, physical, and social (Ashforth & Kreiner, 1999). Many stigmas are associated with these three forms of stigmas. Of particular importance to this chapter are the stigmas associated with social class. Social class stigmas manifest in moral, physical, and social forms. When considering the components and forms of stigmas, it comes as no shock that there is an inextricable link between stigma and social class (Smith, 2012).

Both social class and stigma are communicatively constructed and maintained through discourse (Dougherty, 2011; Meisenbach, 2010). As discussed in this chapter, it is through our discourse that we create discursively marked, yet physically unmarked, characteristics of social class. We cannot neglect the material realities of social class, yet it is through discourse that these materials gain relevance. Discourse also serves as a driving force in the creation of stigma and the process of stigmatization. The discursive process of socializing individuals into recognizing and treating the stigma bearers accordingly is termed stigma communication (Smith, 2007). Stigma messages are shared within families; as they gain acceptance, they become stigmatized, rather than one of the individual components of stigma (Bresnahan, Zhuang, Zhu, Anderson, & Nelson, 2016). Thus, we can conclude that families play an important role in how individuals learn to stigmatize others (Goffman, 1963; Link & Phelan, 2001; Smith, 2007). In many situations, family can serve a central role in the sharing and acceptance of stigmas (Flood-Grady & Koenig Kellas, 2019). Therefore, we are socialized into social class and stigmatization.

There are many stigmatizing identities and experiences associated with social class. Research has explored the stigma associated with social class experiences with unemployment (Dougherty, Rick, & Moore, 2017), government assistance (Ranney & Kushman, 1987), and occupation/career choice (Ashforth & Kreiner, 1999; Rivera, 2015). Social classes are imbued with stigmas that diminish and harm the individuals afflicted by the stigmatizing messages. People are "classed" and subjected to the effects of stigmatization. Unfortunately, social class stigmatization can lead to the reinforcement of stigmatized identities and policies (Marston, 2008). The bearers of social class stigma(s) are faced with managing their stigmatized identities (Meisenbach, 2010). Research proposes that stigmatized individuals may deploy one of the following strategies to manage their stigmatized identity: acceptance, avoidance, evading responsibility, reducing offensiveness, denying, and ignoring/displaying (Meisenbach, 2010). It is not yet clear how people from different social classes communicatively manage stigma. Further, research has not yet indicated a way in which individuals can eliminate stigma. This gap in the literature addressing the link between stigma and social class requires further exploration.

In summary, families play a role in the communicative construction and maintenance of social class. The discursive and material implications of the linked association between stigma and social class is important for future scholarly exploration. In particular, it is important to understand how class based stigmatization can result in problematic policies and reinforced stigmatization.

Economic Precarity. Economic precarity is one of the defining differences separating people from different social classes (Gist-Mackey & Guy, 2019), with working class families constantly drawing on familial and social resources to manage that precarity. Because the larger family also tends to live in poverty, these social resources are soon exhausted, causing low income people to spiral into economic hardship (Gist-Mackey & Guy, 2019). Economic hardship and co-rumination impacts parental stress and mental health (Afifi et al., 2015). Families that experience long term economic precarity often develop material and communicative strategies that produce resilience by deemphasizing emotions during bouts of unemployment and emphasizing capacity, such as planning ahead and having alternative skill sets that allows parents to have side jobs (Lucas & Buzzanell, 2004). We also know that the resource gap can change the way in which people develop language. For example, in a study in rural Bangladesh, the authors found that those with adequate access to nutrition had a higher score for language meaning and comprehension at 18 months of age (Saha, et al., 2010). It is important to note, however, that this type of study often privileges the standard language development and meaning systems associated with the middle class, representing a form of class privilege (Johnson, Avineri, & Johnson, 2017). Regardless, it is clear that social class impacts how food security is communicated (Dougherty et al., 2018).

Social Mobility. Education is key to social mobility. However, people whose family has never attended college are unlikely to attend and complete college. One reason is that they are socialized differently within their families (Lareau, 2003). For example, lower class children are exposed to fewer words than middle class children (Johnson et al., 2017) but may make more meaningful use of silence than middle class children (Dougherty, 2011). This difference gains importance in educational settings where classed assumptions privilege middle class language usage (Johnson et al., 2017). For this reason, middle and upper class children generally are advantaged in educational settings. In addition, people from the working classes have access to less developmental resources in college (Dougherty, 2011). They are more likely to hold a part time minimum wage job. Middle and upper class students are more likely to have time and access to network with other students, increasing the likelihood of future high income employment (Stuber, 2006). For this reason, first generation college students require a different type of support than typical college students (Gist-Mackey, Wiley, & Erba, 2018). Successful first generation college students recognize themselves as pioneers in the educational system, making them both recipients and agents of social support.

Demographic Gap

The web-of-power plays out in a society that has also been divided by demographic differences such as race, age, gender, and sexuality. Not surprisingly, these differences become intertwined with social class. To illustrate this phenomenon, in this section we describe race and gender differences in social class.

Race. In the United States, race has been deliberately intertwined with systems of oppression such that for many race and social class are synonymous. Of course, slavery marked African Americans as below any recognized social class. They were treated as only partially human in need of a white caretaker. After the Civil War, other systemic processes were put in place to segregate African Americans. This segregation can be seen in education systems, work systems, religious systems, and housing systems. For example, Massey and Denton (1993) document what they call American Apartheid in which African Americans were segmented into the ghettos in larger U.S. cities. They were prevented from owning property outside of these red zones and were not eligible for home loans inside of these zones. Because of the concentration of poverty and crime in areas where African Americans were forced to live, jobs and businesses fled these areas, leaving little hope for upward mobility. These oppressive systems continue to shape the lives of African Americans.

Lareau (2003) reveals that race and social class are connected in the socialization of children. Children are able to receive social capital from parents, which impacts the children's ability to navigate social spaces. Consistent with Lareau's (2003) concept of socialization and social class in families, Burton, Bonilla-Silva, Ray, Buckelew, and Freeman (2010) express the difficulty some African-Americans families have encountered while being accused of "talking white." This challenge exposes the relationship between language, racial groups and social classes. Dougherty, Rick, and Moore (2017) discuss the imbrication of social class and race in their study exploring stigmas of unemployment. Race played a factor in the study as participants assumed the typical unemployed person was either black or Hispanic and living in the ghetto.

Both race and social class are commonly conjoined and used for comparative purposes. For example, Hart and Risley (1995) conflated race with social class in their investigation of the impact of race and social class on the vocabulary of children. Children from families that were on welfare were found to have a less expansive vocabulary compared to children from families that were higher on the social class spectrum. Of the 42 families represented in the study, 17 were African-African, while a total of 13 African American families were lower class and/or recipients of welfare. Though not all African Americans are from a low social class or socio-economic status, creating studies that focus on racial groups on one particular place of the social class spectrum illustrates the intersecting biases of the researchers who design these studies.

Additional research showcases the difference in the vocabulary maturation of children assigned to a specific social class (Coley, 2002). Similarly, when examining the role of race and social class in the parental involvement in the academic development and reading abilities of kindergartners, race is a factor. With notice to small differences in the data, Coley (2002) found that Asian and White families had more literary engagement with their children as compared to Black families. Furthermore, Hispanic and African-American families were less likely to practice literary engagement with their families, perhaps because of the strong oral traditions that often characterize these families.

Finally, as researchers weave race and the social construction of social class together for academic purposes, oppression is not consistently recognized as an explanation for the placement of groups on the social class spectrum. Additional research should be conducted to further investigate the relationship between social class and race with attention to oppression and the creation of the structure of social class and the impact on families.

Gender. At its core, social class is fundamentally gendered. Women are more likely to live in poverty than men (Hays, 2003), are more likely to be burdened with single parenting than men, and, as previously mentioned, are more likely to experience hardships associated with lower class positions than are men (McCall, 2008).

The ability to have children is treated differently for women from different social classes. Women from the working class are viewed as overly fertile, with poor black women in particular viewed as uncontrollably fertile (Bell, 2009). The discourse of infertility is, conversely, constructed as an experience of middle and upper class white women (Bell, 2009).

In addition, working class women are at the center of family planning and abortion policies. In terms of family planning, much historical and contemporary policy is based on the assumption that poor women, especially poor women of color, are overly fertile and their fertility therefore needs to be carefully controlled (Bell, 2009). In contrast, abortion access is less available to working class and poor women than to middle and upper class women, meaning that carefully planning when, whether, and how to have a family is primarily a privilege of middle and upper class women.

Discourses of mothering is also a classed phenomenon (Byrne, 2006). Not only are women expected to perform the role of mother, they are also expected to perform that role in resource-intensive ways. As a result, lower class women cannot meet the standards of "good" mother and are designated as deficient. "Good mothering" is not just about resource, it is also very much dependent on how mothers talk about resources that are available to them. Because single parent mothers are less likely to have the intensive resources available to two parent families, they are less likely to be perceived as good mothers. Byrne (2006) demonstrates how talk about resources such as education, friendships, and children's fashion are all coded through discourses of race, class, and gender.

Although the research on social class and families is in its infancy, the existing literature does provide important clues as to how class differentiates families, both materially and communicatively. This research also provides interesting theoretical points of departure for researchers interested in pursuing work in this area. In the next section, we explore how social class can be studies beyond the family.

Beyond the Family: Family Communication and Society

There are a number of ways in which social class and communication theorizing can be used to study socially important issues. In this section, we focus on inequality in the criminal justice system and property ownership for black families. The inequity in the criminal justice system has been well documented (Stevenson, 2014), with black men far more likely to face arrest and long periods of incarceration than any other demographic in the U.S. When social class is recognized as a contributing factor, it is in terms of a simple economic issue—the inability of most incarcerated people to afford a lawyer. However, given that social class is a complex process that is woven into a web-of-power that both shapes and is shaped by communication, it would also be important to explore the ways in which the criminal justice system is both produced by and reproduces social class. For example, if people from the working class communicate differently than do people from the middle class, and if middle class communication is privileged in the criminal justice system, then it is likely that the those from the working class will not communicate in a way that will be recognized as legitimate by the criminal justice system. As a result, stigma, financial precarity, and demographic gaps in social class will conspire to lead more African American men toward incarceration for offenses that would not produce incarceration in most other demographic groups. For this reason, African American families need to communicate with young boys on how to engage with police differently than do Caucasian families with young boys. African American families may also be less inclined to call law enforcement when they have a problem due to their unequal treatment within the legal system. To create a more equitable criminal justice system, future research should explore the intersection of social class, race, and gender in the criminal justice system.

Ownership and financial freedom from debt are resource gaps separating families from different social classes. This form of success is tied into social class discourses. Individuals and families who are property owners with little to no debt are typically part of the more prosperous social classes. These financially-secure classes are granted access to power and opportunities that financially precarious classes are not. Not surprisingly, people from the working class tend to define career success in unique ways (Lucas & Buzzanell, 2004) and struggle to achieve dignity for the labor that they perform (Lucas, 2011b). The racial, gender, and other demographic inequalities that intersect with social class may create diverging experiences that require further exploration. Research should seek to understand the diverging phenomenological experiences and hardships people face in efforts to achieve higher social class status. Specifically, exploring the experiences of minority owned business could reveal how individuals manage the movement between financial security and financial precarity.

Implications for Scholars and Practitioners

Within this chapter. we have reviewed the ways in which social class and social mobility engage with family. Social class and mobility uniquely shape the lives of individuals worldwide. Therefore, there is a significant need for family scholars and practitioners to explore the intersections of family, social class, and social mobility. To date, there has been some promising family communication research that addresses social class and mobility, but we need to accelerate this research. Thus, we propose some future directions and considerations for addressing the dearth of research on this topic.

The family serves a central role in socializing ideals, principles, thoughts, and communication patterns. Therefore, family communication researchers should begin to investigate how the family socializes family members into social class. Specifically, how do families talk about class and mobility? In what ways does that familial communication about social class affect family members' decisions past, present, and future? These questions can teach us much about how social class ideologies are challenged and reinforced through discourse.

Family communication scholars should investigate the ways in which family is impacted by disruptions of social class norms. If a family member or unit achieves upward social mobility, how does that affect family communication? This can occur amongst first generation college students. What happens if someone from a higher/lower social class is introduced as a partner or potential new member into a family from a different social class? In what ways is the communication of the new member limited? How does the family's communication patterns change? These questions are important because, as previously discussed, social class and mobility are not fixed. The fluid nature of social class and mobility may apply to family communication phenomena, thus future research should consider these processes. There are numerous ways in which we can address the dearth of research within this topic area with new explorations and by challenging ourselves to incorporate social class into our current research agenda and practices.

Many current research practices fail to account for social class. There are numerous assumptions of literacy, knowledge, and access that are inherently classed. Technology, educational, literacy, and financial gaps oftentimes do not receive consideration in family, unless the research is addressing a marginalized population. Our surveys, questionnaires, manuscripts, and methods of data collection are classed. In many instances, families from other social class groups deem our work inaccessible, unrelatable, or too complex. Therefore, family scholars must mindfully and purposefully inspect the ways in which they infuse social class into research practices and reporting.

References

Afifi, T., Davis, S., Afifi, W., Merrill, A. F., Coveleski, S., & Denes, A. (2015). In the wake of the great recession: Economic uncertainty, communication, and biological stress responses in families. *Human Communication Research, 41*(2), 268–302. doi:10.1111/hcre.12048

APA. (n.d.). Children, youth, families and socioeconomic status. file:///C:/Users/doughertyd/Box%20Sync/social%20class%20readings/Children,%20Youth,%20Families%20and%20Socioeconomic%20Status%20APA.htm

Ashcraft, K., & Mumby, D. (2004). *Reworking gender: A feminist communicology of organization.* Thousand Oaks: Sage.

Ashforth, B. E., & Kreiner, G. E. (1999). "How can you do it?": Dirty work and the challenge of constructing a positive identity. *Academy of Management Review*, *24*(3), 413–434. doi:10.5465/AMR.1999.2202129

Bell, A. (2009). "IT'S way out of my league": Low-income women's experiences of medicalized infertility. *Gender and Society*, *23*(5), 688.

Bourdieu, P. (1984). *Distinction.* London: Routledge.

Bresnahan, M., Zhuang, J., Zhu, Y., Anderson, J., & Nelson, Joshua. (2016). Obesity stigma and negative perceptions of political leadership competence. *American Behavioral Scientist*, *60.* doi:10.1177/0002764216657383.

Burton, L. M., Bonilla-Silva, E., Ray, V., Buckelew, R., & Hordge Freeman, E. (2010). Critical race theories, colorism, and the decade's research on families of color. *Journal of Marriage and Family*, *72*(3), 440–459.

Byrne, B. (1,2). (2006). In search of a "Good Mix": 'Race', class, gender and practices of mothering. *Sociology*, *40*(6), 1001–1017. doi:10.1177/003803850606984

Cloud, D. L. (2005). Fighting words: Labor and the limits of communication at Staley, 1993 to 1996. *Management Communication Quarterly*, *18*(4), 509–542.

Coley, R. J. (2002). *An uneven start: Indicators of inequality in school readiness.* Policy Information Report. Princeton, NJ: Educational Testing Service.

Conley, D. (2008). Reading class between the lines (of this volume): A reflection on why we should stick to folk concepts of social class. In A. Lareau & D. Conley (Eds.), *Social class: How does it work?* (pp. 366–373). New York: Russell Sage Foundation.

Dougherty, D. S. (2011). *The reluctant farmer : An exploration of work, social class, and the production of food.* Leicester : Troubador.

Dougherty, D. S., Rick, J. M., & Moore, P. (2017). Unemployment and social class stigmas. *Journal of Applied Communication Research*, *45*(5), 495–516.

Dougherty, D. S., Schraedley, M. A., Gist-Mackey, A. N., & Wickert, J. (2018). A photovoice study of food (in)security, unemployment, and the discursive-material dialectic. *Communication Monographs*, *85*(4), 443–466. doi:10.1080/03637751.2018.1500700

Flood-Grady, E., & Koenig Kellas, J. (2019). Sense-making, socialization, and stigma: Exploring narratives told in families about mental illness. *Health Communication*, *34*(6), 607–617. https://doi-org.proxy.mul.missouri.edu/10.1080/10410236.2018.1431016

Gist-Mackey, A. N., & Guy, A. (2019) 'You get in a hole, it's like quicksand': A grounded theory analysis of social support amid materially bounded decision-making processes. *Journal of Applied Communication Research.* doi:10.1080/00909882.2019.1617430

Gist-Mackey, A. N., Wiley, M. L., & Erba, J. (2018). "You're doing great. Keep doing what you're doing": Socially supportive communication during first-generation college students' socialization. *Communication Education*, *67*(1), 52–72. doi:10.1080/03634523.2017.1390590

Goffman, E. (1963). *Stigma: Notes on the management of spoiled identity.* New York: Simon & Schuster, Inc.

Hart, B., & Risley, T. R. (1995). *Meaningful differences in the everyday experience of young American children.* Baltimore, MD: Paul H Brookes Publishing.

Hays, S. (2003). *Flat broke with children: Women in the age of welfare reform.* Oxford: Oxford University Press.

Inequality.org (2019). *Facts.* Retrieved from https://inequality.org/facts/

Johnson, E. J., Avineri, N., & Johnson, D. C. (2017). Exposing gaps in/between discourses of linguistic deficits. *International Multilingual Research Journal, 11*(1), 5–22. doi:10.1080/19313152.2016.1258185

Lareau, A. (2003). *Unequal childhoods: Class, race, and family life.* Berkeley: University of California Press.

Link, B. G., & Phelan, J. C. (2001). Conceptualizing stigma. *Annual Review of Sociology, 27*, 363–385.

Lubrano, A. (2004). *Limbo: Blue-collar roots, white-collar dreams.* Hoboken, NJ : Wiley.

Lucas, K. (2011a). Socializing messages in blue-collar families: Communicative pathways to social mobility and reproduction. *Western Journal of Communication, 75*(1), 95–121. doi:10.1080/10570314.2010.536964

Lucas, K. (2011b). The working class promise: A communicative account of mobility-based ambivalences. *Communication Monographs, 78*(3), 347–369. doi:10.1080/03637751.2011.589461

Lucas, K., & Buzzanell, P. M. (2004). Blue-collar work, career, and success: Occupational narratives of *Sisu*. *Journal of Applied Communication Research, 32*(4), 273–292.

Manza, J., & Brooks, C. (2008). Class and politics. In A. Lareau & D. Conley (Eds.), *Social class: How does it work?* (pp. 201–231). New York: Russell Sage Foundation.

Marston, G. (2008). A war on the poor: Constructing welfare and work in the twenty-first century. *Critical Discourse Studies, 5*, 359–370. doi:10.1080/17405900802405312.

Massey, D. S., & Denton, N. A. (1993). *American apartheid: Segregation and the making of the underclass.* Cambridge, MA: Harvard University Press.

McCall, L. (2008). What does class inequality among women look like? A comparison with men and families, 1970–2000. In A. Lareau & D. Conley (Eds.), *Social class: How does it work?* (pp. 293–325). New York: Russell Sage Foundation.

Meisenbach, R. (2010). Stigma management communication: A theory and agenda for applied research on how stigmatized individuals manage moments of stigmatization. *Journal of Applied Communication Research*, 38(3), 268–292. doi:10.1080/00909882.2010.490841

Mumby, D. K. (1998). Power & politics. In F. M. Jablin & L. L. Putnam (Eds.), *The new handbook of organizational communication* (pp. 585–623). Thousand Oaks: Sage.

Odenweller, K. G., & Harris, T. M. (2018). Intergroup socialization: The influence of parents' family communication patterns on adult children's racial prejudice and tolerance. *Communication Quarterly, 66*(5), 501–521. https://doi-org.proxy.mul.missouri.edu/10.1080/01463373.2018.1452766

Osteen, M. (2008). Automobility and amoral space in American film noir. *Journal of Popular Film and Television, 35*(4), 183–192.

Philipsen, G. (1976). Places for speaking in Teamsterville. *Quarterly Journal of Speech, 62*(1), 15–25.

Putnam, L. L. (2004). Dialectical tensions and rhetorical tropes in negotiations. *Organization Studies, 25*, 35–53.

Ranney, C. K., & Kushman, J.E. (1987). Cash equivalence, welfare stigma and food stamps. *Southern Economic Journal, 53*, 1011–1027.

Rivera, K. D. (2015). Emotional taint: Making sense of emotional dirty work at the U.S. border patrol. *Management Communication Quarterly, 29*, 198–228. doi:10.1177/0893318914554090

Saha, K. K., Tofail, F., Frongillo, E. A., Rasmussen, K. M., Arifeen, S. E., Persson, L. Å., ... & Hamadani, J. D. (2010). Household food security is associated with early childhood language development: results from a longitudinal study in rural Bangladesh. Child: Care, health and development, 36(3), 309–316.

Sawhill, I. V. (2013). Family structure: The growing importance of class. Brookings Institute. https://www.brookings.edu/articles/family-structure-the-growing-importance-of-class/

Sheridan, M. A., & McLaughlin, K. A. (2016). Neurological models of the impact of adversity on education. *Current Opinion in Behavioral Sciences, 10*, 108–113. doi:10.1016/j.cobeha.2016.05.013

Shriberg, D. (2013). *School psychology and social justice: Conceptual foundations and tools for practice*. New York, NY: Routledge.

Smith, R. A. (2007). Language of the lost: An explication of stigma communication. *Communication Theory, 17*(4), 462–485. doi:10.1111/j.1468-2885.2007.00307.x

Smith, R. A. (2012). Segmenting an audience into the own, the wise, and normals: A latent class analysis of stigma-related categories. *Communication Research Reports, 29*(4), 257–265. https://doi-org.proxy.mul.missouri.edu/10.1080/08824096.2012.704599

Stevenson, B. (2014). *Just mercy: A story of justice and redemption*. New York, NY: Spiegel and Grau.

Stuber, J. M. (2006). Talk of class: The discursive repertoires of White working-and upper-middle-class college students. *Journal of Contemporary Ethnography, 35*(3), 285–318.

U.S. Bureau of Labor Statistics. (n.d.). Retrieved from https://www.bls.gov/

Wang, T. R. (2014). "I'm the only person from where I'm from to go to college": Understanding the memorable messages first-generation college students receive from parents. *Journal of Family Communication, 14*(3), 270–290. https://doi-org.proxy.mul.missouri.edu/10.1080/15267431.2014.908195

Watt, P. (2008). "Underclass" and "ordinary people" discourses: Representing/Re-Presenting council tenants in a housing campaign. *Critical Discourse Studies, 5*(4), 345–357.

7. *Immigration and Family Communication: Resilience, Solidarity, and Thriving*

JENNIFER A. KAM, ROSELIA MENDEZ MURILLO, AND MONICA CORNEJO

In 2017, the UN Population Division estimated that the world consisted of 258 million people (3.4% of the world's population) who were born outside their country of residence (i.e., foreign born) or who did not have citizenship in their country of residence (MPI, 2017b). Clearly, immigration is a worldwide experience, but a close look at the United States, in particular, also reveals that the nation is largely made up of immigrants. With respect to recent immigrants, the Pew Research Center reported that in 2017 the United States consisted of approximately 43.7 million immigrants in 2016, "accounting for about one-fifth of the world's migrants in 2016" and approximately 13.5% of the U.S. population (López, Bialik, & Radford, 2018, para #1). Thus, immigrants form a significant portion of the U.S. population. When we focus on immigrant families, 18 million children (i.e., 17 years old or younger) live in a household with at least one immigrant parent—that is 26% of the 70 million children who reside in the United States (Zong, Batalova, & Hallock, 2018).

In popular press and academic writing, the term, *immigration*, can refer to voluntarily relocating to another country to seek better opportunities (Ogbu & Simons, 1998). Voluntary immigration is distinct from involuntary immigration, the latter of which refers to being forced to leave one's country to avoid, for example, a crisis, "war, persecution, natural disasters" (Schwartz, Unger, Zamboanga, & Szapocznik, 2010, p. 240). Some sources, however, use the term, *immigration*, in a broader sense to include voluntary and involuntary immigrants, such as "naturalized citizens, lawful permanent residents, certain legal nonimmigrants (e.g., persons on student or work visas), those admitted under refugee or asylee status" and persons residing in the country without authorization (MPI, 2017a, para #2). In this chapter, we use the terms *immigration* and *immigrants* broadly, but when possible distinguish between immigrants' experiences based on their voluntary and involuntary relocation, racial/ethnic identity, and documentation status. Immigrants are a heterogeneous group of people. The reasons for relocating to another country, the conditions under which they relocate, whether they are authorized to remain in a country, their cultural backgrounds, their ethnic/racial identities, their education level, their gender identity, and their socio-economic status are merely a few factors that contribute to immigrants' diverse experiences. Those diverse experiences, in turn, affect immigrants' sense of self, family communication, and well-being (Ogbu & Simons, 1998; Schwartz et al., 2010).

Immigration often results in experiences that require family communication to manage them. Although there are many experiences to consider, this chapter focuses on two immigration-related experiences that can have a substantial impact on the well-being of immigrant families and that have garnered widespread media coverage: (a) *being undocumented (or having a family member who is undocumented)*, and (b) *family separation and reunification*. With respect to undocumented immigration status, family communication contributes to children's understanding of what it means to be undocumented, shapes how children cope with stress from being undocumented or having an undocumented family member, and teaches children how to talk about their own or a family member's undocumented status and with whom (Kam, Pérez Torres, & Steuber Fazio, 2018a; Kam, Steuber Fazio, & Mendez Murillo, 2018b). For families who have been separated because of deportation or stepwise migration, family communication is necessary to maintain one's relationship from a distance (if possible) or to reconnect if reunification occurs (Suárez-Orozco, Bang, & Kim, 2011). Both immigration-related experiences have garnered attention outside the field of communication, but we still know little about how family members manage these experiences, as well as the effects of these experiences on family communication processes and well-being.

In this chapter, we discuss the work that has been conducted within and outside the field that has considered family communication and relational processes surrounding undocumented immigration status and family separation-reunification. We summarize the key theoretical approaches to understanding the role of family communication in managing these immigration-related experiences, as well as the effects of such experiences on families. We then consider how family communication in these two experiences might affect children of immigrants' attitudes and behaviors outside the family. Lastly, we end by exploring implications for scholars and practitioners who are interested in immigration and family communication.

Undocumented Immigration Status and Family Separation-Reunification

Some immigrants may never experience fear of deportation for themselves or a family member, and they may never have to live apart from a parent(s) because of deportation or stepwise migration. Nonetheless, past research suggests that these two experiences impact many immigrant families, particularly Latinx and Asian immigrant families of low socio-economic status (Krogstad, Passel, & Cohn, 2018; Suárez-Orozco et al., 2011). Thus, this section describes the main theoretical frameworks used to study these two experiences with respect to family communication and relationships, focusing first on undocumented immigration status.

Undocumented Immigration Status

Approximately 10.7 million immigrants in the United States are undocumented, a number that has decreased over the past decade (12.2 million in 2007; Krogstad et al., 2018). Undocumented immigrants are non-U.S. citizens or non-U.S. nationals who come to the United States without obtaining authorization or who come to the United States *with* authorization, but who remain in the United States after their authorization expires (Internal Revenue Service, August 27, 2017). Most undocumented immigrants have lived in the United States for over 10 years (Krogstad et al., 2018). They relocate to the United States for many reasons, some of which include escaping violence in their native country, pursuing career or educational opportunities, or reuniting with family members (Artiga & Ubri, 2017; Salas, Ayon, & Gurrola, 2013).

Stress, Resilience, and Thriving: The Role of Family Communication. To date, we have limited knowledge of family communication in relation to undocumented immigration because few studies have been conducted in this area. The studies that have attempted to shed light on such processes have often adopted a stress-resilience-thriving framework. They examine the stressors that immigrants face because of their undocumented status; the effects of such stressors on their identity, academic well-being, mental health, and physical health; and how undocumented immigrants cope with their stress through family communication and other means (Gonzales, Suárez-Orozco, & Dedios-Sanguineti, 2013; Kam et al., 2018a; Kam & Merolla, 2018).

Using a stress-resilience-thriving framework (Feeney & Collins, 2014; Fergus & Zimmerman, 2005), Kam and colleagues suggested that undocumented immigrants and their families have internal assets and protective resources that can attenuate the negative effects of stress and contribute to their resilience (Kam et al., 2018a). More specifically, *resilience* is the ability to positively adapt to adversity (Afifi, Merrill, & Davis, 2016); however, undocumented immigrants and their families can do more than merely recover from adversity. Undocumented immigrants and their families can flourish in the face of adversity and become stronger from such experiences, a process known as *thriving* (Feeney & Collins, 2015).

In the United States, undocumented immigrants face numerous stressors, such as fear of detainment or deportation for self and family members, chronic uncertainty regarding their future well-being, negative stereotypes against them (e.g., criminals), discrimination, severe financial strain, and limited opportunities for employment, education, and healthcare (Gonzales, 2011; Kam et al., 2018a; Rendón García, 2019; Yoshikawa, Suárez-Orozco, & Gonzales, 2017). Such stressors impact the ways in which immigrant families communicate with each other. Yet at the same time, undocumented immigrants can draw upon family communication as a coping strategy to manage the stress from being undocumented.

Guided by resilience theory and thriving, we described a multilevel model of coping, focusing particularly on individual-level assets (i.e., psychological and individual actions that they use to manage stress and thrive) and family-level resources (i.e., family communication that helps them manage the stress and thrive; Kam et al., 2018a), which can also be extended to non-family members (e.g., teachers, school counselors, co-workers; Kam & Merolla, 2018), community-level resources (e.g., neighborhood groups, social activist; Vesely, Leticq, & Goodman, 2017), and institution-level resources (e.g., schools, universities, corporations; non-profit organizations, Kam et al., 2018a, 2018b; Kam & Merolla, 2018). Similarly, Enriquez, Morales Hernandez, Millan, and Vazquez Vera (2019) proposed a multilevel model focusing on university (institutional level), state, and federal policies that have the potential to affect undocumented college students. Thus, undocumented immigrants' academic, relational, mental, and physical well-being is affected by individual, interpersonal-, community-, institutional-, state-, and federal-level experiences (Enriquez et al., 2019; Kam et al., 2018a, 2018b).

A focus on family communication, in particular, has revealed several ways in which immigrants manage the stress from being undocumented through communication with family members. Semi-structured interviews with undocumented Mexican students in high school revealed that they coped through family communication (Kam et al., 2018a). According to the students, parents, aunts, and uncles conveyed messages to ensure the safety of the students. For example, family members advised students not to talk to anyone about their undocumented status, to earn good grades in school, to avoid getting into fights, to avoid alcohol and other drug use, and to avoid police offers. Students reported that their parents also made plans with their children and extended family members to protect the children should a parent be detained or deported. Kam et al. (2018a) also found that students worked with their family as a team to manage the financial strain associated with being undocumented. Nevertheless, some students thought that their family members intentionally did not discuss their undocumented experiences to protect the students from experiencing emotional contagion. Rendón García (2019) found similar results when interviewing Latina mothers in mostly mixed-status families. Mothers also emphasized the importance of protection in similar ways to what students reported in Kam et al. (2018a). Although some mothers openly discussed their undocumented immigration status with their children, others avoided the topic because of low communication efficacy, fear of emotional contagion, or uncertainty regarding whether their children could keep the information private.

In addition to the family communication identified in Kam et al. (2018a), Kam and Merolla (2018) examined how hope communication from a parent(s) increased high school documented and undocumented Latinx immigrants' intentions to attend college. The more often parents talked to the students about the students' goals, discussed pathways for accomplishing their goals, and encouraged confidence in being able to pursue such pathways, the more likely the students were to report greater intentions of attending college in the middle and at the end of the academic year. Although we do not know whether intentions led to actual college attendance and retention, Kam and Merolla (2018) point to family communication as an important source of thriving to consider when trying to promote academic mobility for Latinx immigrants in the United States.

Communication Privacy Management Theory: Interior and Exterior Boundaries. In addition to identifying stressors and sources of resilience and thriving, scholars have considered the privacy management of undocumented families either within the family or outside the family. Several studies have considered the factors that motivate immigrants to discuss their undocumented experiences with non-family members (Kam et al., 2018b; Kam, Gasiorek, Pines, & Steuber Fazio, 2018c; Patler & Pirtle, 2018), as well as instances when parents did not tell their children that the children were undocumented (Abrego, 2011; Gonzales, 2011). Clearly, communication privacy management theory (CPM; Petronio, 2002) can help us further understand how undocumented immigrants manage the information they share about their immigration status, as well as the impact that such decisions and actions have on their families.

CPM offers a boundary metaphor (i.e., exterior and interior) to describe how families manage information. The exterior boundary refers to a family's rules and norms for sharing information outside the family. For undocumented families, these rules and norms dictate whether non-family members are allowed to have access to private information about their undocumented status and related experiences, to what extent, and for what purpose. For example, Kam et al. (2018b) used CPM to explicate undocumented Mexican high school students' decisions to talk to non-family members about the students' undocumented status and related experiences. Their findings suggest that students' exterior boundaries were permeable when students required support, felt they could trust and feel safe with the person, felt accepted by the person, or felt empowered. These findings illustrate how undocumented families manage the information they share with non-family members.

CPM also suggests that people have interior boundaries that dictate who within a family has access to private information (Petronio, 2010). The interior boundaries may explain why some undocumented parents do not tell their children of the children's undocumented status. Prior research (e.g., Abrego, 2011; Gonzales, 2011) suggests that, often, this discovery occurs in adolescence as undocumented youth transition into adulthood and approach important milestones. For some adolescents, this discovery results in negative emotions (e.g., frustration, anger, despair) and resentment toward their parent(s).

To shed light on the effects that disclosure has on undocumented youth's family relationships and identity, Cornejo (2019) explored this phenomenon among college students (majority Latinx) with Deferred Action for Childhood Arrivals (DACA).[1] She found that for some DACA college students, their parents' disclosure had little to no effect on their family relationships. For others, their parents' disclosure spurred resentment toward the parent(s), and students experienced identity confusion. By contrast, others interpreted their parents' disclosure more positively, reporting gratitude for their parents' sacrifices coming to the United States. When exploring the content of disclosures, some students reported learning of their undocumented status in high school when they wanted to apply for scholarships, awards, and travel opportunities that required documentation. Their parent(s) had to inform the students that they were ineligible because of the students' undocumented status. When the students learned of their own undocumented status, some students also reported that their parents helped them make sense of what it means to be undocumented, focused on the students' safety, and explained their migration journey to the United States.

Family Separation and Reunification

Having an undocumented parent(s) means children face the ongoing threat of having their parent(s) detained or deported, and if the child is undocumented, they also fear deportation for themselves and their parent(s) (Kam et al., 2018a). Furthermore, the recent separation of immigrant families at the United States-Mexico border in May 2018 that has been widely covered by popular media further emphasizes the possibility that families might be separated because of their undocumented status. Nevertheless, less covered by popular media today is the fact that immigrant families also experience separation because of a process known as stepwise migration (Orellana, Thome, Chee, & Lam, 2001).

Stepwise migration can occur in many ways. It may occur if one or two parents move to the United States first, while one or more children remain in their native country with a relative. Alternatively, one or more children might move to the United States first and live with a relative, while the parent(s) remains in their native country (Hernandez, 2013). Lastly, a parent and one or more children might move to the United States, while the other parent and possibly siblings remain in their native country. Families may remain separated for weeks, months, or years until the parent(s) can afford to bring their children to that country and be reunited. Being separated because of stepwise migration or because of detention or deportation is likely to be an incredibly challenging, traumatic experience that can significantly and negatively impact identity, family communication, relational quality, and overall well-being. Nonetheless, a stress-resilience-thriving framework suggests that internal assets and protective resources can buffer the negative effects of stress or help people flourish in the face of adversity (Feeney & Collins, 2014; Fergus & Zimmerman, 2005). Thus, the following section discusses how separation can negatively affect identity and family relationships, but certain family communication processes such as relational maintenance might serve as a protective resource for separated families.

The Effects of Separation on Family Communication and Relationships. Suárez-Orozco, Todorova, and Louie (2002) described the separation phase as a process in which, "families undergo profound transformations that are often complicated by extended periods of separation between loved ones" (p. 625). Thus, the disruption of family structures is inevitable. At times, children may associate their parents' decision to migrate without them as a lack of love (Black, 2005) and some have experienced anger and resentment (Schapiro, Kools, Weiss, & Brindis, 2013). Furthermore, Suárez-Orozco, Bang, and Kim (2010) found that children in families who had been separated for four or more years from their mothers reported higher symptoms of both depression and anxiety compared to those who were not separated from their mothers.

Although family members may wait months to several years to be reunited, some might never be reunited. Bacallao and Smokowski (2007) found that families who had been separated for six months or less had the least trouble adapting to the departure of a family member. Longer separations usually resulted in a reconstruction of family roles. For example, children became more attached to the parent that stayed behind, learned to admire this parent as a single parent, and detached themselves from the parent in the United States. By contrast, some children experienced positive aspects of separation such as improved family relationships (Aguilera-Guzmán, Salgado de Snyder, Romero, & Medina-Mora, 2004). Although there is limited research on the fathers' perspective, an ethnographic study found that fathers felt closer to their children because of the migration experience (Dreby, 2006).

Relational Maintenance at a Distance. Relational maintenance can be particularly challenging when separation occurs with children who are too young to comprehend the separation or too young to have a conversation with the geographically separated parent (Suárez-Orozco et al., 2002). Nevertheless, specific forms of communication and cognitive activities may serve as protective factors for family members separated by distance (Merolla, 2010). Drawing from Merolla (2012), maintenance behaviors during separation fall under three broad categories: ***intrapersonal*** (e.g., thinking about the other family member and their relationship), ***dyadic*** (e.g., positive face-to-face and phone/computer-mediated communication between the separated family members), and ***network*** (e.g., social support from extended family and friends). Although these maintenance behaviors are crucial during separation (i.e., introspective strategies), enacting them before (i.e., prospective strategies) and after (i.e., retrospective strategies) reunification might also influence the well-being of the relationship (Merolla, 2010). To maintain the parent-child relationship, parents can discuss the significance of their sacrifice by emphasizing the benefits and opportunities that will arise from the separation (Suárez-Orozco et al., 2002). Research in the context of long-distance romantic partners has shown that different forms of intrapersonal, dyadic, and network maintenance behaviors are related to greater partner intimacy and relationship satisfaction, as well as lower stress levels (Merolla, 2012).

The Importance of Family Communication in the Reunification Process. Although the reunification process might seem like the end of family stress due to the separation, a new wave of stress and renegotiating of family roles arises when family members are reunited. Depending on the length of the separation, the parent and children might feel like strangers when reuniting (Suárez-Orozco et al., 2002). Thus, parents and children must develop a new bond and begin to build trust. This might be especially difficult if the family has grown in size or if stepsiblings or stepparents now form part of the family dynamics (Smith, Lalonde, & Johnson, 2004). In this case, children might feel isolated or betrayed by their parents. Furthermore, children may feel distraught after they are reunited with their parents because they miss the family members and life they left in their native country (Suárez-Orozco et al., 2002).

The reunification process can be incredibly challenging for family relationships and well-being. Such experiences, however, are not necessarily permanent or inevitable. In a five-year longitudinal study, Suárez-Orozco et al. (2010) found that, although participants reported higher levels of anxiety and depression in their initial period of reunification, those symptoms had leveled out by the fifth year. Knobloch, Pustateri, Ebata, and McGlaughlin (2015) found positive opportunities in children separated within the military context. Although military deployment contributed to relational turbulence, children reported higher levels of family cohesion, independence, and preparedness for future separations. Although, military children might not have the same experiences as immigrant children, their separation experiences might have some parallels. These findings highlight the challenges of reunification, but it gives hope to children and parents who have been separated. Family communication scholars can examine the types of communication patterns prior to, during, and following separation to develop strategies for smoother reunification processes.

Beyond the Family: Family Communication and Society

Family communication surrounding undocumented immigration status and family separation-reunification might affect children's attitudes and behaviors outside the family. Children who are undocumented or who have a family member who is undocumented often live in fear that they or a family member will be deported, and they often experience stigmatization and discrimination

(Yoshikawa et al., 2017). Thus, family communication can involve protective messages that advise children not to talk about their family's undocumented status or related experiences with non-family members (Kam et al., 2018b). All of these protective messages, while potentially effective at preventing detention and deportation, might create feelings of distrust toward people outside the family. Indeed, Jefferies (2014) found that undocumented immigrants rarely discussed their status and related experience with non-family members.

Although family members' protective messages may create distrust in others, these protective messages might also have positive outcomes for youth. For example, undocumented college students must learn how to navigate higher education by self-advocating for academic opportunities (Hernandez et al., 2010). For these students, the experiences they had as children—seeing their parents struggle due to their parents' undocumented status—pushed them to be highly successful in their studies, and it changed their attitudes toward the opportunities they had received. Thus, prior family communication messages can influence undocumented youth's attitudes towards academic institutions.

Furthermore, family communication of immigration status and an emphasis to continue on the "right path" can instill in youth the desire to participate in civic engagement activities (e.g., volunteering for community-based programs; Perez et al., 2010; Philbin & Ayon, 2016). Some undocumented youth are motivated to volunteer in their communities because they want to develop a sense of belongingness. The positive messages received from parents can encourage undocumented youth to push for a legislative solution that allows undocumented immigrants, including their parents, to obtain a pathway to citizenship. Thus, family communication cannot only change youths' attitudes at the micro-level, but it can influence youths' attitudes and behaviors at the larger macro-level.

In regards to family separation-reunification, such experiences may allow children to be more resilient toward other stressors (Knobloch et al., 2015). Through family communication, children and their families learn to renegotiate their roles (Suarez et al., 2010). Consequently, children learn to shoulder more responsibility than normal, which in turn, could increase independence and resilience. Knobloch and colleagues found that children reported feeling better prepared for future separations. Although speculative, it is possible that the resilience and thriving developed through managing separation-reunification can lead to resilience and thriving in other contexts, such as youth's transition to adulthood or maintaining friendships or a romantic relationship. This is an area that could benefit from further examination.

Implications for Scholars and Practitioners

A great deal of work is still needed to understand how immigrant families utilize communication to manage their experiences with being undocumented or their experiences with separation-reunification. Family communication scholarship can shed light on important protective resources for immigrant families, as well as communication processes that can help them gain access to resources outside the family. Such insights could be of great utility for key stakeholders at the different levels (e.g., peers, teachers, school counselors, professors, staff, college/university policies, state policies, federal policies) that affect the well-being of immigrant families. Thus, this section explores avenues for future research and implications of such work.

Implications for Family Communication Research

Family communication is central to the well-being of children who are undocumented and/or who have a family member who is undocumented. One type of family that has been overlooked by communication scholars is *mixed-status families*—families that consist of undocumented and documented members (i.e., citizens or legal permanent residents—"non-U.S. citizens who are lawfully authorized to live permanently within the United States"; Artiga & Ubri, 2017; Homeland Security, 2019). Mixed-status families experience salient differences in their identities, given that some members are at a greater disadvantage than others. Thus, a question emerges: do documented family members feel uncomfortable and avoid talking to undocumented family members about certain experiences (e.g., visiting grandparents in another country) that highlight the undocumented family members' disadvantages? Family communication scholars might use theories on privacy management to understand when, why, and how mixed-status families communicate with each other about their advantaged and disadvantaged positions.

In addition, communication research is needed to understand how mixed-status families manage their salient differences, yet also maintain a shared family identity. Soliz (2007) refers to shared family identity as the minimization of intergroup distinctions such that family members perceive themselves as having a common ingroup identity. Afifi, Basinger, and Kam (2019) recently theorized that identification with others in the form of ingroup membership is likely to lead to communal coping—appraising a stressor as jointly owned and taking joint action to manage the stressor. Thus, promoting a shared family identity might also lead mixed-status families to engage in communal coping to manage the stress from being undocumented. Although communal coping is not always beneficial, particularly when it leads to emotional contagion, the undocumented high school students in Kam et al.'s (2018a) study reported that working together was essential to the family's success. Thus, family communication scholars might examine the communication strategies that promote shared family identity, and in turn, communal coping. They might pursue the following questions: How do mixed-status families promote shared family identity? Does shared family identity not only lead to working together as a family, but also directly lead to greater relational quality and overall well-being?

Shared family identity can also inform our understanding of separation-reunification. When a parent and child live in separate countries because of stepwise migration or deportation, to what extent do they have a shared family identity? What communicative behaviors promote shared family identity, and does shared family identity enhance separated families' relational quality and individual well-being? Although we argued that the relational maintenance strategies set forth by Merolla (2010) are likely to attenuate the distressing nature of family separation-reunification, relational maintenance strategies might also enhance separated families' shared family identity. For example, if primary caregivers speak highly of the separated parent and emphasize how much the separated parent loves the child, might the child feel a greater sense of shared family identity compared to children whose primary caregivers do not convey such messages about the parent? Currently, we are unaware of any studies that have examined such relational maintenance strategies with respect to stepwise migration or separation from deportation. Thus, research is needed to test whether Merolla's (2010) relational maintenance strategies can serve as protective resources for separated immigrant families.

In addition to relational maintenance strategies, family communication scholars might consider whether apologies and communicating forgiveness can help immigrant families heal from the trauma of separation. Forgiveness is defined as a decrease in negative emotion and motivation to retaliate, along with an increase in positive emotion and desire for relational repair (McCullough, Worthington, & Rachal, 1997). Forgiveness is an essential component to relational maintenance and has been found to support positive family functioning (Hoyt, Fincham, McCullough, Maio, & Davila, 2006) and good physical health (Lawler et al., 2005). Yet, apologies and forgiveness have not been explored as a protective factor among children separated from their parents due to migration. Exploring apologies and forgiveness (e.g., why they occur, how they are communicated, their effects) makes good sense from theoretical and applied perspectives.

Practical Implications

Understanding family communication surrounding undocumented immigration and separation-reunification is crucial to informing the development of effective resources for immigrant families. Given that family communication can serve as a protective resource or it can exacerbate the stressful nature of being undocumented or separated, immigrant families might benefit from learning how they can, for example, effectively cope together, maintain their relationship from a distance, or communicate in ways that can help them reconnect upon reuniting. The findings established from family communication research that addresses such issues could inform trained marriage and family therapists working in schools, in counseling and psychological services at two- and four-year colleges, and at non-profit organizations geared toward helping immigrant populations.

More specifically, studying privacy management is important because family's exterior privacy boundaries can affect whether undocumented immigrants or separated families seek support outside the family. Jefferies (2014) found that undocumented immigrants are often afraid to discuss their situation with non-family members, which inhibits their ability to access support from peers, mentors, and advocates. If parents prohibit their children from discussing their undocumented status or separation with non-family members, children might be less inclined to talk to a school counselor or mental health profession to manage their stress. They might also miss out on certain opportunities (e.g., how to apply to college or finding financial aid). Thus, family communication research can help identify ways we can break down barriers that prevent immigrant families from accessing resources. We do not advocate for complete disclosure, but there may be certain situations and under certain circumstances in which undocumented immigrant children might have to seek resources outside the family.

Furthermore, broken family attachments can heighten children's trauma and hinder their ability to navigate traumatic experiences (e.g., Santa-Maria & Cornille, 2007). Consequently, children who are separated from their family may be more prone to mental health disorders (Rojas-Flores, Clements, Hwang Koo, & London, 2017). Specifically, Rojas-Flores et al. (2017) found that previously detained or deported parents reported higher rates of post-traumatic stress disorder (PTSD) symptoms among their children when compared to documented parents or parents who had no prior engagements with immigration enforcement. By implementing a multi-agent approach, that is, obtaining the perspective of children, parents, teachers, and clinicians', Rojas-Flores et al.'s study was able to garner a more holistic understanding of the psychological repercussions of parental detention and deportation on

U.S. Latinx born children. These multiple perspectives shed light on the negative mental health consequences of detached families and can serve as an important resource for family clinical interventions.

Concluding Remarks

To shed light on the important role that communication plays among immigrant families, this chapter took a close look at undocumented immigration status and family separation-reunification. Although these experiences may be exceedingly difficult, family communication may serve as a source of resilience and thriving for immigrant families (e.g., Kam et al., 2018a). Unfortunately, few studies have examined family communication processes in relation to undocumented immigration and separation-reunification. Hopefully, however, this chapter has provided a convincing argument for conducting such research by emphasizing the important effects that family communication can have on the well-being of immigrant families.

Note

1. Deferred Action for Childhood Arrivals (DACA) is a federal executive order that allows certain immigrants (e.g., relocated to the United States at 15 years old or younger, resided in the United States since 2007, have not been convicted of a felony or certain misdemeanors) the ability to obtain a social security number, a work permit, and relief from deportation. The program expires every two years and renewal is not guaranteed.

References

Abrego, L. J. (2011). Legal consciousness of undocumented Latinos: Fear and stigma as barriers to claims-making for first-and 1.5-generation immigrants. *Law & Society Review*, *45*, 337–370. doi:10.1111/j.1540-5893.2011.00435.x

Afifi, T., Basinger, E., & Kam, J. A. (2019, November). *The extended theoretical model of communal coping (TMCC): Understanding the properties and functionality of communal coping*. Paper to be presented at the National Communication Association, Baltimore, MD.

Afifi, T. D., Merrill, A. F., & Davis, S. (2016). The theory of resilience and relational load. *Personal Relationships*, *23*, 663–683. doi:10.1111/pere.12159

Aguilera-Guzmán, R. M., de Snyder, V. N. S., Romero, M., & Medina-Mora, M. E. (2004). Paternal absence and international migration: Stressors and compensators associated with the mental health of Mexican teenagers of rural origin. *Adolescence*, *39*, 711–724.

Artiga, S., & Ubri, P. (2017). *Living in an immigrant family in America: How fear and toxic stress are affecting daily life. Well-being, and health.* Menlo Park, CA: Kaiser Family Foundation.

Bacallao, M. L., & Smokowski, P. R. (2007). The costs of getting ahead: Mexican family system changes after immigration. *Family Relations, 56*, 52–66. doi:10.1111/j.1741-3729.2007.00439.x

Black, A. E. (2005). *The separation and reunification of recently immigrated Mexican families* (Doctoral dissertation). Minneapolios, MN: Walden University.

Cornejo, M. (2019). *Discovering one's undocumented immigration status: The perspectives of college students with Deferred Action for Childhood Arrivals (DACA)* (Unpublished master's thesis). University of California, Santa Barbara, United States.

Dreby, J. (2006). Honor and virtue: Mexican parenting in the transnational context. *Gender and Society, 20*(1), 32–59. doi:10.1177/0891243205282660

Enriquez, L. E., Morales Hernandez, M., Millán, D., & Vazquez Vera, D. (2019). Mediating illegality: Federal, state, and institutional policies in the educational experiences of undocumented college students. *Law and Social Inquiry*. Published online first on March 18, 2019. doi:10.1017/lsi.2018.16

Feeney, B. C., & Collins, N. L. (2014). A theoretical perspective on the importance of social connections for thriving. In M. Mikulincer & P. R. Shaver (Eds.), *The Herzliya series on personality and social psychology. Mechanisms of social connection: From brain to group* (pp. 291–314). Washington, DC: American Psychological Association.

Feeney, B. C., & Collins, N. L. (2015). A new look at social support: A theoretical perspective on thriving through relationships. *Personality and Social Psychology Review, 19*, 113–147. doi:10.1177/1088868314544222

Fergus, S., & Zimmerman, M. A. (2005). Adolescent resilience: A framework for understanding healthy development in the face of risk. *Annual Review of Public Health, 26*, 399–419. doi:10.1146/annurev.publhealth.26.021304.144357

Gonzales, R. G. (2011). Learning to be illegal: Undocumented youth and shifting legal contexts in the transition to adulthood. *American Sociological Review, 76*, 602–619. doi:10.1177/0003122411411901

Gonzales, R. G., Suárez-Orozco, C., & Dedios-Sanguineti, M. C. (2013). No place to belong: Contextualizing concepts of mental health among undocumented immigrant youth in the United States. *American Behavioral Scientist, 57*, 1173–1198. https://doi.org/10.1177/0002764213487349

Hernández, M. G. (2013). Migrating alone or rejoining the family? Implications of migration strategies and family separations for Latino adolescents. *Research in Human Development, 10*, 332–352. doi:10.1080/15427609.2013.846048

Hernandez, S., Hernandez Jr, I., Gadson, R., Huftalin, D., Ortiz, A. M., White, M. C., & Yocum-Gaffney, D. (2010). Sharing their secrets: Undocumented students' personal stories of fear, drive, and survival. *New Directions for Student Services, 131*, 67–84. doi:10.1002/ss.368

Homeland Security. (2019). Lawful permanent residents (LPR). Retrieved from https://www.dhs.gov/immigration-statistics/lawful-permanent-residents.

Hoyt, W. T., Fincham, F. D., McCullough, M. E., Maio, G., & Davila, J. (2006). Responses to interpersonal transgressions in families: Forgiveness, forgivability, and relationship-specific effects. *Journal of Personality and Social Psychology*, *89*, 375–394. doi:10.1037/0022-3514.89.3.375

Internal Revenue Service. (2017). *Immigration terms and definitions involving aliens.* Retrieved from https://www.irs.gov/individuals/international-taxpayers/immigration-terms-and-definitions-involving-aliens

Jefferies, J. (2014). Fear of deportation in high school: Implications for breaking the circle of silence surrounding migration status. *Journal of Latinos and Education*, *13*, 278–295. doi:10.1080/15348431.2014.887469

Kam, J. A., & Merolla, A. J. (2018). Hope communication as a predictor of documented and undocumented Latina/o high school students' college intentions across an academic year. *Communication Monographs*, *85*, 399–422. doi:10.1080/03637751.2018.1463101

Kam, J. A., Pérez Torres, D., & Steuber Fazio, K. (2018a). Identifying individual-and family-level coping strategies as sources of resilience and thriving for undocumented youth of Mexican origin. *Journal of Applied Communication Research*, *46*, 641–664. doi:10.1080/00909882.2018.1528373

Kam, J. A., Steuber Fazio, K., & Mendez Murillo, R. (2018b). Privacy rules for revealing one's undocumented status to nonfamily members: Exploring the perspectives of undocumented youth of Mexican origin. *Journal of Social and Personal Relationships.* Published online first on December 6, 2018. doi:10.1177/0265407518815980

Kam, J. A., Gasiorek, J., Pines, R., & Steuber Fazio, K. (2018c). Latina/o adolescents' family undocumented-status disclosures directed at school counselors: A latent transition analysis. *Journal of Counseling Psychology*, *65*, 267–279. doi:10.1037/cou0000259

Knobloch, L. K., Pusateri, K. B., Ebata, A. T., & McGlaughlin, P. C. (2015). Experiences of military youth during a family member's deployment: Changes, challenges, and opportunities. *Youth & Society*, *47*, 319–342. doi:10.1177/0044118X12462040

Krogstad, J., Passel, J., & Cohn, D. (2018, November 28). 5 facts about illegal immigration in the U.S. *Pew Research Center.* Retrieved from http://www.pewresearch.org/fact-tank/2018/11/28/5-facts-about-illegal-immigration-in-the-u-s/.

Lawler, K. A., Younger, J. W., Piferi, R. L., Jobe, R. L., Edmondson, K. A., & Jones, W. H. (2005). The unique effects of forgiveness on health: An exploration of pathways. *Journal of Behavioral Medicine*, *28*, 157–167. doi:10.1007/s10865-005-3665-2

López, G., Bialik, K., & Radford, J. (2018, November 30). Key findings about U.S. immigrants. *Pew Research Center.* Retrieved from http://www.pewresearch.org/fact-tank/2018/11/30/key-findings-about-u-s-immigrants/.

McCullough, M. E., Worthington, Jr. E. L., & Rachal, K. C. (1997). Interpersonal forgiving in close relationships. *Journal of Personality and Social Psychology*, *73*, 321–336. doi:10.1037/0022-3514.73.2.321

Merolla, A. J. (2010). Relational maintenance and noncopresence reconsidered: Conceptualizing geographic separation in close relationships. *Communication Theory, 20*, 169–193. doi:10.1111/j.1468-2885.2010.01359.x

Merolla, A. J. (2012). Connecting here and there: A model of long-distance relationship maintenance. *Personal Relationships, 19*(4), 775–795. doi:10.1111/j.1475-6811.2011.01392.x

Migration Policy Institute. (2017a). Tabulation of data from U.S. Census Bureau, 2017 American Community Survey (ACS) and 1990 Decennial Census; 1990 data were accessed from Steven Ruggles, J. Trent Alexander, Katie Genadek, Ronald Goeken, Matthew B. Schroeder, and Matthew Sobek, Integrated Public Use Microdata Series: Version 5.0 [Machine-readable database] (Minneapolis: University of Minnesota, 2010). Retrieved from https://www.migrationpolicy.org/programs/data-hub/charts/children-immigrant-families

Migration Policy Institute. (2017b). Tabulation of data from the United Nations, Department of Economic and Social Affairs (2017), Trends in International Migrant Stock: Migrants by Destination and Origin (United Nations database, POP/DB/MIG/Stock/Rev.2017). Retrieved from https://www.migrationpolicy.org/programs/data-hub/charts/immigrant-and-emigrant-populations-country-origin-and-destination?width=1000&height=850&iframe=true.

Ogbu, J. U., & Simons, H. D. (1998). Voluntary and involuntary minorities: A cultural-ecological theory of school performance with some implications for education. *Anthropology and Education Quarterly, 29*, 155–188. doi:10.1525/aeq.1998.29.2.155

Orellana, M. F., Thorne, B., Chee, A., & Lam, W. S. E. (2001). Transnational childhoods: The participation of children in processes of family migration. *Social Problems, 48*, 572–591. doi:10.1525/sp.2001.48.4.572

Patler, C., & Pirtle, W. L. (2018). From undocumented to lawfully present: Do changes to legal status impact psychological wellbeing among Latino immigrant young adults? *Social Science and Medicine, 199*, 39–48. doi:10.1016/j.socscimed.2017.03.009

Petronio, S. (2002). *Boundaries of privacy: Dialectics of disclosure*. Albany, NY: SUNY Press.

Petronio, S. (2010). Communication privacy management theory: What do we know about family privacy regulation? *Journal of Family Theory and Review, 2*, 175–196. doi:10.1111/j.1756-2589.2010.00052.x

Philbin, S. P., & Ayon, C. (2016). Luchamos por nuestros hijos: Latino immigrant parents strive to protect their children from the deleterious effects of anti-immigration policies. *Children and Youth Services Review, 63*, 128–135. doi:10.1016/j.childyouth.2016.02.019

Rendón García, S. A. (2019). "No vamos a tapar el sol con un dedo": Maternal communication concerning immigration status. *Journal of Latinx Psychology*. Published online first on April 18, 2019. http://dx.doi.org/10.1037/lat0000131.

Rojas-Flores, L., Clements, M. L., Hwang Koo, J., & London, J. (2017). Trauma and psychological distress in Latino citizen children following parental detention and deportation. *Psychological Trauma: Theory, Research, Practice, and Policy, 9*, 352. doi:10.1037/tra0000177

Salas, L. M., Ayon, C., & Gurrola, M. (2013). Estamos traumados: The impact of anti-immigrant sentiment and policies on the mental health of Mexican immigrant families. *Journal of Community Psychology, 41*, 1005–1020.

Santa-Maria, M. L., & Cornille, T. (2007). Traumatic stress, family separations, and attachment among Latin American immigrants. *Traumatology, 13*, 26–31. doi:10.1177/1534765607302278

Schapiro, N. A., Kools, S. M., Weiss, S. J., & Brindis, C. D. (2013). Separation and reunification: The experiences of adolescents living in transnational families. *Current Problems in Pediatric and Adolescent Health Care, 43*, 48–68. doi:10.1016/j.cppeds.2012.12.001

Schwartz, S. J., Unger, J. B., Zamboanga, B. L., & Szapocznik, J. (2010). Rethinking the concept of acculturation: Implications for theory and research. *American Psychologist, 65*, 237–251. doi:10.1037/a0019330

Smith, A., Lalonde, R. N., & Johnson, S. (2004). Serial migration and its implications for the parent-child relationship: A retrospective analysis of the experiences of the children of Caribbean immigrants. *Cultural Diversity and Ethnic Minority Psychology, 10*, 107. doi:10.1037/1099-9809.10.2.107

Soliz, J. (2007). Communicative predictors of a shared family identity: Comparison of grandchildren's perceptions of family-of-origin grandparents and step grandparents. *Journal of Family Communication, 7*, 177–194. doi:10.1080/15267430701221636

Suárez-Orozco, C., Bang, H. J., & Kim, H. Y. (2010). Transnational familyhood: the experience of separations and reunification for youth immigrant. *Journal of Adolescent Research, 20*, 1–37.

Suárez-Orozco, C., Bang, H. J., & Kim, H. Y. (2011). I felt like my heart was staying behind: Psychological implications of family separations and reunifications for immigrant youth. *Journal of Adolescent Research, 26*, 222–257. doi:10.1177/0743558410376830

Suárez-Orozco, C., Gaytán, F. X., Bang, H. J., Pakes, J., O'Connor, E., & Rhodes, J. (2010). Academic trajectories of newcomer immigrant youth. *Developmental Psychology, 46*, 602–618. doi:10.1037/a0018201

Suárez-Orozco, C., Todorova, I. L., & Louie, J. (2002). Making up for lost time: The experience of separation and reunification among immigrant families. *Family Process, 41*, 625–643. doi:10.1111/j.1545-5300.2002.00625.x

Vesely, C. K., Letiecq, B. L., & Goodman, R. D. (2017). Immigrant family resilience in context: Using a community-based approach to build a new conceptual model. *Journal of Family Theory & Review, 9*, 93–110. doi:10.1111/jftr.12177

Yoshikawa, H., Suárez-Orozco, C., & Gonzales, R. G. (2017). Unauthorized status and youth development in the United States: Consensus statement of the society for research on adolescence. *Journal of Research on Adolescence, 27*, 4–19. doi:10.1111/jora.12272

Zong, J., Batalova, J., & Hallock, J. (2018, February 8). Frequently requested statistics on immigrants and immigration in the United States. *Migration Policy Institute*. Retrieved from https://www.migrationpolicy.org/article/frequently-requested-statistics-immigrants-and-immigration-united-states#Children

8. *Examining Communication and Identity Within Refugee Families*

Aparna Hebbani and Mairead MacKinnon

Historically, millions of people worldwide have been forced to flee from their home country and become refugees, defined by the Office of the United Nations High Commissioner for Refugees [UNHCR] (2018) as, "someone who has been forced to flee his or her country because of persecution, war, or violence. A refugee has a well-founded fear of persecution for reasons of race, religion, nationality, political opinion or membership in a particular social group."

According to UNHCR (2015), an estimated 63 million people have been displaced from their home countries—this is needless to say a huge number of displaced persons looking for resettlement. As an example, Australia has been instrumental in resettling refugees as a signatory to the 1951 UN Refugee Convention and the 1967 Refugee Protocol; in the past, it has been ranked among the top three countries in the world for refugee settlement (RCOA, 2016; UNHCR, 2014). In 2014–2015, the time period in which the current research took place, Australia granted over 13,750 humanitarian visas (DIBP, 2014), and this number has slightly declined by a thousand since then (RCOA, 2018).

Immigration data also shows that in most cases, refugees have relatively large families, so resettlement in the new home country happens across generations. In fact, according to Australia's Department of Immigration and Border Protection (2013), refugee families account for almost 40% of the total refugee movement. In many refugee families, it is often the case that parents spend years and sometimes decades in refugee camps (in a transit or neighbouring country), where their children are born. Research also indicates that upon migration, children acculturate quicker to new cultures than their parents (Hebbani, Obijiofor & Bristed, 2012; Renzaho, Dhingra, &

Georgeou, 2017; Santisteban & Mitrani, 2003) with children learning the host country language and sometimes stepping in as interpreters for their parents.

Australia created its first Department of Immigration in 1945 (Tavan & Neumann, 2009), a system built within the parameters of the *White Australia* policy.[1] Since then, thousands of people from across the world have sought refuge in Australia as a result of fleeing various wars, natural disasters, and oppressive regimes. While those seeking refuge in the mid-1900s were predominantly from European nations fleeing World War II (WWII), this was followed by another wave of refugees escaping the atrocities in South-East Asia. Then, the latter part of the 20th century saw refugees from countries in the African, Middle-Eastern, and South Asian continents fleeing civil war, famine, terrorism, and religious persecution (RCOA, 2012).

Thus, although Australia has been taking refugees for numerous decades, the waves of refugees who have come to Australia are from different countries from across the world, thereby technically resulting in Australia being a multicultural nation. The Government's policy though has been historically somewhat selective in who they grant access. Even Caucasian Europeans who came post-WWII were subjected to racism by Caucasian Australians (Collins, 2003). The following waves of migrants were then targeted (i.e., South-East Asians, then Africans, and Middle-Easterners, and so on).

While earlier refugee cohorts were predominantly of Christian faith, some of the later waves brought with them refugees from Christian and Muslim faiths, who were fleeing religious persecution in countries such as South Sudan, Afghanistan, Iran, Somalia, Ethiopia, and Myanmar. As per 2016 Census data, 52% of Australians cited their religious affiliation as Christianity (various denominations, but 50% of those were Catholic). The same dataset also shows that the next largest religion in Australia was Islam, with 2.6% of the population citing they were Muslim. Over time, greater numbers of Australians are becoming less religious, with a third of the population citing in the 2016 census that they had no religion (30%) (ABS, 2018).

The past two decades has seen an intake of refugees from African nations and South-East Asia—most of whom belong to the Christian and Muslim faith who have fled their home country against their will. As per settlement reports for 2015–2016, almost 50% of those granted refugee status (~19,000) were affiliated with various Christian denominations (ABS, 2018).

These humanitarian refugees now call Australia home, and over time, they are granted Australian citizenship. Despite this, however, settlement for refugees is sometimes challenging, settling down in a new and unfamiliar culture that is quite different than one's place of origin in terms of cultural do's and don'ts, language, traditions, food, and more.

How does this disrupted (and at times traumatic) life trajectory coupled by settling in a culturally distant country impact the refugee family unit and their identity formation? There is a dearth of research in existant family communication literature on refugee family identity and communication (Akkoor, 2014; Turner & West, 2018). This chapter discusses how religion, citizenship, and language proficiency intersect to shape identity among refugee families and how cultural identity is transmitted to the next generation. The next section presents a brief overview of literature on interrelated concepts of identity and self-identity.

Synthesis of Literature

Now more than ever, the number of refugees and displaced persons are at record levels. Global conflicts have led to unprecedented movement and displacement of people from their home countries to neighboring countries and beyond. This movement brings with it major change to one's identity whether it be citizenship, culture, language, or religion.

Varied Facets of Identity

The concept of identity has been studied across various disciplines and diverse groups. One can have multiple (and conflicting) identities whether it be racial, ethnic, religious, or other. Refugees are unique in that they have often been born in one country, spent time in various transit countries, and now live in a third country of settlement, not by choice but due to forced displacement. This may differ for parents and children whether they are born in their parent's home country, in a camp or transit country or their new country of settlement. This can lead to one speaking various languages or adopting various cultural or religious identities. Therefore, "the globalised subject is an individual with multiple, shifting identities and a person whose identity is socially, spatially and historically defined" (Rutter, Cooley, Reynolds, & Sheldon, 2007, p. 134). Identity is also "transient, a reflection on where you are now, a fleeting moment in a biography of the self or the group, only partially connected to where you might have come from, and where you might be going" (Tilley, 2006, p. 9). This definition especially resonates in the case of refugees who may be displaced in a transit country (country of asylum) or refugee camp (Hiruy, 2009).

Ethnic identity is a term often used in discussions surrounding refugee identity. Ethnic identity is defined as "the subjective sense of ethnic group membership that involves self-labeling, sense of belonging, preference for the group, positive evaluation of the ethnic group, ethnic knowledge, and involvement in ethnic group activities" (Cokley, 2007, p. 225). Phinney and Ong (2007, p. 271) describe ethnic identity as deriving from "a sense of peoplehood within a group, a culture, and a particular setting," whereas Phinney, Horenczyk, Liebkind, and Vedder (2001) understand ethnic identity as a sense of belonging with one's heritage/ethic culture and the continuance of that specific culture's values and practices; they go on to say that, "ethnic identity becomes salient as part of the [broader] acculturation process that takes place when immigrants come to a new society" (p. 494).

Refugees often come from minority groups or persecuted minority groups (i.e. the Christian Karen fleeing the Buddhist military regime in Myanmar, or Yazidis fleeing the Syrian and ISIS atrocities). These ethnic minority groups often settle in similar ethnic enclaves in their new country of settlement, attend the same churches, schools and so on. While past research has been concerned with how to measure ethnic identity (Helms, 2007; Phinney & Ong, 2007) or the label of 'refugee' in forming identity (Roberson, 1992; Zetter, 1991), much less research has focused on identities within the refugee family unit and how cultural identity is transmitted to the next generation.

Refugee identity is dependent on many factors such as legal status, gender, age (older people may hold onto certain aspects of their home identity while younger people adapt and change), length of stay in the country of settlement (over time identities may change), language proficiency (ability to speak the language of the new country may expedite a change of identity), and religion (may grow stronger or weaker with migration stresses). These identities can sometimes be conflicting. For instance, Valentine, Sporton, and Nielsen (2009) found young Somali refugees in Denmark could "enact" a Danish identity (by speaking and dressing Danish) but did not feel they belong to Denmark as they were also Muslim and black. They argue that it is "this intersection of their race and faith identities which defines them as outside the nation" (Valentine et al., 2009, p. 244).

In a UK-based study, refugee participants were asked about various parts of their identity. Most were eager to hold onto aspects of their home culture such as language, food, dress, and values (Rutter et al., 2007). Most identified themselves as having a British or a dual identity (i.e., mix of British and other) and also rejected a "refugee" identity. Most (all but two) spoke their native language at home and almost everyone encouraged their children to speak this language at home (albeit sometimes unsuccessfully).

Phinney et al. (2001) explain that ethic identity is a "dynamic construct which evolves and changes in response to developmental and contextual factors" (p. 496). Therefore, how one defines their identity (self-identity) may also be dependent on that person's (or group's) identity being accepted by the larger community (Hiruy, 2009; Valentine et al., 2009; Van Liempt, 2011). These authors provide a good example:

> … a Somali refugee who has UK citizenship may identify as British, yet this may be of little consequence if residents of their wider community do not recognise them as British but, rather, label them an 'outsider' and subject them to racist harassment. (Valentine et al., 2009, p. 237)

This identity is relational and dependent upon host society/migrant relations (Ehrkamp, 2006).

Refugee children, who may have been born in a transit country, refugee camp, or country of resettlement, often have a unique experience in their new country where their home and school life are drastically different, and they are trying to bridge cultural gaps. Often children are trying to fit in and be accepted in one particular environment (and speak the language of that environment), but at times, they also act as cultural/language interpreters at home for their parents who may be struggling with learning the local language (Fantino & Colak, 2001). For many refugee children, "you are what you speak, and what you speak is where you are" (Valentine et al., 2009, p. 242).

As part of ensuring cultural transmission and maintenance, refugee parents often consciously or subconsciously want to transmit aspects of their cultural identity to their children via their home language, food, dress, religious aspects, and so on. We are interested in how parents navigate not only their own changing identity but also how they play an influential role in shaping their children's identity as well. There can be an intergenerational disconnect within the family unit when negotiating and navigating the identity space so it may not always be smooth sailing. Children may be less receptive to their parents' home cultural norms and more adaptive to their new home culture as a result of increased social contact with the local population via schools, friends, and so on, or may downright rebel against their home culture, in line with Berry's domain of assimilation instead of integration or bicultural identity, wherein they absorb their "heritage/home culture" and "national/host culture" (Berry, 1997; Berry, Phinney, Sam, & Vedder, 2006).

Citizenship. Citizenship is another facet which is sometimes considered the basic requirement in gaining a national identity to the country in which one lives. It is argued that "belonging to a nation is not just about citizenship per se (i.e. rights and responsibilities); it is about 'the emotions that such memberships evoke'" (Yuval-Davis et al., 2005, p. 526 in Valentine et al., 2009, p. 246). So, while having citizenship of one country, one may or may not feel the emotional membership to their nationality or national identity, and this may differ between children and their parents. Children more often feel much stronger attachment to their new country of settlement than their parents who have spent time elsewhere and hold differing identities. Ager and Strang (2008) argue that citizenship is a key part of integration. They say "full citizenship is an essential prerequisite for integration and full participation in civic life" (p. 174). The permanency of citizenship is key in making one feel settled, integrated, and safe. Refugees, though, do not choose to leave (for a multitude of reasons); therefore, Ager and Strang note that settling into a new culture and becoming bicultural or adopting a new nationhood can be difficult if they do not feel they have equality to other native-born citizens.

Religion. Religion can play a major part in forming one's identity and is often the sole self-descriptor for some people. Past research shows some refugee groups become more religious and religion becomes a more important part of their lives when they resettle in a new country (McGown, 1999; Van Liempt, 2011). Religion provides a comfort for many experiencing drastic changes in migration including trauma, losing family members, experiencing poverty, and more. Van Liempt (2011, p. 576) argues, "religion thus provides an important anchor within their broader experience of dislocation." Rousseau, Rufagari, Bagilishya, and Measham (2004, p. 1103) describe the importance of faith to identity, "Faith also appears to offer protection against change in an immutably divided world in which adaptation is perceived as a survival mechanism, a superficial change that does not affect innermost identity." There can also be a disconnect between parents holding onto their religion and hoping their children do as well, while children are often less religious or even reject a religion altogether in their new settlement context (see Cadge & Ecklund, 2007).

Language maintenance. Learning the host country language is central to refugee settlement and integration (Ager & Strang, 2008; Heinemann, 2017). There are three pathways that refugees adopt when settling in a new country: (1) keep their first language, (2) adopt the language of the host society, or (3) adopt the host language, but also maintain their home language. Hatoss and Sheely (2009, p. 127) argue, "From the linguistic point of view, a successful adjustment means the acquisition of the language of the host society (in the context of the current paper, English), and the maintenance of the mother tongue for identity, cultural, and other purposes." Issues can arise, however, when there is a disconnect between generations about who learns which language and at which pace (Hebbani et al., 2012; Santisteban & Mitrani, 2003). A lack of host language acquisition can lead to parents losing leadership and authority (Santisteban & Mitrani, 2003) and feeling like their parental role has been diminished (Hebbani et al., 2012).

Beyond the Family: Family, Communication and Society

As we think of refugee settlement, one must be mindful of the context in which refugee settlement in Australia has taken place (past and present) and acknowledge that settlement does not happen in a vacuum. Settlement in Australia has taken place amidst a tumultuous socio-political landscape for decades, with an unwelcoming media which dehumanizes refugees and asylum seekers (Bleiker, Campbell, Hutchison & Nicholson, 2013). By representing refugees and asylum seekers poorly, the media and government rhetoric surrounding these groups can have major consequences for public opinion, restrictive immigration policies, and refugees' own sense of ethic and national identity. In the next section, we focus on presenting a brief overview of related findings from our Australia-based research study.

In 2015, wanting to examine identity within the refugee family unit, we interviewed 47 parents from refugee backgrounds (from Ethiopia, the Democratic Republic of Congo, and Myanmar) who resettled in Australia. Out of 47 parents interviewed, all but one participant identified themselves as being Christian (one participant was Muslim). In total, these 47 participants had 278 children,[2] of which 45% were born in either a transit country or refugee camp, 34% were born in their country of origin, and 20% were born upon arrival in Australia. This indicates two things of particular relevance to this chapter: (a) refugee families in general are somewhat larger than families in the West, and (b) 79% of children were born overseas. Although we did not gather primary data from children in this particular study, the two points mentioned above gives us an idea of how their current identity may have been shaped by their disrupted life journey.

Given this context, it is plausible to hypothesize that refugee families (especially children) would struggle with formulating their identity settling in a vastly different culture, or, on the other hand, one may speculate that these families would be extremely resilient in settlement having been through so many difficulties in life.

On the whole, findings from our study indicated that the latter was true—most parents perceived that their families were integrating well. Parents were happy that their children had developed a bicultural identity. In fact, many parents *wanted* their children to have a bicultural identity—this was true across the three country groups we studied. This is in line with Phinney et al.'s (2001) explanation of integrated/bicultural identity, versus separated, marginalized, or assimilated identities.

An Ethiopian father of five children spoke of how satisfied he was that his children were learning both cultures at the same time, "I take them to

Ethiopian community events, we take them to the church, so they learn the Ethiopian culture. At the same time, they learn Australian culture. So we are happy with that, so everything is going well." Similarly, a mother from Myanmar rationalized her thought process to accept the fact that her children will absorb Australian culture when she said, "We have to accept what they [children] are going to become [Australian] because we are in Australia, so I'm happy they are being Australian, yeah." Parents' narratives also revealed the importance they placed on transmitting religion, language, dress, and food habits to their children as part of shaping their identity.

Role of Religion on Self and Children's Identity

Religiosity in Australia is declining (as the numbers quoted earlier in this chapter), but we found that religion played an *integral* part of most refugee parents' lives in Australia, which is in line with past research (see McGown, 1999; Van Liempt, 2011). Identifying themselves as being either Orthodox Christians or practicing Baptists, partaking in religious activities was almost mandatory in all families we met. Practically all parents ensured that everyone (children included) attended church services on Sundays; in some cases, children went to Sunday school as well. Children, especially girls, had to wear "appropriate" clothing for church (for more details see Hebbani, Obijiofor & MacKinnon, 2018). Many parents depended on the support that their church pastor or other church members from their community provided. Most children also attended K-12 schools with affiliation to Christian denominations. Just how integral a role religion played in our participants' lives is summed up by a father from Myanmar, "Church is a priority on Sunday because God has helped us."

Importance of Language in Shaping Identity within the Family Unit

Knowing the important role that language plays in refugee settlement, parents placed tremendous emphasis on ensuring that children learned the language of their home country (i.e., English), but at the same time, ensuring that they also learned their mother tongue (either Karen, Mizo, Falam Chin, Karenni, Amharic, Arabic, French, or Swahili) which was central to a refugee family's identity. One can comprehend why this may be the case with years spent in a transit country or refugee camp (up to 31 years for one participant and an average of 10 years for all participants) and 45% of children being born in a transit country/refugee camp with a language different to their home country, as one parent from Myanmar said, "I don't want to let my children forget their own language."

Parents accepted that their children would learn English due to social contact with Australians at school and in the community and had no qualms about this. In fact, at times, the children who became quite proficient in English (at a faster rate than their parents) stepped in and acted as interpreters for their parents who may have had relatively low English language proficiency.

But when it came to language spoken at home and within the family, almost all parents we spoke to insisted their mother tongue be the primary language spoken at home to prevent language loss. One mother from Myanmar explained how this was a strict rule in their home, "I tell them [3 daughters] to only speak Karen at home," and her husband continued, "If they talk in English too much, I say, 'Hey, are you Karen or are you white people?' "

So switching language depending on domain (at home or outside) was one strategy parents employed to ensure the next generation did not lose touch with their linguistic roots, "I want my children to speak in our language [Karenni] at home, but outside, they can speak English very well." This also ensured that children were bilingual so they could successfully communicate with relatives still in their home country as well as follow church services which are conducted in the mother tongue.

Differences in Identity among Generations

While most children were seen as having a bicultural or Australian identity, two-thirds of parents also saw themselves as being bicultural or Australian. Only a handful of parents identified themselves with only their country of origin. Having/not having Australian citizenship was often mentioned by some in having an impact on whether or not they identified themselves as Australians. Some participants who had been granted Australian citizenship mentioned that as the pivotal turning point to becoming "Australian." Here are some quotes which highlighted how citizenship outcomes affected their identity, "I'm Burmese at the moment, not Australian. Only Burmese. Yes, because I've been here only for a short time. I'm not a citizen yet, I'm not Australian yet." Similarly, one father from Myanmar who was waiting for the outcome of his citizenship application said that on receipt of citizenship, he would call themselves as "Australian" but until then, he was a Karen Australian. As a mother from Myanmar put it, "I feel as [if] I'm a little bit Australian at the moment because I already got the Australian citizenship."

There were a few parents who were exemplars of bicultural identity and their quotes speak volumes about successful settlement and integration. One father from Myanmar called himself a "Karen Kangaroo" while an Ethiopian mother saw herself as, "integrated 50/50 as been here a long time (we are half Aussie); I sometimes feel like I belong somewhere in between—we just can't sit around Ethiopians drinking coffee—we need to take part in more integration." One Congolese father saw himself as both, "I see myself as Congolese Australian and African. Even God knows my colour will never change. I'll always remain Congolese." Interestingly, none of the participants ever talked about having a "refugee identity."

Overall, we found that refugee families are settling well, integrating into Australia (contrary to what is portrayed in the media or in the political rhetoric). Refugee families appear to be highly resilient, and perhaps their strong identification with religion does indeed help them navigate through various adversities into their new host country. While there may be instances of intergenerational conflict like in any other family (domestic or migrant), it appears that refugee families show that they can overcome all odds and still be a cohesive family unit. The refugee family's identity is highly intertwined with their religion and language.

Implications for Scholars and Practitioners

Having a positive self-identity is important for wellbeing, and "individuals derive positive self-attitudes from belonging to groups that are meaningful to them" (Phinney & Ong, 2007, p. 275). Therefore, studying identity and how it is shaped in newly settled refugees is important for the wellbeing (Bergquist, Soliz, Everhart, Braithwaite, & Kreimer, 2018) and positive resettlement of such groups.

When refugee parents' identities are in alignment with that of their children, this results in less intergenerational conflict and makes for happier settlement/family unit. Refugees are cognizant that this is their new country and this is where the future of their family lies, so they are supportive of integration and accept a blend of both cultures. Indeed, they could be exemplars of resilience who—despite having a disrupted life trajectory—have (in most part) a positive attitude.

Refugee settlement agencies and organizations should consider the importance of family harmony in the services and information they provide to refugees who are resettling in a new country. For the most part, these agencies normally assist refugees with employment, driving lessons, starting businesses, housing, and other aspects of holistic settlement, and some agencies are expanding to offer formal and informal support services focused on family and cultural settlement. Such services should strive to provide accurate information pre- and post-migration in order to ease families through resettlement. Information about acculturation and its impact on parenting and changing parenting roles in a culturally different environment would aid in positive family wellbeing perhaps via focused parenting workshops and family counselling services that take into account cultural differences amongst the various country groups. Such cultural orientation is currently missing from the International Organization for Migration's (IOM) Australian Cultural Orientation (AUSCO) Programme. While this programme provides refugees with practical information about life in Australia, it lacks in-depth information about parenting. This orientation could better help set refugee families up to sustain family identity and support family communication.

Future research should consider gathering holistic data from the entire family unit (i.e., both generations) and also probe further the role and importance of religiosity. Unfortunately, this was outside the scope of our study. We also had a predominantly Christian cohort in our study simply because of the country groups included in our study, hence future scholars could examine the role and importance of religion among refugees from other religious backgrounds. Most importantly, knowing and understanding that identity is complex, fluid, and can change dynamically depending on various contexts and life experiences, a longitudinal study is warrented to study the refugee family unit's identity.

In conclusion, whereas numerous psychology, sociology, and intercultural communication scholars have researched, theorized, and created a significant corpus of literature on immigrant acculturation, identity, and settlement, much scope remains with respect to the refugee population and family unit. For instance, eminent psychology researchers such as John Berry, David Sam, Jean Phinney, and Colleen Ward have formulated numerous theories of intercultural relations/communication, and other communication scholars such as Mary Fitzpatrick, Elizabeth Suter, Dawn Braithwaite, and Leslie Baxter (to name a few) have added to the body of knowledge on family communication by creating scales to measure family communication or researching families. Other scholars such as Chitra Akkoor have advocated the need to conduct more research on other family types such as refugee family units. This paper attempted to embark on that research trajectory by adding to the literature on identity within the refugee family unit.

Notes

1. For a brief overview of the history of immigration in Australia please see Udah, Singh, & Chamberlain (2019).
2. These could be either biological children, or children to whom they are legal guardians.

References

Ager, A., & Strang, A. (2008). Understanding integration: A conceptual framework. Journal of refugee studies, 21(2), 166–191.

Akkoor, C. (2014). "Is he my real uncle?" Reconstructing family in the diaspora. In L. Baxter (Ed.), *Remaking 'family' communicatively* (pp. 229–246). New York: Peter Lang.

Australian Bureau of Statistics [ABS]. (2018). *Religion in Australia: 2016 census data summary.* Retrieved from http://www.abs.gov.au/ausstats/abs@.nsf/Lookup/by%20Subject/2071.0~2016~Main%20Features~Religion%20Data%20Summary~70

Bleiker, R., Campbell, D., Hutchison, E., & Nicholson, X. (2013). The visual dehumanisation of refugees. Australian Journal of Political Science, 48(4), 398–416.

Bergquist, G., Soliz, J., Everhart, K., Braithwaite, D. O., & Kreimer, L. (2018). Investigating layers of identity and identity gaps in refugee resettlement experiences in the Midwestern United States. *Western Journal of Communication, 3,* 1–20.

Berry, J. W. (1997). Immigration, acculturation, and adaptation. *Applied Psychology: An International Review, 46*(1), 5–68. doi:10.1111/j.1464-0597.1997.tb01087.x

Berry, J. W., Phinney, J. S., Sam, D. L., & Vedder, P. (2006). Immigrant youth: Acculturation, identity, and adaptation. *Applied Psychology, 55,* 303–332. doi:10.1111/j.1464-0597.2006.00256.x

Cadge, W., & Ecklund, E. (2007). Immigration and religion. *Annual Review of Sociology, 33,* 359–379. doi:10.1146/annurev.soc.33.040406.131707

Cokley, K. (2007). Critical issues in the measurement of ethnic and racial identity: A referendum on the state of the field. *Journal of Counseling Psychology, 54*(3), 224–234. doi:10.1037/0022-0167.54.3.224

Collins, J. (2003). *Immigration and immigrant settlement in Australia: Political responses, discourses and new challenges.* Malmo, Sweden: School of International Migration and Ethnic Relations.

Department of Immigration and Border Protection [DIBP]. (2013). *Migration programme statistics.* Belconnen, Australia: Commonwealth of Australia.

Department of Immigration and Border Protection [DIBP]. (2014). *Annual report: 2013–14.* Retrieved from https://www.homeaffairs.gov.au/reports-and-pubs/Annualreports/dibp-annual-report-2013-14.pdf

Ehrkamp, P. (2006). "We Turks are no Germans": assimilation discourses and the dialectical construction of identities in Germany. *Environment and Planning A, 38*(9), 1673–1692. doi:10.1068/a38148

Fantino, A. M., & Colak, A. (2001). Refugee children in Canada: Searching for identity. *Child Welfare, 80*(5), 587–596.

Hatoss, A., & Sheely, T. (2009). Language maintenance and identity among Sudanese-Australian refugee-background youth. *Journal of Multilingual and Multicultural Development, 30*(2), 127–144. doi:10.1080/01434630802510113

Hebbani, A. G., Obijiofor, L., & Bristed, H. (2012). Acculturation challenges that confront Sudanese former refugees in Australia. *Journal of Intercultural Communication, 28*(2), 1–18.

Hebbani, A., Obijiofor, L., & MacKinnon, M. (2018, May). *Examining intergenerational cultural transmission in refugee families: A study of Congolese, Burmese, and Ethiopian refugee families resettled in Australia*. Paper presented at the International Communication Association Preconference: Inclusivity and Family Communication Research: Advances and Innovations from across the Discipline, Prague, Czech Republic.

Heinemann, A. M. (2017). The making of 'good citizens': German courses for migrants and refugees. *Studies in the Education of Adults*, *49*(2), 177–195. doi:10.1080/02660830.2018.1453115

Helms, J. E. (2007). Some better practices for measuring racial and ethnic identity constructs. Journal of Counseling Psychology, 54(3), 235.

Hiruy, K. (2009). *Finding home far away from home: place attachment, place-identity, belonging and resettlement among African-Australians in Hobart* (Doctoral dissertation). Tasmania, AUS: University of Tasmania.

McGown, R. B. (1999). *Muslims in the Diaspora: The Somali communities of London and Toronto*. Toronto, ON: University of Toronto Press.

Phinney, J. S., Horenczyk, G., Liebkind, K., & Vedder, P. (2001). Ethnic identity, immigration, and well-being: An interactional perspective. *Journal of Social Issues*, *57*, 493–510.

Phinney, J. S., & Ong, A. D. (2007). Conceptualization and measurement of ethnic identity: Current status and future directions. *Journal of Counseling Psychology*, *54*(3), 271–281. doi:10.1037/0022-0167.54.3.271

Refugee Council of Australia [RCOA]. (2012). *History of Australia's refugee program*. Retrieved from https://www.refugeecouncil.org.au/getfacts/seekingsafety/refugee-humanitarian-program/history-australias-refugee-program/.

RCOA. (2016). *UNHCR global trends 2015: How Australia compares with the world*. Retrieved from http://www.refugeecouncil.org.au/how-many-refugees/

RCOA. (2018). *How generous is Australia's Refugee Program compared to other countries? An analysis of UNHCR's 2018 Global Refugee Statistics*. Retrieved from https://www.refugeecouncil.org.au/2018-global-trends/

Renzaho, A. M., Dhingra, N., & Georgeou, N. (2017). Youth as contested sites of culture: The intergenerational acculturation gap amongst new migrant communities-Parental and young adult perspectives. *PloS one*, *12*(2), e0170700. doi:10.1371/journal.pone.0170700

Roberson, M. K. (1992). Birth, transformation, and death of refugee identity: Women and girls of the Intifada. *Women & Therapy*, *13*(1–2), 35–52. doi:10.1300/J015V13N01_05

Rousseau, C., Rufagari, M. C., Bagilishya, D., & Measham, T. (2004). Remaking family life: Strategies for re-establishing continuity among Congolese refugees during the family reunification process. *Social Science & Medicine*, *59*(5), 1095–1108. doi:10.1016/j.socscimed.2003.12.011

Rutter, J., Cooley, L., Reynolds, S., & Sheldon, R. (2007). *From refugee to citizen: 'Standing on my own two feet'. A research report on integration, 'Britishness' and *citizenship*. Report for the Metropolitan Support Trust and the Institute of Public Policy Research. London, UK.

Santisteban, D. A., & Mitrani, V. B. (2003). The influence of acculturation processes on the family. In K. M. Chun, P. Balls Organista, & G. Marín (Eds.), *Acculturation: Advances in theory, measurement, and applied research* (pp. 121–135). Washington, DC: American Psychological Association.

Tavan, G., & Neumann, K. (2009). *Does history matter?: Making and debating citizenship, immigration and refugee policy in Australia and New Zealand*. Canberra: ANU Press.

Tilley, C. (2006). Introduction: Identity, place, landscape and heritage. *Journal of Material Culture, 11*(1/2), 7–32. doi:10.1177/1359183506062990

Turner, L., & West, R. (2018). Invited essay: Investigating family voices from the margins. *Journal of Family Communication, 18*(2), 85–91. doi:10.1080/15267431.2018.1435548

Udah, H., Singh, P., & Chamberlain, S. (2019). Settlement and employment outcomes of black African immigrants in Southeast Queensland, Australia. *Asian and Pacific Migration Journal*. doi:10.1177/0117196819830247

United Nations High Commissioner for Refugees [UNHCR]. (2014). *UNHCR global trends 2013: War's human cost*. Retrieved from http://www.unhcr.org/5399a14f9.html.

UNHCR. (2015). *UNHCR global trends 2015: Figures at a glance*. Retrieved from http://www.unhcr.org/en-au/figures-at-a-glance.html.

UNHCR. (2018). *Refugee facts: What is a refugee*. Retrieved from https://www.unrefugees.org/refugee-facts/what-is-a-refugee/.

Valentine, G., Sporton, D., & Nielsen, K. B. (2009). Identities and belonging: A study of Somali refugee and asylum seekers living in the UK and Denmark. *Environment and Planning D: Society and Space, 27*(2), 234–250. doi:10.1068/d3407

Van Liempt, I. (2011). Young Dutch Somalis in the UK: Citizenship, identities and belonging in a transnational triangle. *Mobilities, 6*(4), 569–583. doi:10.1080/17450101.2011.603948

Yuval-Davis, N., Anthias, F., & Kofman, E. (2005). Secure borders and safe haven and the gendered politics of belonging: Beyond social cohesion. Ethnic and racial studies, 28(3), 513–535.

Zetter, R. (1991). Labelling refugees: Forming and transforming a bureaucratic identity. *Journal of Refugee Studies, 4*(1), 39–62. doi:10.1093/jrs/4.1.39

9. *Illness Identity Within the Family—And Beyond*

Angela L. Palmer-Wackerly and Heather L. Voorhees

Psychologists and sociologists have long studied the concept of "identity," and several communication scholars have explored how one's sense of self influences one's communicative behavior—and vice versa. But only in the past several decades have we begun researching how identity is related to illness, or *illness identity*, and how serious illness can change a person's sense of self. Illness identity has been defined in varied ways. For example, Charmaz and Rosenfeld (2010) use the term to represent the incorporation of chronic illness or disability into one's sense of self through physical impairments, emotional reactions, and cognitive beliefs about the illness. Yanos, Roe and Lysaker (2010) define illness identity as "the set of roles and attitudes that people have developed about themselves in relation to their understanding of [illness]" (p. 74). Researchers have studied illness identity within chronic illness (e.g., Charmaz, 1995; Oris et al., 2018) and within specific illness contexts, such as asthma (Adams, Pill, & Jones, 1997), cancer (Miller, 2015), diabetes (Oris et al., 2016), HIV (Baumgartner, 2007), mental illness (Jordan, Patel, & Bentley, 2017), and Parkinson's disease (Martin, 2016). While the majority of illness identity research has focused on individual, personal, or self-identity, researchers have long recognized that illnesses are also relational (Ballard-Reisch & Letner, 2003); not only can illness have a profound effect on one's family, but the family can influence how patients and others understand and experience their illness. Thus, in the following chapter, we present an overview of illness identity research within the context of family, illness identity beyond the family, and future research directions.

Connecting Illness Identity to Family Communication

Understanding Illness Identity

The modern-day understanding of "identity" was popularized by psychologist E.H. Erikson (1959), who defined it as the degree to which individuals incorporate various aspects of themselves into a coherent sense of self, which directs their everyday lives. Communication scholars have used at least two key theories to understand identity. Social Identity Theory (Tajfel & Turner, 1979) states that individuals form their identities based on memberships in multiple social groups, and that such memberships impact how people see themselves, how they behave, and what they believe. Communication Theory of Identity (Hecht, 1993) understands a person's identity as four individual, yet related and often overlapping, frames: personal (how you see yourself), relational (how your relationships shape and reflect the way you see yourself), communal (your sense of belonging to a larger group), and enacted (the way you physically or verbally demonstrate your sense of self). Using these and other theories, communication scholars have since posited that identity and health are closely linked, and have worked to outline how identity influences individuals' health behaviors, decisions, and values (Hecht & Choi, 2012). The term *illness identity* not only encompasses a person's opinions and feelings about their disease and treatment, but also how that illness changes the way they think about themselves (Charmaz, 1995). Further, illness identity encompasses how *others* understand a person's identity in relation to their illness. People with whom you have a relationship—family, friends, co-workers, healthcare professionals, etc.—have a sense of who you are within that relationship, and if a serious or chronic illness threatens their image of you, maintaining or repairing others' sense of your identity can be a struggle (Little, Paul, Jordens, & Sayers, 2002). It has been shown that patients want more information about potential identity changes when they are first diagnosed, in order to better cope with their disease (Karnilowicz, 2011).

Nearly 40% of Americans will be diagnosed with cancer at some point during their lifetimes (National Institutes of Health, 2016); approximately 86 million Americans are living with some form of cardiovascular disease or the after-effects of a stroke (American Heart Association, 2014); and half of all American adults cope with at least one chronic illness (Ward, Schiller, & Goodman, 2014), which is an ongoing, incurable condition such as diabetes, Crohn's disease, rheumatoid arthritis, or psoriasis. Serious illness touches many families, and the process of (not) accepting that illness into personal and relational identities can influence how a family communicates and functions. For example, when a partner supports an individual through an illness, that partner is reaffirming the patient's relational identity by acknowledging the patient's important role in the family (Charmaz, 1995). But if a patient is confused about or threatened by an illness's impact on his or her relational identity, he or she may not feel comfortable with, or entitled to, seeking support (Miller, 2015). Further, identity is shaped by "our understanding of what others expect us to do" (Combs & Freedman, 2016, p. 213), so when a patient's symptoms or treatments prevent them from participating in the family the way they once did, it can change familial roles and relational identities.

Invisible illnesses, or those that are not readily physically apparent to others, present a unique nuance to illness identity, in that patients with diagnoses of multiple sclerosis or irritable bowel syndrome, for example, can sometimes choose to conceal their illness, which can lower the illness' impact on their overall sense of self (Quinn & Earnshaw, 2011). Parents of children with invisible disabilities, such as autism or learning disabilities, tend to identify their children as both "normal" *and* "disabled," rather than allowing one label to dominate that child's identity (Harry, Rueda, & Kalyanpur, 1999). Additionally, research has shown that development and acceptance of an illness identity is shaped by factors like patient age, gender, race, and ethnicity (e.g., Hausmann, Ren, & Sevick, 2010; Iida, Stephens, Rook, Franks, & Salem, 2010).

Illness Identity and Families

Social support has been shown to facilitate adjustment to illness through increased empathy, respect, and constructive discussions (Funch & Marshall, 1983), and patients experiencing serious or chronic illness often rely on loved ones for support. Patients want family members to allow them to express their worries and fears honestly while also feeling valued, loved, and cared for. Emotional support (expressions of caring, concern, and empathy) has been particularly important in facilitating patients' psychological adjustment to illness (e.g., Gotcher, 1993). Support has also been shown to increase individuals' adherence to community healthful norms, perceptions of personal control, and intent to choose healthful behaviors later (Goldsmith & Albrecht, 2011).

Thus, researchers have explored how illness and illness identity influence supportive communication within families, including between parents and children, siblings, and spouses. In one study, HIV-positive parents of children ages 10 to 18 often struggled to be transparent and honest with their children about HIV and AIDS prevention and symptoms, because openly talking about their HIV or AIDS diagnoses seemed at odds with their desired identities of being responsible parents (Edwards, Donovan-Kicken, & Reis, 2014).

Women who are diagnosed with breast cancer in middle-age can experience shifts in their relational identities with their mothers; aging mothers tend to depend on their middle-aged daughters for various types of support, but a middle-aged daughter's cancer diagnosis presents an opportunity for the mothers to support the daughter (Oktay & Walter, 1991). Likewise, within marriages, one person's cancer experience can shape how they and their spouses understand their overall marriage by either amplifying, clarifying, or threatening their shared "couple identity" of the relationship itself (Miller & Caughlin, 2013).

Another type of support, called *decisional support*, is when loved ones assist patients with treatment decisions. Krieger et al. (2015) found that when a patient and a family member framed cancer illness identity in different ways—either "my cancer" or "our cancer"—the relationship experienced tension, and complicated treatment decision-making. Palmer-Wackerly et al. (2018) extended this work by connecting patients' cancer identity to their decision-making about cancer clinical trials. Patients were found to either enroll in or decline clinical trials based on how well the cancer trial aligned or conflicted with their cancer illness identity, including if they viewed themselves as sick or healthy and/or how their illness intersected with other key identities (e.g., mom, Christian, grandmother).

Support is not always effective, however. For example, in cases of disability, individuals complain of others offering assistance in patronizing ways that are more about making themselves feel better than genuinely caring for another (i.e., asking to help push a wheelchair) (Braithwaite & Japp, 2005). Thus, individuals with visible illness or disability struggle with communicating that they are "able" to perform tasks to others who see them as "not able" to perform tasks, and social support is not always desired. In contrast, individuals with hidden illnesses may desire support but do not want others to see them differently. In other cases, individuals with illness or disability may know exactly what type of help they want, such as physical assistance with lifting or moving something (Braithwaite & Japp, 2005). In certain illness contexts, it is often difficult for supportive others to know what support to offer when patients themselves are not sure what support they desire.

Though scholars have learned much about illness identity in the past several decades, there are still gaps in our knowledge of how and why illness may change a person's identity, and how that illness identity may influence a person's relationships. This is a burgeoning area of research, and we have much to learn about how specific illnesses affect illness identity acceptance, how demographics like age and gender may influence illness identity, and how family support (or lack thereof) can impact one's illness identity.

Beyond the Family: Illness Identity and Society

While family communication and illness identity can mutually influence each other, societal communication can also mutually influence illness identity and family communication. For example, social support can be perceived as more effective when all parties share similar social identities, or membership within similar groups (Haslam, Jetten, O'Brien, & Jacobs, 2004). In the case of traumatic brain injury, patients' identity strength and well-being were increased through support from family and others in their social network (Jones et al., 2011). Likewise, social identity has been shown to operate as a coping resource in that members of disadvantaged groups tend to help each other through emotional, informational, and tangible resources to "collectively resist" stigma and discrimination (Haslam, Jetten, Postmes, & Haslam, 2009, p. 13) by rejecting negative stereotypes and reaffirming positive evaluations of themselves in contexts, such as epilepsy (e.g., Jacoby, Snape, & Baker, 2005) and stroke (Shadden & Agan, 2004). Further, as Harwood and Sparks (2003) argue, individuals who strongly identify with a social group at risk for certain diseases (e.g., cervical cancer, breast cancer) are more likely to engage in preventative health practices, such as pap smears or mammograms.

Self-help support groups, both face-to-face and online, have been associated with positive health benefits for its participants through such activities as sharing information, giving diverse perspectives, encouraging hope, allowing venting, sharing humor, and relating with similar others (Braithwaite, Waldron, & Finn, 1999), especially for individuals who struggle with a hidden illness, such as infertility, or who have trouble finding similar others (Malik & Coulson, 2010). Online support groups can also create collective illness identities (e.g., people with eating disorders), in which participants frame experiences in ways that enhance trust, bonding, and group cohesion (Koski, 2014). Formal computer-mediated support group interventions that combine educational and emotional support for members (e.g., Comprehensive Health Enhancement Support System [CHESS] for women with breast cancer) have resulted in significant increases of perceived social support, quality of life, and self-efficacy in disease management as well as a significant decrease in depression (Rains & Young, 2009). However, face-to-face support group participants often complain of low attendance. One reason for avoiding these social situations is the fear of confronting evidence of future selves as immobile or physically weaker (Braithwaite & Japp, 2005). Likewise, individuals may compare themselves to others and feel like their illness experience is not as legitimate as others with worse conditions (e.g., terminal cancer vs. cancer survivor; infertility before children [primary infertility] vs. after children [secondary infertility]). Some support groups recognize the key role families play in constructing illness identity and offer either separate forums for the unique needs of caregivers (Hornillos & Crespo, 2012) or combined forums where patients and family members can discuss comprehensive illness needs (Paige, Damiani, Flood-Grady, & Krieger, 2019).

Social Legitimacy of Illness Identity

Social legitimacy is an interdisciplinary term that has been defined as "how certain forces continue to make and impose certain exclusions and inclusions within the social order, in effect giving legitimacy to … and thus constituting that very social order" (Prasad, 2007, p. 3492). In this way, legitimacy is seen as given by powerful structures in their validation of dominant ideas. For the purpose of relating social legitimacy to illness identity, we define social legitimacy as a perceived social acceptance or recognition of the severity of an illness. Thus, social legitimacy has implications for illness identity (trans) formation and acceptance within families through macro-level factors, such as *language*, *culture*, and *stigma*.

Language. Illness identity influences how individuals prefer to receive (and even interpret) support from their family and friends. To give effective support, people with a certain illness and people without that illness must share a common language with a common understanding (Bowker, 1996). Although patients often use similar language to explain a disease (i.e., cancer), the meaning behind the term may differ. For example, Bowker (1996) described others' tendency to frame cancer as a battle when discussing her cancer experiences with her. She, however, did not like the term "battle," as it meant to her that cancer would be relentless and never-ending. Another study showed that rural cancer patients interpreted metaphors differently in relation to cancer treatment risk, which may affect treatment decision-making (Krieger, Parrott, & Nussbaum, 2011). For example, health care providers often use metaphors to explain illnesses and treatments to patients, but metaphors may have different meanings to different people. One experiment involving rural, middle-aged women (Krieger et al., 2011) showed that participants were more likely to express higher intentions of participating in a clinical trial when they heard the trial described with the metaphor *Randomization is like the sex of a baby. The possibility of a boy is the same as the possibility of a girl* (p. 9), than when they heard the standard clinical metaphor of *Randomization is like the flip of a coin. The possibility of getting heads is the same as the possibility of getting tails* (p. 8). To this particular audience, the "sex of a baby" metaphor was more culturally grounded, and therefore more relatable and meaningful to their lives. These results show the importance of affect in information-processing of language, with the latter having a negative cultural connotation of gambling and chance with one's life, and the former a positive cultural connotation of family.

Culture. Cultural groups have shown how families can influence societal understanding of illness identity. Culture has been defined in more than 300 ways; however, an intergroup perspective on culture and communication involves moving away from fixed categories (e.g., gender, race, ethnicity) to examining how communication creates and maintains membership in communities (Hecht, Jackson, & Pitts, 2005). Different cultural groups, defined as groups that share similar everyday behavior, explain illness through explanatory models (EMs) consisting of different causes, symptoms, treatments, and effects (Shaw, Armin, Torres, Orzech, & Vivian, 2012, p. 69). EMs can influence treatment decision-making through understanding of risk and treatment adherence (Lee & Vang, 2010). For example, in *The Spirit Catches You and You Fall Down* (Fadiman, 1997), a Hmong family in California understood their daughter Lia's epilepsy to be a privileged medical/spiritual condition that brought her in closer contact with spirits; however, they also blamed an older daughter for causing the onset of Lia's epilepsy by slamming the door too loudly, which caused spirits to abandon Lia's body. Doctors predicted Lia, who became permanently disabled at nearly 5 years old, would live a few months at most; however, she lived to be 30 years old and remained a central part of all family celebrations. As one of her physicians described, "We saw her life ending when she was 5, but her mother's unconditional love taught me the value of life" (Magagnini, 2012). Thus, how families define illness identity for loved ones can change how others outside the family, including health care providers, view patients' personal and relational illness identity.

Stigma. One key barrier to social legitimacy for individuals and families experiencing illness, however, is stigma. Stigma has been defined as "an attribute that is deeply discrediting" (Goffman, 1963, p. 3) with individuals being perceived as "tainted" and "discounted" (p. 3). Stigma can be applied by others, but also by the self (Defenbaugh, 2013). All illness can be viewed as stigmatizing, especially terminal illness (Harwood & Sparks, 2003); however, some may be more so than others. For people with stigmatized illnesses, such as sexually-transmitted infections or mental illnesses, anticipated stigma (the negative treatment people expect to receive from others) and internalized stigma (negative beliefs about oneself, often learned from family, peers, or media) can increase their psychological distress (Quinn and Earnshaw, 2013). Meisenbach (2010) developed Stigma Management Communication theory, which helps to explain how people perceive and react to stigma, including stigmatized illness. This theory posits three main tenets: (a) stigmas are constructed via communication and managed through the perceptions of both stigmatized and non-stigmatized individuals; (b) stigmas are created and changed by ever-shifting perceptions and experiences; and (c) stigmas vary in breadth and depth. Schneider (2003) noted that individuals with stigmatizing illness identities strategically interact with others about their illness when facing larger structural or cultural forces, using tactics such as distancing (i.e., separating oneself from his or her illness), rejecting (i.e., failure to relate the meanings of the illness to oneself while also acknowledging the illness meanings for others), and normalizing (i.e., challenging the meanings of an illness). For example, HIV-positive patients in Saskatoon, Canada, who embraced a positive illness identity often took on the role of community "helper," educating others about HIV and openly sharing their personal experiences (Hatala et al., 2018). Alternatively, Bergquist (2018) found that family stigma and community stigma about mental health led to an increase in self-stigma about mental health, which predicted lower perceived importance of seeking help from health care professionals. Likewise, values associated with rural identity—stoicism, control, and self-reliance—were related to higher stigma from the self, family, community, and public about mental health. Faith-based community organizations, such as churches, have also been shown to perpetuate stigma around certain conditions, such as mental illness (Bryant, Moore, Willis, & Hadden, 2015) and HIV (Hartwig, 2013), resulting in social isolation, depression, and shame for patients and families with those illnesses. Thus, stigma from a variety of sources affects how individuals construct meaning of their illness in their self-concept, their relationships, and their social groups.

Implications for Scholars, Practitioners, and Families

The purpose of above sections is to connect illness identity to family communication to show that our understanding of illness is created, maintained, and influenced by the communication within families, as well as by communication occurring outside the family. Below, we outline promising areas for future researchers and clinicians to help families cope with the realities of illness identities.

Conceptual Clarification: Health Identity versus Illness Identity

Health has been defined as the absence of illness, which is understood as "normalcy" (Defenbaugh, 2013), and health identity has been used in juxtaposition to illness identity. However, just because an individual has an illness, does not mean that that they view themselves as unhealthy (Palmer-Wackerly et al., 2018), especially when considering identity transformations that occur during chronic illness. In other words, a medical diagnosis may not be an individual's only evaluation of health; their subjective interpretations of how their bodies *feel* and how their illnesses are *managed* might be better predictors of whether people identify as healthy or ill (Roberto and McCann, 2011). People with chronic illness must learn to adapt to their illness because it is most likely a permanent condition (e.g., diabetes, alcoholism, heart disease) (Hayden, 1993); thus, the chronic illness context requires patients to incorporate elements of their medical condition into their overall identity if they are to manage their disease and relationships effectively. Thus, the more disruptive to their lives an illness or limitation is, the more central "health" becomes to individuals' personal identities (Roberto & McCann, 2011). This salience leads individuals with chronic illness to redefine themselves in order to accept their changed personal and social reality, which often involves a loss of some kind (Hayden, 1993). More research is needed to understand how, when, and why people shift back and forth from considering themselves "healthy" to identifying as "ill," and what effect these shifts may have on their illness identity, relationships, and overall well-being. More research in this area could help clinicians in working with patients and families who are struggling to cope with chronic illness, particularly illnesses involving a high degree of uncertainty, complexity, unpredictability, and rarity. More research could also help families understand that "illness" can be experienced in different, multiple, and contradictory ways and to give each other the space to grieve their losses, negotiate new meanings about illness and health, and find new relationships and identities, thus improving their relationships and quality of life.

Theoretical Development: Communication across the Illness Trajectory and Lifespan

To improve individuals' quality of life, lower healthcare costs, and improve treatment decision-making, it is important to understand how individuals' illness identity is changed and managed across the illness trajectory and lifespan. Inherent in this theoretical development is research that shows that illness need not exist in our physical bodies to still become part of our illness identity. For example, one area of illness identity and family research focuses on the pre-identity of cancer, or *previvors*, who are defined as "survivors of a predisposition to cancer but who haven't had the disease" (Facing Our Risk of Cancer Empowered [FORCE], 2009). In one study, researchers found that previvors have unique medical, personal, and social information needs (such as preventative treatment decisions) that change across four stages: pre-testing, post-testing, pre-management, and post-management (Dean et al., 2017). Illness identities can also stretch through multiple generations via health legacies, where stories of family members' diagnosis and management can affect future generations' health communication and behavioral choices (Alemán & Helfrich, 2010). The rise of genetic testing—both in medical settings and via mass-market, at-home kits—is making family medical histories more salient to a broader population, and is changing how individuals think about health and illness prevention. Future studies should explore how genetic medical information impacts family communication about health and illness, and what impact family health histories may have on individuals' current and future health choices. Information gleaned from such studies could aid families in more thoughtfully understanding and discussing their medical histories, and could help genetic counselors offer more effective and personalized advice.

As chronic illness becomes more common, the fluidity of illness identity is also becoming increasingly important. For example, there is much we need to learn about how age affects illness identity. There has been some research around the illness identity of pediatric patients (e.g. Luyckx et al., 2018; Waldron, Malpus, Shearing, Sanchez, & Murray, 2017), but scholars have called for more studies examining how age at diagnosis influences illness identity development (Oris et al., 2016). This type of research could help parents of pediatric patients better understand their child's illness experience, and communicate more effectively and sensitively. Beyond chronological age, we should continue studying how one's illness identity changes and evolves over the course of illness duration. For instance, infertility treatment can occur over several years, which can affect how patients and partners understand their infertility, accompanying needs and treatment goals, but also how they want to communicate with health care providers about their infertility across the treatment trajectory (Palmer-Wackerly, Voorhees, D'Souza, & Weeks, 2019). Likewise, as individuals move from cancer patient to cancer survivor, both patient and caregiver illness identities change, with patients worried about the cancer returning, couples renegotiating their roles, and caregivers sometimes mourning the loss of their caregiver role (Miller & Caughlin, 2013). Future researchers should take a longitudinal look at illness identity, to study how it may evolve, and what impact that evolution has on a person's communicative and health behavior.

Operationalization of Illness Identity

Much of extant illness identity research is qualitative, exploring unique, multiple and conflicting experiences of individuals and families. However, quantitative and mixed-methods research is also needed to explain, generalize, and predict aspects of illness identity uncovered in qualitative studies. For instance, though qualitative research has demonstrated that accepting an illness identity can result in lower stress and higher overall well-being, it is not clear if the relationship between illness identity and physical health is causal—and, if it is, which variable (illness identity acceptance or physical/mental health) causes the other (Oris et al., 2018). In other words, does the joint pain and fatigue brought by rheumatoid arthritis cause an otherwise healthy 23-year-old patient to adopt an illness identity of feeling older and helpless, or does the identity threat posed by rheumatoid arthritis make joint pain and fatigue physically and mentally feel more severe? The relationship between illness identity, family, and behavior also needs to be explored more fully. Because loved ones often play a vital role in patient education, symptom management, and treatment decisions, more research is needed to determine what role illness identity and family support play in patient-provider communication (Ballard-Reisch & Letner, 2003) and health outcomes (Palmer-Wackerly et al., 2018).

To our knowledge, only one scale attempts to *explicitly* measure illness identity. Oris et al. (2016) developed and validated the Illness Identity Questionnaire, a 26-item scale that measures individuals in four factors of personal illness acceptance: engulfment, rejection, acceptance, and enrichment. Much more work needs to be done to understand how illness identity relates to physical and psychological functioning before this scale can be useful to clinicians (Oris et al., 2016); however, as this work continues to be developed, it is promising in its ability to help patients and families understand and take ownership of their illness experiences.

Additional research is also needed to extend the explanatory and predictive knowledge of illness identity, including relational and communal identity, along with its antecedents and outcomes. For example, April and colleagues (2019) found that the severity of a chronic illness diagnosis predicted a significant change in patients' relational illness identity, which in turn lowered patient psychosocial well-being. However, this relationship only occurred if patients perceive their relational identity change as negative. Interestingly, severity of diagnosis did not predict personal or communal identity. Paige et al. (2019) examined chronic obstructive pulmonary disease (COPD) illness identity, which is understudied in health communication research, and found that a COPD diagnosis was associated with rural patients' acceptance of a communal COPD identity, which in turn was associated with patients' perceptions of online related support as helpful to their coping efforts (Paige et al., 2019). Thus, much more quantitative and mixed-methods work needs to be done to explore, understand, measure, explain, and predict illness identity and its influence on treatment outcomes and overall well-being. This work is particularly important and becomes increasingly complex considering that individuals are living longer and often have multiple diagnosed chronic illnesses.

Conclusion

Chronic illness affects the health and economic well-being of every country in the world. As a result, the United Nations made chronic illness a key focus in its 2011 meeting (U.S. Institute of Medicine, 2012). In the U.S., approximately half of all adults (117 million people) are struggling with chronic illness (Ward et al., 2014); one in four Americans are living with two or more such conditions (U.S. Institute of Medicine, 2012). The two most common chronic health illnesses, heart disease and cancer, account for nearly half of all deaths in the U.S. (Ward et al., 2014). Other non-life-threatening diseases, such as arthritis, diabetes, and obesity, are leading causes of disability and significantly disrupt individuals' quality of life. As a result, chronic illness is responsible for 84% of our nation's health care costs (Johnson, Hayes, Brown, Hoo, & Ethier, 2014), and the U.S. Institute of Medicine (2012) concluded that improving quality of life for chronically ill individuals has not been given the research funding or attention that it requires to improve control of chronic illness and overall patient well-being.

Thus, this chapter explored the importance of illness identity as it relates to the support for, and social legitimacy of, illness, and overall patient and family well-being. Because families are often participants in loved ones' illness experiences, we focused on the influence of family communication within illness identity. We offered an overview of the various ways communication scholars have studied illness identity and its influence on communicative behavior within and outside of family relationships, and we identified future research avenues that can offer new perspectives on personal, relational, and communal illness identity. Over the past several decades, we have increasingly learned much about the emotional, spiritual, mental, and social ramifications of illness, and we are constantly expanding our understanding of illness identity. Just as clinicians and scientists continue to search for treatments and cures, communication researchers must continue to study how, when, and why illness mutually affects one's identity, relationships, family roles, disclosure, support-seeking, and coping efforts—in short, the lived experience of illness.

References

Adams, S., Pill, R., & Jones, A. (1997). Medication, chronic illness and identity: The perspective of people with asthma. *Social Science & Medicine, 45*, 189–201. https://doi.org/10.1016/S0277-9536(96)00333-4

Alemán, M. W., & Helfrich, K. W. (2010). Inheriting the narratives of dementia: A collaborative tale of a daughter and mother. *Journal of Family Communication, 10*, 7–23. https://doi.org/10.1080/15267430903385784

American Heart Association Statistics Committee and Stroke Statistics Committee. (2014). *Heart disease and stroke statistics—2015 update: A report from the American Heart Association.* https://www.ahajournals.org/doi/10.1161/CIR.0000000000000152

April, M., Soliz, J., Brock, R. L., & Palmer-Wackerly, A. L. (2019). Perceived severity of chronic illness diagnosis and psychosocial well-being: Exploring magnitude and affective dimensions of change in layers of identity. Paper presented to the Health Communication division at the 2019 annual meeting of the National Communication Association, Baltimore, MD.

Ballard-Reisch, D. S., & Letner, J. A. (2003). Centering families in cancer communication research: Acknowledging the impact of support, culture and process on client/provider communication in cancer management. *Patient Education and Counseling, 50*, 61–66. doi:10.1016/S0738-3991(03)00082-X

Baumgartner, L. M. (2007). The incorporation of the HIV/AIDS identity into the self over time. *Qualitative Health Research, 17*, 919–931. https://doi.org/10.1177%2F1049732307305881

Bergquist, G. (2018). Mental health care and sociocultural context: Understanding intersections of stigma socialization and mental health care service use in rural areas. *ETD Collection for University of Nebraska – Lincoln*, 1–284.

Bowker, J. (1996). Cancer, individual process, and control: A case study in metaphor analysis. *Health Communication, 8*, 91–104. doi:10.1207/s15327027hc0801_5

Braithwaite, D. O., & Japp, P. (2005). "They make us miserable in the name of helping us": Communication of personas with visible and invisible disabilities. In E. B. Ray (Ed.), *Health communication in practice: A case study approach* (pp. 171–179). Mahwah, NJ: Lawrence Erlbaum Associates, Publishers.

Braithwaite, D. O., Waldron, V. R., & Finn, J. (1999). Communication of social support in computer-mediated groups for people with disabilities. *Health Communication, 11*, 123.

Bryant, K., Moore, T., Willis, N., & Hadden, K. (2015). Development of a faith-based stress management intervention in a rural African American community. *Progress in Community Health Partnerships : Research, Education, and Action, 9*, 423–430. https://doi.org/10.1353/cpr.2015.0060

Charmaz, K. (1995). The body, identity, and self: Adapting to impairment. *Sociological Quarterly, 36*, 657–680. https://doi.org/10.1111/j.1533-8525.1995.tb00459.x

Charmaz, K., & Rosenfeld, D. (2010). Chronic illness. In W.C. Cockerham (Ed.), *The New Blackwell Companion to medical sociology* (pp. 312–333). Oxford, UK: Wiley-Blackwell.

Combs, G., & Freedman, J. (2016). Narrative therapy's relational understanding of identity. *Family Process, 55*, 211–224. https://doi.org/10.1111/famp.12216

Dean, M., Scherr, C. L., Clements, M., Koruo, R., Martinez, J., & Ross, A. (2017). "When information is not enough": A model for understanding BRCA-positive previvors' information needs regarding hereditary breast and ovarian cancer risk. *Patient Education and Counseling, 100*, 1738–1743. https://doi.org/10.1016/j.pec.2017.03.013

Defenbaugh, N. L. (2013). Revealing and concealing ill identity: A performance narrative of IBD disclosure. *Health Communication, 28*, 159–169. doi:10.1080/10410236.2012.666712

Edwards, L. L., Donovan-Kicken, E., & Reis, J. S. (2014). Communicating in complex situations: A normative approach to HIV-related talk among parents who are HIV+. *Health Communication, 29*, 364–374. https://doi.org/10.1080/10410236.2012.757715

Erikson, E. H. (1959). *Identity and the life cycle: Selected papers.* New York: International Universities Press.

Facing Our Cancer Risk Empowered [FORCE]. (2009). *What is a previvor?* Retrieved April 8, 2019, from https://www.facingourrisk.org/understanding-brca-and-hboc/publications/newsletter/archives/2009winter/what-is-previvor.php

Fadiman, A. (1997). *The spirit catches you and you fall down: A Hmong child, her American doctors, and the collision of two cultures* (1st ed.). New York: Farrar, Straus, and Giroux.

Funch, D., & Marshall, J. (1983). The role of stress, social support and age in survival from breast cancer. *Journal of Psychosomatic Research, 27*, 77–83.

Goffman, E. (1963). *Stigma; notes on the management of spoiled identity.* Englewood Cliffs, NJ: Prentice-Hall.

Goldsmith, D. J., & Albrecht, T. L. (2011). Social support, social networks, and health. In T. L. Thompson, R. L. Parrott, & J. F. Nussbaum (Eds.), *Handbook of health communication* (2nd ed., pp. 335–348). New York, NY: Routledge.

Gotcher, J. M. (1993). The effects of family communication on psychosocial adjustment of cancer patients. *Journal of Applied Communication Research, 21*, 176–188.

Harris, J., Bowen, D. J., Badr, H., Hannon, P., Hay, J., & Sterba, K. R. (2009). Family communication during the cancer experience. *Journal of Health Communication, 14*, 76–84. http://doi.org/10.1080/10810730902806844

Harry, B., Rueda, R., & Kalyanpur, M. (1999). Cultural reciprocity in sociocultural perspective: Adapting the normalization principle for family collaboration. *Exceptional Children, 66*, 123–136. https://doi.org/10.1177%2F001440299906600108

Hartwig, K. A. (2013). Faith-based community health interventions: Incorporating cultural ecology, the social ecological framework, and gender analysis. In G. L. Kreps,

D. K. Kim, & A. Singhal (Eds.), *Health Communication: Strategies for Developing Global Health Programs* (pp. 244–261). New York: Peter Lang Publishing, Inc.

Harwood, J., & Sparks, L. (2003). Social identity and health: An intergroup communication approach to cancer. *Health Communication, 15*, 145–159.

Haslam, S. A., Jetten, J., O'Brien, A., & Jacobs, E. (2004). Social identity, social influence and reactions to potentially stressful tasks: Support for the self-categorization model of stress. *Stress and Health*, 20(1), 3–9. http://doi.org/10.1002/smi.995

Haslam, S. A., Jetten, J., Postmes, T., & Haslam, C. (2009). Social identity, health and well-being: An emerging agenda for applied psychology. *Applied Psychology, 58*(1), 1–23. https://doi.org/10.1111/j.1464-0597.2008.00379.x

Hatala, A. R., Bird-Naytowhow, K., Pearl, T., Peterson, J., del Canto, S., Rooke, E., … Tait, P. (2018). Being and becoming a helper: Illness disclosure and identity transformations among Indigenous people living with HIV or AIDS in Saskatoon, Saskatchewan. *Qualitative Health Research, 28*, 1099–1111. https://doi.org/10.1177%2F1049732318764394

Hausmann, L. R., Ren, D., & Sevick, M. A. (2010). Racial differences in diabetes-related psychosocial factors and glycemic control in patients with type 2 diabetes. *Patient Preference and Adherence, 4*, 291.

Hayden, S. (1993). Chronically ill and "feeling fine": A study of communication and chronic illness. *Journal of Applied Communication Research, 21*, 263.

Hecht, M. L. (1993). 2002—A research odyssey: Toward the development of a communication theory of identity. *Communication Monographs, 60*, 76–82. https://doi.org/10.1080/03637759309376297

Hecht, M. L., & Choi, H. (2012). The communication theory of identity as a framework for health message design. In H. Cho (Ed.), *Health communication message design: Theory and practice* (pp. 137–151). Thousand Oaks, CA: SAGE Publications.

Hecht, M. L., Jackson, R. L., & Pitts, M. (2005). Culture: Intersections of intergroup and identity theories. In J. Harwood & H. Giles (Eds.), *Intergroup communication: Multiple perspectives* (pp. 21–42). New York: Peter Lang.

Hornillos, C., & Crespo, M. (2012). Support groups for caregivers of Alzheimer patients: A historical review. *Dementia, 11*, 155–169. https://doi.org/10.1177/1471301211421258

Iida, M., Stephens, M. A. P., Rook, K. S., Franks, M. M., & Salem, J. K. (2010). When the going gets tough, does support get going? Determinants of spousal support provision to type 2 diabetic patients. *Personality and Social Psychology Bulletin, 36*, 780–791. https://doi.org/10.1177%2F0146167210369897

Institute of Medicine. 2012. Living Well with Chronic Illness: A Call for Public Health Action. Washington, DC: The National Academies Press. https://doi.org/10.17226/13272.

Jacoby, A., Snape, D., & Baker, G. A. (2005). Epilepsy and social identity: The stigma of a chronic neurological disorder. *The Lancet Neurology, 4*, 171–178. http://doi.org/10.1016/S1474-4422(05)01014-8

Johnson, N. B., Hayes, L. D., Brown, K., Hoo, E. C., & Ethier, K. A. (2014). CDC National Health Report: leading causes of morbidity and mortality and associated behavioral risk and protective factors—United States, 2005–2013.

Jones, J., Haslam, S. A., Jetten, J., Williams, W. H., Morris, R., & Saroyan, S. (2011). That which doesn't kill us can make us stronger (and more satisfied with life): The contribution of personal and social changes to well-being after acquired brain injury. *Psychology & Health, 26*, 353–369.

Jordan, J., Patel, N., & Bentley, K. J. (2017). Emerging adult identity following adolescent experiences with psychotropic medications: A retrospective study. *Journal of Human Behavior in the Social Environment, 27*, 694–705. https://doi.org/10.1080/10911359.2017.1327390

Karnilowicz, W. (2011). Identity and psychological ownership in chronic illness and disease state. *European Journal of Cancer Care, 20*, 276–282. https://doi.org/10.1111/j.1365-2354.2010.01220.x

Koski, J. P. (2014). "I'm just a walking eating disorder": The mobilisation and construction of a collective illness identity in eating disorder support groups. *Sociology of Health & Illness, 36*, 75–90. https://doi-org.libproxy.unl.edu/10.1111/1467-9566.12044

Krieger, J. L., Palmer-Wackerly, A. L., Krok-Schoen, J. L., Dailey, P. M., Wojno, J. C., Schoenberg, N., … Dignan, M. (2015). Caregiver perceptions of their influence on cancer treatment decision-making: Intersections of language, identity, and illness. *Journal of Language and Social Psychology, 34*(6), 640–656. https://doi.org/10.1177/0261927X15587556

Krieger, J. L., Parrott, R. L., & Nussbaum, J. F. (2011). Metaphor use and health literacy: A pilot study of strategies to explain randomization in cancer clinical trials. *Journal of Health Communication, 16*, 3–16. doi:10.1080/10810730.2010.529494

Lee, H., & Vang, S. (2010). Barriers to cancer screening in Hmong Americans: The influence of health care accessibility, culture, and cancer literacy. *Journal of Community Health, 35*(3), 302–314. doi:10.1007/s10900-010-9228-7

Little, M., Paul, K., Jordens, C. F. C., & Sayers, E. J. (2002). Survivorship and discourses of identity. *Psycho-Oncology, 11*, 170–178. https://doi.org/10.1002/pon.549

Luyckx, K., Oris, L., Raymaekers, K., Rassart, J., Moons, P., Verdyck, L., … Mark, R. E. (2018). Illness identity in young adults with refractory epilepsy. *Epilepsy & Behavior, 80*, 48–55. https://doi.org/10.1016/j.yebeh.2017.12.036

Magagnini, S. (2012, September 16). Lia Lee dies; daughter of Hmong refugees changed American views of medicine. *The Washington Post.* Retrieved from https://www.washingtonpost.com/national/health-science/lia-lee-dies-daughter-of-hmong-refugees-changed-american-views-of-medicine/2012/09/16/44f1a9e4-0011-11e2-9367-4e1bafb958db_story.html?utm_term=.7fbfb7c6091b

Malik, S. H., & Coulson, N. S. (2010). Coping with infertility online: An examination of self-help mechanisms in an online infertility support group. *Patient Education and Counseling, 81*, 315–318.

Martin, S. C. (2016). The experience and communicative management of identity threats among people with Parkinson's disease: Implications for health communication theory and practice. *Communication Monographs, 83*, 303–325. https://doi.org/10.1080/03637751.2016.1146407

Meisenbach, R. (2010). Stigma Management Communication: A theory and agenda for applied research on how individuals manage moments of stigmatized identity. *Journal of Applied Communication Research, 38*(3), 268–292. https://doi-org.libproxy.unl.edu/10.1080/00909882.2010.490841

Miller, L. (2015). 'People don't understand that it is not easy being a cancer survivor': Communicating and negotiating identity throughout cancer survivorship. *Southern Communication Journal, 80*(1), 1–19. https://doi.org/10.1080/1041794X.2014.936971

Miller, L. E., & Caughlin, J. P. (2013). 'We're going to be survivors': Couples' identity challenges during and after cancer treatment. *Communication Monographs, 80*(1), 63–82. http://dx.doi.org/10.1080/03637751.2012.739703

National Institutes of Health. (2016). https://www.cancer.gov/about cancer/understanding/statistics. Accessed April 9, 2017.

Oktay, J. S., & Walter, C. A. (1991). *Breast cancer in the life course: Women's experiences.* New York: Springer.

Oris, L., Luyckx, K., Rassart, J., Goubert, L., Goossens, E., Apers, S., ... Moons, P. (2018). Illness identity in adults with a chronic illness. *Journal of Clinical Psychology in Medical Settings, 25*, 429–440. https://doi.org/10.1007/s10880-018-9552-0

Oris, L., Rassart, J., Prikken, S., Verschueren, M., Goubert, L., Moons, P., ... Luyckx, K. (2016). Illness identity in adolescents and emerging adults with type 1 diabetes: Introducing the Illness Identity Questionnaire. *Diabetes Care, 39*, 757–763. https://doi.org/10.2337/dc15-2559

Paige, S. R., Damiani, R. E., Flood-Grady, E., & Krieger, J. L. (2019, March). The perceived availability of online social support: Exploring the contributions of illness and rural identities in respiratory health. Accepted for presentation at the 2019 College of Journalism and Communications Research Symposium, Gainesville, FL.

Palmer-Wackerly, A. L., Dailey, P. M., Krok-Schoen, J. L., Rhodes, N. D., & Krieger, J. L. (2018). Patient perceptions of illness identity in cancer clinical trial decision-making. *Health Communication, 33*, 1045–1054. https://doi.org/10.1080/10410236.2017.1331189

Palmer-Wackerly, A. L., Voorhees, H. L., D'Souza, S., & Weeks, E. (2019). Infertility patient-provider communication and (dis)continuity of care: An exploration of illness identity transitions. *Patient Education and Counseling, 102*(4), 804–809. https://doi.org/10.1016/j.pec.2018.12.003

Prasad, N. P. (2007). Medicine, power and social legitimacy: A socio-historical appraisal of health systems in contemporary India. *Economic and Political Weekly, 42*, 3491–3498.

Quinn, D. M., & Earnshaw, V. A. (2011). Understanding concealable stigmatized identities: The role of identity in psychological, physical, and behavioral outcomes. *Social Issues and Policy Review*, *5*, 160–190. https://doi.org/10.1111/j.1751-2409.2011.01029.x

Quinn, D. M., & Earnshaw, V. A. (2013). Concealable stigmatized identities and psychological well-being. *Social and Personality Psychology Compass*, *7*, 40–51. https://doi.org/10.1111/spc3.12005

Rains, S. A., & Young, V. (2009). A meta-analysis of research on formal computer-mediated support groups: Examining group characteristics and health outcomes. Human communication research, 35(3), 309–336. https://doi.org/10.1111/j.1468-2958.2009.01353.x

Roberto, K. A., & McCann, B. R. (2011). Everyday health and identity management among older women with chronic health conditions. *Journal of Aging Studies*, *25*, 94–100.

Schneider, B. (2003). Narratives of Schizophrenia: Constructing a Positive Identity. *Canadian Journal of Communication*, *28*, 185–201. https://doi.org/10.22230/cjc.2003v28n2a1358

Shadden, B. B., & Agan, J. P. (2004). Renegotiation of identity: The social context of aphasia support groups. *Topics in Language Disorders*, *24*, 174–186.

Shaw, S. J., Armin, J., Torres, C. H., Orzech, K. M., & Vivian, J. (2012). Chronic disease self-management and health literacy in four ethnic groups. *Journal of Health Communication*, *17*, 67–81. doi:10.1080/10810730.2012.712623

Tajfel, H., & Turner, J. F. (1979). An integrative theory of intergroup conflict. *The Social Psychology of Intergroup Relations*, *22*, 74.

Waldron, R., Malpus, Z., Shearing, V., Sanchez, M., & Murray, C. D. (2017). Illness, normality and identity: The experience of heart transplant as a young adult. *Disability and Rehabilitation*, *39*, 1976–1982. https://doi.org/10.1080/09638288.2016.1213896

Ward, B. W., Schiller, J. S., & Goodman, R. A. (2014). Multiple chronic conditions among us adults: A 2012 update. *Preventing Chronic Disease*, *11*. https://dx.doi.org/10.5888%2Fpcd11.130389

Yanos, P. T., Roe, D., & Lysaker, P. H. (2010). The impact of illness identity on recovery from severe mental illness. *American Journal of Psychiatric Rehabilitation*, *13*, 73–93. https://doi.org/10.1080/15487761003756860

10. *Adoptee Identity, Belonging, and Communication with Birth and Adoptive Families*

Colleen Warner Colaner and LaShawnda Kilgore

Adoption involves the transfer of parental rights from biological to legal parents. This legal transfer has ripples in individual and relationship realms that are felt for generations. Each one of these child placements touches the life course of numerous members of the adoptive and birth families, including current and future family members, thus touching the lives of millions of individuals worldwide (Galvin & Colaner, 2013). Adoptees find themselves between two families for the duration of their life. This liminal family membership can create "layers of differentness" as adoptees grapple with abilities, appearances, and traits that may depart from their adoptive nuclear family (Grotevant, 1997, p. 4).

Historically, adoption was shrouded in secrecy, with adoptees being told very little—if at all—about their adoption (Galvin & Colaner, 2013). Thus, biological families were largely unknown to adoptees. This had a number of negative outcomes, even in the most loving and well-adjusted adoptive families. The reality was that adoptees yearned to know answers to fundamental questions of identity as they sought to make sense of their belonging and differentness in relation to their adoptive parents.

Open adoption emerged in response to (a) adoptees' desires to know more about their past and (b) birth parents' desires to remain connected to their children after placement. Open adoption allowed for connections between birth and adoptive parents to best support the child's needs for identity and belonging. Open adoption has been associated with a number of positive outcomes for adoptees, birth parents, and adoptive parents (Grotevant,

McRoy, Wrobel, & Ayers-Lopez, 2013). However, open adoption relationships require considerable collaboration, negotiation, and emotional distance regulation. These relationships are created and maintained through talk, thus placing communication at the center of these complex relational webs (Colaner & Scharp, 2016).

While open adoption has the potential to meet adoptees' identity needs, the function of open adoption can potentially reinforce the child's differentness in the adoptive and genetic family. Because adoption in general and open adoption in particular involves the linking of two families, adoptees naturally find numerous instances of difference in their legal and genetic families. In the following pages, we first pull from adoption research to delineate individual, contextual, and familial differences embedded in the adoption experience before discussing communication practices that allow adoptive families to transcend these differences. Second, we offer suggestions for how adoption reveals possibilities for reconsidering family membership and belonging in new ways, centering children between families with collaborative rather than competitive orientations. Finally, we offer implications for adoption scholars and practitioners by emphasizing the important role of communication education to promote family connections.

Layers of Difference in the Adoption Experience

Adoptees exist between families for their entire life. They are products of legal and biological families, but not fully either, prompting complex identity work and creating potential differences in the family memberships. The extent to which adoptees experience differences in their family relationships emerges as a product of individual, familial, and contextual characteristics. We discuss each of these characteristics below.

Individual Characteristics of Adoption Difference

Differences stemming from one's adoption status may be more prominent for some than for others due to individual characteristics. (Colaner & Soliz, 2015). Tolerance for uncertainty and adoption curiosity are trait features that trigger some adoptees' reflection about their adoption (Grotevant, Dunbar, Kohler, & Esau, 2000). Those with low tolerance for uncertainty and high adoption curiosity will be more apt to seek out and interact with birth families to explore the meaning of their adoption for their definition of self, and thus will be more likely to feel the degree to which they differ from members of their adoptive and genetic families.

In interview and focus group research with adult adoptees, this pull between birth and adoptive parents has been apparent. Adoptees often report sensing ways that they differ from their adoptive families, which prompts an innate desire to know their birth parents' characteristics as a way to better understand their own characteristics, proclivities, and appearance (Colaner, Halliwell, & Guignon, 2014). One woman, for example, described her need to study her adoption records to make sense of her genetic roots (Colaner & Kranstuber, 2010). She recalled spending hours of her childhood pouring over the thin folder of records that accompanied her adoption placement, looking for clues that would help her better understand herself. When she sought out her biological parents in adulthood, she discovered that her mother had an extensive brain injury and her father was deceased. After decades of wondering and searching, she found herself with her birth parents' identities but without a path to gain more information or insight. Without a way to better understand her genetic origins, she attempted to resign herself to uncertainty, saying, "I just kind of think that I am going to wander the earth forever just kind of wondering" (p. 246). Another adult adoptee in that study reflected on her permanent lack of information about her birth family, saying, "They didn't know my mom's name or anything about her .... I would just wonder a little bit about what she looked like or what happened. I never really asked because I didn't think they really knew either" (p. 246). In response to this permanent lack of information, individuals created fantasy versions of their biological families to better understand their own identity. One woman envisioned that her birth mother was either Judy Garland, Gloria Estefan, or Karen Carpenter based on her own talent for singing. Another imagined every woman she saw in public with blonde hair as possibly her mother, drawing on the one characteristic she knew to make sense of her identity and belonging.

Adoptees have presented varying responses to this liminal space between belonging and differentness. Some individuals without information about their biological background became preoccupied with their adoption status, attributing the bulk of the highs and lows in their life and family relationships to their adoption status (Colaner, 2014). These individuals tended to be highly dissatisfied with their adoption, not as connected with their adoptive parents, and exhibited lower levels of self-esteem (Colaner & Soliz, 2015). Individuals also noted the myriad ways they did not fit into their adoptive family, thus emphasizing the differences. One woman compared herself to her adoptive parents saying, "Jeepers, I really don't fit in with these people" (Colaner et al., 2014, p. 483). Another in that study emphasized the differences between her and her sister, saying, "We were both just completely different people. And ... we're both raised by the same parents, and we both came out so completely different" (p. 483). Emphasizing the lack of belonging served to heighten the differences between the self and the adoptive family.

Alternately, many adoptees emphasized belongingness in their adoptive family in the face of differences. These individuals credit their adoptive parents as creating their unique identity, thus de-emphasizing their biology and focusing instead on their socialization in the adoptive home. One said, for example, "My entire identity, who I know I am … is … formed by my adoptive parents" (Colaner et al., 2014, p. 477). Similarly, another adoptee assumed a role as the family historian in her adoptive family as a way to emphasize connection. Despite a lack of genetic connectedness to her family, this adoptee became central to the adoptive family's identity by functioning as the family expert and gatekeeper of family ancestry. This was particularly important further up the family tree, as she explained, "I see it as the way that I make myself a part of the family. You know, I know all of my aunts and uncles, you know, feel like I am a part of the family, like no doubt about it. But … you know, once those branches get a little farther and farther out, I … I want to feel like I'm a part of that by helping to bring it together, I guess" (Colaner et al., 2014, p. 478). Thus, connection in an adoptive family lessened the potential differences by emphasizing belongingness.

Connection with an adoptive family may lessen the differences, but the pull between the families is an inevitable component of adoption experience. Gravitating to one family unit over another is a natural human response to suppress the feelings of difference, but doing so has relational implications. Analysis of data from adult adoptees revealed that the more adoptees identified with their birth mother, the less they identify with the adoptive parents (Colaner, Horstman, & Rittenour, 2018). Even though adoptees are intimately connected to both families and report moderate to strong levels of attachment to each family, these family identifications may be at odds with one another.

Familial Considerations of Adoption Difference

Difference is embedded into the adoption experience in multiple ways. Not only is the child suspended between two families, but the families themselves exist on the margins of how society defines family. Adoptive families fall prey to the *deficit comparison model*, in which complex family forms are compared to the standard North American family form, consisting of heterosexual marriage, biological connectedness, and shared ethnic/racial identification (Ganong & Coleman, 2018), with the societal assumption that this nuclear family form is the standard to which all other family forms should be compared (Baxter, 2014). Adoptive families, given that they lack biological connectedness, fall short of the standard, and can thus be stigmatized as being a lesser family form (Suter, 2014). Adoptive families offer legal justification for their family relationship, showing court degrees and revised birth certificates listing adoptive parents as mother and/or father (Galvin, 2006). Yet, adoptive parents and siblings face intrusive questions that call the family's legitimacy into question (Suter & Ballard, 2009), such as "How much did you pay for her" (p. 115) and "Do you love them as much as if you had *your own*?" (p. 115). Adoptive families at times are perceived as and feel more "family-like" than family, stuck in a liminal space of connected yet not fully viewed as a legitimate family unit in society.

Similarly, birth families face ambiguous loss upon placement of a child into adoption. The adopted child is both theirs and not theirs. Birth families face day-to-day life without the biological child, even if they are able to stay connected through an open adoption relationship. Birth parents rely on adoptive parents who function as the gatekeepers of the open adoption relationship while their children are in their formative years, regulating how, when, and who in the birth family communicates with the adoptive family (Colaner & Scharp, 2016). The birth family bears the emotional, mental, and spiritual scars of relinquishment—and the mother the physical scars of birth—that linger long past the placement (Brodzinsky & Smith, 2014). The adoptive and biological families involved in the adoption continue to exist on the margins of societal assumptions of what a family should be, thus embodying family difference long term.

Contextual Factors of Adoption Difference

In addition to the differences embedded into the structure of adoption relationships, certain adoption scenarios add additional complexity, including transracial adoption and trauma, discussed in turn below.

The Transracial Adoption Paradox. Adoption often comes with diverse and at times competing identities. In the case of transracial adoption, differences expand beyond group belongingness within families to racial identification. Transracial adoption most often occurs with white parents adopting minority children (Galvin, 2003). In this scenario, the minority child functions largely within majority-white spaces, including neighborhoods, social groups, schools, and places of worship. As a function of existing in their parents' majority-white communities, most children of transracial adoption report having few individuals in their day-to-day interactions who share their racial ingroup, particularly within their closest circles. Thus, transracial adoptees tend to have the values, privileges, and opportunities of children in white families as a product of their predominately-white racial socialization (Docan-Morgan, 2011).

However, the child cannot fully be a member of the race identity group of their White parents (Nelson & Colaner, 2018). The child's skin tone prohibits the child from fully existing in these majority-white structures in ways similar to their white peers. Transracially adopted children face racial biases and prejudices in public spaces long occupied by their White parents. At the same time, the adoptee does not fully exist in the racial minority identity group of his or her biology. Children of transracial adoption are often unfamiliar with elements of culture attached to their race due to lack of exposure and socialization in their racial majority home. Transracially adopted children often feel out of place when interacting with individuals from their racial ingroup. Scholars have termed this liminal space between biological race and socially-derived racial identification as the *transracial adoption paradox* (Richard, 2003). Adoptive parents attempt to mitigate the child's experience of this paradox by providing racial socialization in the form of cultural heritage camps, social events with others in the child's racial ingroup, or linking the child with racial mentors. Even still, the paradox remains, and for some adoptees is experienced as a feeling of *cultural homelessness*, described as not fully fitting into any racial group (Vivero & Jenkins, 1999). Thus, transracial adoptees exist in the liminal space between racial identities, further emphasizing their disconnection from their biological family and their difference in their legal family.

Adoption-Related Trauma. Adoption trauma can also cause differences to emerge in adoptive family functioning and adoptee wellbeing. Trauma is defined as "the experience of multiple, chronic, and prolonged developmentally adverse events, most often of an interpersonal nature" (van der Kolk, 2005, p. 402). Adoptees face numerous mental and biological health risks based on early fetal, birth, and infant bonding experiences. Although many adoptees tend to adjust quite well, adoptees face complex developmental tasks to make sense of early experiences as they integrate into adoptive family systems (Von Korff, Grotevant, & McRoy, 2006).

Adoption and trauma are interconnected in a variety of ways. Foster youth experience the greatest risks for trauma, as they are removed from the care of their parents and guardians largely due to neglect and/or abuse (Greeson et al., 2011). Children adopted internationally are also at risk for attachment trauma, depending on the nature of their pre-adoptive experiences and timing of placement with their adoptive family (Purvis, Cross, Parris, & Dansereau, 2013). Domestic infant adoption is also intertwined with adoption-related trauma based on attachment and fetal experiences, as we detail below. Across these adoption pathways, children may experience attachment disruptions, early adverse experiences, and/or intergenerational trauma that may relate to developmental difficulties long term.

Historically, practitioners and scholars assumed that babies were resilient and unaffected by early adversity, given that they were unlikely to remember experiences in infancy (Purvis et al., 2013). However, recent research is creating new layers of understanding about the long-lasting effects of early trauma and infant mental health (Shonkoff & Levitt, 2010). Experiencing trauma at any age can have lasting impacts on an individual, but for children under the age of 3, trauma drastically affects and even impedes their development (Frigerio, Ceppi, Rusconi, Giorda, Raggi, & Fearon, 2009). Childhood trauma—also known as adverse childhood experiences (ACE)—comprises of physical, sexual or emotional abuse, physical or emotional neglect, parental mental illness, substance dependence, incarceration, parental separation or divorce, or domestic violence (Felitti et al., 2019). There is a strong relationship between exposure to ACE and seven of the ten leading causes of death in adults. Considering the role of trauma in adoption highlights important long-term implications of early experiences.

An attachment disruption can be a form of early developmental trauma for adoptees. Bowlby's (1980) attachment theory provides a foundation for understanding how important it is to a child's development to have a secure attachment to caregivers. During the first years of life, an attachment relationship varies in its degree of security, depending on the sensitivity and responsiveness of the infant's caregiver (Bowlby, 1980). The attachment figure alternately serves two key functions: he or she provides (1) a haven of safety and comfort to which the infant can turn in times of distress or threat, and (2) a secure base for exploration of the environment in the absence of danger.

Attachment with a maternal figure begins in utero. Mothers who exhibit positive behaviors with the fetus, such as warmth, interest, and connection tend to have children with more secure attachment styles and optimal child development outcomes (Alhusen, Hayat, & Gross, 2013). Mother attunement to child wellbeing begins prior to birth and is stable over time. Pre-birth attachment is evidenced in mother caregiving behaviors such as mind-mindedness of infant mental health states (McMahon, Camberis, Berry, & Gibson, 2016). We also see evidence of fetal attachment to mother post-birth. We have long known that infants show preference for their biological mothers' voice in experimental laboratory studies, opting to suck on a rubber nipple that plays a recording of their mothers' voice over one that plays a recording of the voice of another woman (DeCasper & Fifer, 1980). Evidence suggests that other senses demonstrate infant connectedness to mothers based on pre-birth experiences. Infants are able to smell their biological mother's breast-milk and distinguish that mother from other humans (Nishitani et al., 2009). Infants also show preferences for the foods their mother ate during gestation (Mennella, Jagnow, & Beauchamp, 2001) and the sounds they heard while in the womb (Hepper, 1991). The pregnant woman and her fetus are intimately connected, such that the fetus experiences everything that the women does.

Children connected to families through adoption may also be more likely to experience birth-related difficulties. Low-intervention birthing practices and baby-friendly hospitals—designated by the World Health Organization as medical procedures encouraging breastfeeding within 1 hour of birth, giving only breast milk, rooming in, breastfeeding on demand, no pacifiers, and information on breastfeeding support—have recognized the important bonding processes that begin upon birth (Rowe-Murray & Fisher, 2002). Breastfeeding prompts biological bonding for mothers and newborns, with effects on obesity and immune system functioning (León-Cava, Lutter, Ross, & Martin, 2002). These birth and feeding practices are often unavailable to families formed through adoption. Although infants are able to re-attach to new caregivers, especially in the first two years of life, adoption involves an attachment disruption from the first caregiver. Thus, adoption begins with a form of trauma that should be at the forefront of adoptive parents' caregiving (Purvis et al., 2013).

Intergenerational trauma research also gives glimpses into how the biological mothers' adverse experiences can be associated with changes in fetal development and biological functioning later in life (Gray, Jones, Theall, Glackin, & Drury, 2017). Just as the fetus experiences the tastes, sounds, and smells of the mother during gestation, the pregnant mothers' adverse experiences are also shared with the fetus. For example, babies born to Dutch mothers who survived famine during World War II showed higher levels of heart disease, diabetes, and obesity in adulthood (Roseboom, van Der Meulen, Ravelli, Osmond, Barker, & Bleker, 2001), Pregnant mothers living in New York City who survived the 9/11 World Trade Center attack tended to have babies with a biological marker of susceptibly to post-traumatic stress disorder (PTSD); this correlation is strongest in children with mothers who survived the attack while in their third trimester (Yehuda et al., 2005). Children born from mothers who experience high rates of relationship conflict while pregnant also tend to exhibit biological markers of this conflict in their nervous system (Graham, Ablow, & Measelle, 2010). Epigenetics research provides some evidence that transmission of physiological markers of trauma may even precede pregnancy, such as the offspring of Holocaust survivors showing similar DNA methylation as their parents even when mothers became pregnant after the end of the war (Yehuda et al., 2016). The legacy of stress, trauma, and difficulty from birth family to adoptee, even in the face of an adoption intervention, is long-lasting.

Fetal origin scholars theorize that this pre-birth learning sends messages to the developing biological systems about the world the child is about to enter. This learning is functional from an evolutionary standpoint, as the biological processes develop in ways to maximize survival of the fetus post-birth based on the best prediction of the world as a dangerous or safe place (Paul, 2010). While the bulk of this research has been done outside of the context of adoption, there are important implications to consider for adoptees. Extrapolating these studies to adoption points to the importance of considering the long-term consequences of birth mother experiences. While reasons for placement vary considerably (Clutter, 2014), situations in which stressful, unstable, insecure, and potentially violent features of the birth mothers' life prompted the decision to place a child in an adoptive home may be consequential long term. Investigating the relationship birth mothers' ACE scores and infant mental health, for example, is an important next step for adoption research. The effect fetal attunement for post-adoption development remains murky. As trauma researchers begin to learn more about the association between trauma, the body, and the brain, new pathways to support adoptees' health and wellbeing will emerge.

Communication Practices to Transcend Adoption Differences

Collaborative communication practices play an important role in helping adoptees feel supported and unconstrained between two family groups, thus reducing the negative tone of adoption-related differences. Adoption has always involved a birth and an adoptive family, but recent shifts to opening up connections between the families via open adoption has created more intentionality about meeting the child's developmental needs (Grotevant et al., 2000). Open adoption relationships function best when adoptive and birth parents work together to meet the developmental needs of the child (Grotevant et al., 2013). These collaborative relationships offer connections between families that can embrace and support adoptees with open and responsive communication behaviors.

Collaborative communication involves birth and adoptive parents interacting with one another without ownership of or entitlement to the child but rather allows the adoptee to exist freely between the two families. One adoptee described this dual membership by saying, "I suppose insofar as my adoptive parents have shaped me, that I in turn shaped them in ways that would echo my birth parents" (Colaner et al., 2014, p. 481). She viewed her identity as a product of both her adoptive and birth families simultaneously. Another adoptee described how her adoptive and birth father interacted with one another, celebrating her accomplishments and expressing pride in the person she became. She viewed this collaboration as providing multiple layers of support that allowed her to view her dual membership in both families as a positive and not limiting experience. This collaborative relationship embodies what Gritter urged when he said of open adoption, "We should not be asking who this child belongs to but who belongs to this child" (Syversen, 2019, p. 111).

Adoption communication openness (ACO) is a specific communication practice that encourages adoptees to exist more comfortably within adoption relationships (Colaner & Soliz, 2015). ACO is open, direct, empathic, and sensitive communication used to support children's emotions about adoption. Adoptive parents practicing ACO invite conversations about adoption, providing a nonjudgmental environment for the child to seek information and process feelings about the adoption. ACO encourages development of an adoptive identity, relates to adoptees' feelings of self-esteem, and reduces feelings of adoption difference. Research reveals that feeling close to one's birth mother related to decreased feelings of closeness with adoptive parents (Colaner et al., 2018). At the same time, adoptees felt closer to their birth parents when they had adoptive parents who were high in ACO, suggesting that adoptive parents' communication behaviors play a role in adoptees' ability to connect with birth parents. Alternately, adoptive parents' lack of willingness to talk about birth parents contributed to adoptees feeling trapped between families (Colaner et al., 2014, 2018). Adoptive parents report saying that their child is able to ask questions about adoption at any time (Colaner & Scharp, 2016), but ACO is not a passive quality of the family dynamic. Adoptees reported not asking their adoptive parents questions because they sensed the adoptive parents' discomfort with the topic or because the adoptive parent never brought adoption up as a topic of conversation. ACO requires that adoptive parents actively cultivate an environment in which adoption is an acceptable topic, model adoption talk in interactions with and around the child, and respond to the child's comments, needs, and questions with empathy, active listening, and compassion.

Beyond the Family: Family Communication and Society

In light of the multiple forms of differences embedded into adoptive relationships, adoption provides an important model of connectedness, with implications for other family forms. Adoption relationships center the child between birth and adoptive parents. In healthy open adoption relationships, birth and adoptive parents work collaboratively to meet the child's information, developmental, and identity needs (Grotevant et al., 2013). Such collaborative relationships offer a glimpse into the importance of centering children's experiences without controlling children's developmental growth toward the preferred interests of the parents. The collaborative model central to adoption can serve as a model across a range of parent-child relationships.

US parenting norms have strong roots in a sense of ownership of children, with children positioned as products of parents (Tsabary, 2016). Western culture is dominated by individualism, with emphasis on the self as a unique individual positioned independently from a group (Watson, 2012). A highly individualistic orientation emphasizes achievement as a personal (as opposed to a group) recognition (Kim, 2002). Applied to parenting practices, these Western, individualistic values of control and individual achievement can serve to position the parent as greater than and the authority over the child (Freeman & Mathison, 2009). Rather than honoring the child's autonomy as a human being, the child serves to further extend the parent's will, making the parent fuller and more complete (Tsabary, 2016).

Western-based notions of parenting position children as belonging to one set of parents. This orientation does not allow children to exist between families, as ownership has to be negotiated in relation to specific individuals. U.S. legal practices grant parent rights to at most two parents in the majority of states (Althouse, 2008), positioning the family unit as an exclusive entity regulating a child's livelihood. However, children across a range of family structures are connected to multiple parental units, such as in post-divorce families, blended families, queer families, families formed through reproductive technology, and voluntary kin arrangements (Baxter, 2014). Delegating parental rights to one family unit priorities parental control over child autonomy. Freeman and Mathison (2009) assert that societal values that position children as under-developed, incomplete humans in need of regulation undercut respect for children's experiences, desires, and self-sufficiency. However, prioritizing children's autonomy over parental control provides ways to consider how children may be constrained by relegating parental rights to just familial unit. Centrally locating a child among multiple caregivers may be a central feature of highly functional complex family structures in the modern era.

Adoption highlights a familial model in which children connect across families. When an adoptee cannot peacefully co-exist between families, their experience of adoption-related difference can be exacerbated and charged with negativity, tension, and discomfort (Colaner et al., 2014). Western values embodied in such an individualistic family orientation may exacerbate the experience of difference in the adoption experience by forcing an adoptee to adhere to one family unit over multiple identifications and make an impossible choice to prioritize one family membership over the other. The inability to co-exist in multiple family memberships in a communal orientation, then, subjugates adoptees to an uncomfortable liminal space of not quite belonging to either family unit.

Shifting away from a child ownership mentality offers opportunities for embracing difference as a productive component of the adoption experience. Adoptive family relationships prompting us to rethink ownership in the parent-child bond, embracing parenting values that are communal in nature, involving multiple generations and family units caring for the child and distributing parental tasks among a larger group of people (Kim, 2002). Shifting away from individualism and control in childrearing de-centers perceptions of ownership, reframing the question of belongingness from who owns the child to who belongs to the child.

Open adoption practices in particular places children at the center of two families, thus stretching family definitions and typical family processes housed in Western ideals. Open adoption allows us to understand families differently, embracing the possibility of what family can be in a more communal space. Rather than children positioned as products of parental control and subjected to parental ownership, adoptees have the opportunity to exist within a web of multiple caregivers. To the degree that adoptive and birth parents collaborate to meet the child's developmental needs, open adoption provides an opportunity to embrace the communal possibilities for children, with implications for a wide variety of parent-child relationships.

Implications for Scholars and Practitioners

Family communication processes naturally lend themselves toward intervention (Kam & Miller-Day, 2017). There is considerable potential for scholarly and practical advancements in the field of adoption. Family communication research on adoption has the potential to culminate in an adoptive parent-focused and communication-based preventative intervention education program. Rigorous adoption communication trainings and interventions should—in addition to being research-based—also be evidence-tested. Longitudinal research would be necessary to gauge the effectiveness of the training over time. Programs such as the Trust Based Relational Intervention (TBRI) show promise for the healing function of relationships for children who have experienced relationship adversity (Purvis et al., 2013). Creating and implementing a communication-based, trauma-informed adoption interventions that takes into account fetal origins, attachment disruption, and genetic pre-dispositions could greatly serve the adoption community in promoting positive outcomes for adopted youth.

The myth of infant resilience no longer serves the adoption community. Fundamental physiological changes occur when children are exposed to complex, developmental trauma (van der Kolk, 2014). Children experiencing prebirth stressors, attachment disruptions, and intergenerational trauma tend to exhibit insufficient self-regulation behaviors rooted brain development, specifically an overactive limbic system and delayed prefrontal cortex (Purvis et al., 2013). A lack of self-regulation, such as decreased impulse control, emotional imbalance, and hyperactivity, can be misinterpreted as misbehavior at home and school, when in reality the child may be dysregulated from unresolved trauma occurring in early fetal and infant development. Increasingly understanding the degree to which intergenerational trauma and fetal trauma (in addition to genetic factors) affects the adoptees' lived experiences can shed light on the complex landscape affecting long-term adoption effects. This type of work will require complex, longitudinal research studies that draw in data from birth parent experiences before, during, and after the child gestation. This work will also require creative and intentional translation to help parents, teachers, medical doctors, and mental health practitioners with insight to best serve the adopted population.

Love is not enough to address complex adoption-related trauma. Children who are placed into adoptive families need to create safe and healthy connections in order to heal from their trauma. Family communication scholars have important work to contribute in this area by revealing the restorative function of safe, supportive, healthy relationships after the experience of trauma. Family communication theories can intersect with attachment therapies to provide foundational support for adoptees. This work can fruitfully combine with practices from child-centered play therapists and pediatric neurobiologists to offer adoptive parents crucial information to promote early and ongoing bonding and healing for children with difficult early experiences. Importantly, "traumatized individuals recover in the context of relationships: with families, loved ones, AA meeting, veterans; organizations, religious communities, or professional therapists" (van der Kolk, 2014, p. 212). Understanding the role parental relationships play in the healing of adoption trauma is an important avenue to explore. Relationships that provide physical and emotional safety can lead to reconnecting with human beings and healing.

References

Alhusen, J. L., Hayat, M. J., & Gross, D. (2013). A longitudinal study of maternal attachment and infant developmental outcomes. *Archives of Women's Mental Health, 16*, 521–529. doi:10.2007/s00737-013-0357-8

Althouse, L. N. (2008). Three's company-how American law can recognize a third social parent in same-sex headed families. *Hastings Women's Law Journal, 19*, 171.

Baxter, L. A. (2014). *Remaking "family" communicatively.* New York: Peter Lang.

Bowlby, J. (1980). *Loss: Sadness and depression.* New York: Basic Books.

Brodzinsky, D., & Smith, S. L. (2014). Post-placement adjustment and the needs of birthmothers who place an infant for adoption. *Adoption Quarterly, 17*, 165–184. doi:10.1080/10926755.2014.891551

Clutter, L. B. (2014). Adult birth mothers who made open infant adoption placements after adolescent unplanned pregnancy. *Journal of Obstetric, Gynecologic & Neonatal Nursing, 43*, 190–199.

Colaner, C. W. (2014). Measuring adoptive identity: Validation of the adoptive identity work scale *Adoption Quarterly, 17*, 1–24. doi:10.1080/10926755.2014.891546

Colaner, C. W., Halliwell, D., &Guignon, P. (2014). "What do you say to your mother when your mother's standing beside you?" Birth and adoptive family contributions to adoptive identity via relational identity and relational–relational identity gaps. *Communication Monographs, 81*, 469–494. doi:10.1080/03637751.2014.955808

Colaner, C. W., Horstman, H. K., & Rittenour, C. E. (2018). Negotiating adoptive and birth shared family identity: A social identity complexity approach. *Western Journal of Communication, 82*, 393–415. doi:10.1080/10570314.2017.1384564

Colaner, C. W., & Kranstuber, H. (2010). "Forever kind of wondering": Communicatively managing uncertainty in adoptive families. *Journal of Family Communication, 10*, 236–255. doi:10.1080/15267431003682435

Colaner, C. W., & Scharp, K. M. (2016). Maintaining open adoption relationships: Practitioner insights on adoptive parents' regulation of adoption kinship networks. *Communication Studies, 67*, 359–378. doi:10.1080/10510974.2016.1164208

Colaner, C. W., & Soliz, J. (2015). A communication-based approach to adoptive identity: Theoretical and empirical support. *Communication Research*, 1–27. doi:10.1177/0093650215577860

DeCasper, A. J., & Fifer, W. P. (1980). Of human bonding: Newborns prefer their mothers' voices. *Science, 208*, 1174–1176.

Docan-Morgan, S. (2011). "They don't know what it's like to be in my shoes": Topic avoidance about race in transracially adoptive families. *Journal of Social and Personal Relationships, 28*, 336–355. doi:10.1177/0265407510382177

Felitti, V. J., Anda, R. F., Nordenberg, D., Williamson, D. F., Spitz, A. M., Edwards, V., … Marks, J. S. (2019). Relationship of childhood abuse and household dysfunction to many of the leading causes of death in adults: The Adverse Childhood Experiences (ACE) Study. *American Journal of Preventive Medicine, 56*, 774–786.

Freeman, M., & Mathison, S. (2009). *Researching children's voices*. New York: Guilford Press.

Frigerio, A., Ceppi, E., Rusconi, M., Giorda, R., Raggi, M. E., & Fearon, P. (2009). The role played by the interaction between genetic factors and attachment in the stress response in infancy. *Journal of Child Psychology and Psychiatry, 50*, 1513–1522.

Galvin, K. (2003). International and transracial adoption: A communication research agenda. *Journal of Family Communication, 3*, 237–259. doi:10.1207/S15327698JFC0304_5

Galvin, K. (2006). Diversity's impact on defining the family. In L. H. Turner & R. West (Eds.), *The family communication sourcebook* (pp. 3–19). Thousand Oaks, CA: Sage.

Galvin, K., & Colaner, C. W. (2013). Created through law and language: Communicative complexities of adoptive families. In K. Floyd & M. T. Morman (Eds.), *Widening the family circle* (2nd ed., pp. 191–209). Thousand Oaks, CA: Sage.

Ganong, L., & Coleman, M. (2018). Studying stepfamilies: Four eras of family scholarship. *Family Process, 57*, 7–24.

Graham, A. M., Ablow, J. C., & Measelle, J. R. (2010). Interparental relationship dynamics and cardiac vagal functioning in infancy. *Infant Behavior and Development, 33*, 530–544.

Gray, S. A., Jones, C. W., Theall, K. P., Glackin, E., & Drury, S. S. (2017). Thinking across generations: unique contributions of maternal early life and prenatal stress to infant physiology. *Journal of the American Academy of Child & Adolescent Psychiatry, 56*, 922–929.

Greeson, J. K. P., Briggs, E. C., Kisiel, C. L., Layne, C. M., Ake, G. S., Ko, S. J. … Fairbank, J. A. (2011). Complex trauma and mental health in children and adolescents placed in foster care: Findings from the National Child Traumatic Stress Network. *Child Welfare, 90*, 91–108.

Grotevant, H. D. (1997). Coming to terms with adoption: The construction of identity from adolescence into adulthood. *Adoption Quarterly*, 1, 3–27. doi:10.1300/J145v01n01_02

Grotevant, H. D., Dunbar, N., Kohler, J. K., & Esau, A. M. L. (2000). Adoptive identity: How contexts within and beyond the family shape developmental pathways. *Family Relations, 49*, 379–387. doi:10.1111/j.1741-3729.2000.00379.x

Grotevant, H. D., McRoy, R. G., Wrobel, G. M., & Ayers-Lopez, S. (2013). Contact between adoptive and birth families: Perspectives from the Minnesota/Texas Adoption Research Project. *Child Development Perspectives, 7*, 193–198. doi:10.1111/cdep.12039

Hepper, P. G. (1991). An examination of fetal learning before and after birth. *The Irish Journal of Psychology, 12*, 95–107.

Kam, J. A., & Miller-Day, M. (2017). Introduction to special issue. *Journal of Family Communication, 17*, 1–14.

Kim, M.-S. (2002). *Non-western perspectives on human communication.* Thousand Oaks, CA: Sage.

León-Cava, N., Lutter, C., Ross, J., & Martin, L. (2002). *Quantifying the benefits of breastfeeding: A summary of the evidence.* Washington, DC: Pan American Health Organization, 3.

McMahon, C., Camberis, A. L., Berry, S., & Gibson, F. (2016). Maternal mind-mindedness: Relations with maternal–fetal attachment and stability in the first two years of life: Findings from an Australian prospective study. *Infant Mental Health Journal, 37*, 17–28.

Mennella, J. A., Jagnow, C. P., & Beauchamp, G. K. (2001). Prenatal and postnatal flavor learning by human infants. *Pediatrics, 107*, 1–6.

Nelson, L. R., & Colaner, C. W. (2018). Becoming a transracial family: Communicatively negotiating divergent identities in families formed through transracial adoption. *Journal of Family Communication, 18*, 51–67. doi:10.1080/15267431.2017.1396987

Nishitani, S., Miyamura, T., Tagawa, M., Sumi, M., Takase, R., Doi, H., … Shinohara, K. (2009). The calming effect of a maternal breast milk odor on the human newborn infant. *Neuroscience Research, 63*, 66–71.

Paul, A. M. (2010). *Origins: How the nine months before birth shape the rest of our lives.* New York, NY: Simon & Schuster.

Purvis, K. B., Cross, D. R., Parris, S. R., & Dansereau, D. F. (2013). Trust-based relational intervention (TBRI): A systemic approach to complex developmental trauma. *Child and Youth Services, 34*, 360–386. https://doi-org.proxy.mul.missouri.edu/10.1080/0145935X.2013.859906

Richard, M. L. (2003). The transracial adoption paradox: History, research, and counseling implications of cultural socialization. *The Counseling Psychologist, 31*, 711–744. doi:10.1177/0011000003258087

Roseboom, T. J., van Der Meulen, J. H., Ravelli, A. C., Osmond, C., Barker, D. J., & Bleker, O. P. (2001). Effects of prenatal exposure to the Dutch famine on adult disease in later life: An overview. *Twin Research and Human Genetics, 4*, 293–298.

Rowe-Murray, H. J., & Fisher, J. R. (2002). Baby friendly hospital practices: Cesarean section is a persistent barrier to early initiation of breastfeeding. *Birth, 29*, 124–131.

Shonkoff, J. P., & Levitt P. (2010). Neuroscience and the future of early childhood policy: Moving from why to what and how. *Neuron, 67*, 689–691.

Suter, E. A. (2014). The adopted family. In L. A. Baxter (Ed.), *Remaking "family" communicatively* (pp. 137–156). New York, NY: Peter Lang.

Suter, E. A., &Ballard, R. L. (2009). "How much did you pay for her?": Decision-making criteria underlying adoptive parents' responses to inappropriate remarks. *Journal of Family Communication, 9*, 107–125. doi:10.1080/15267430902773253

Syversen, B. (2019). *Mustard seed faith: A journey through infertility, miscarriages, adoption, and faith.* Nashville, TN: Harper Collins Publishers.

Tsabary, S. (2016). *The awakened family.* New York: Penguin.

van der Kolk, B. (2005). Developmental trauma disorder: Towards a rational diagnosis for children with complex trauma histories. *Psychiatric Annals, 33*, 401–408.

van der Kolk, B. A. (2014). *The body keeps the score: brain, mind, and body in the healing of trauma.* New York: New York.

Vivero, V. N., & Jenkins, S. R. (1999). Existential hazards of the multicultural individual: Defining and understanding "cultural homelessness". *Cultural Diversity and Ethnic Minority Psychology, 5*, 6.

Von Korff, L., Grotevant, H. D., & McRoy, R. G. (2006). Openness arrangements and psychological adjustment in adolescent adoptees. *Journal of Family Psychology, 20*, 531.

Watson, B. (2012). Intercultural and cross-cultural communication In A. Kurylo (Ed.), *Inter/cultural Communication* (pp. 25–45). Thousand Oaks, CA: Sage.

Yehuda, R., Daskalakis, N. P., Bierer, L. M., Bader, H. N., Klengel, T., Holsboer, F., & Binder, E. B. (2016). Holocaust exposure induced intergenerational effects on FKBP5 methylation. *Biological Psychiatry, 80*, 372–380.

Yehuda, R., Engel, S. M., Brand, S. R., Seckl, J., Marcus, S. M., & Berkowitz, G. S. (2005). Transgenerational effects of posttraumatic stress disorder in babies of mothers exposed to the World Trade Center attacks during pregnancy. *The Journal of Clinical Endocrinology & Metabolism, 90*, 4115–4118.

11. Communicating Family: Identity and Difference in the Context of Foster Care

LESLIE R. NELSON AND LINDSEY J. THOMAS

Family, for many, is a taken-for-granted concept, with biological or legal connections carrying assumptions of care and love. However, family, and the social capital that familial relationships often provide, is not guaranteed. The present chapter illuminates communication and formative processes of one such complicated family form: the foster family. This chapter provides an overview of foster care and foster family dynamics, reviews extant foster-focused and communication-related literature, offers insights into the ways that communication in and about foster families might influence broader society and culture, and provides future considerations in regard to foster care-related communication research and practice.

In 2017, an estimated 2.7 million children resided in residential care, and more than 440,000 youth lived in the US foster care system alone (Adoption and Foster Care Analysis Reporting System, henceforth AFCARS, 2018; Petrowski, Cappa, & Gross, 2017). The structure and policy of foster care systems vary by state and country. In the US, the federal government publishes resources (e.g., policy guidelines, demographics, studies and suggestions) aimed toward increasing (former) fostered youths' well-being. These resources are generally followed across state departments of Child Welfare Services (CWS), which are charged with monitoring the well-being of children and, if needed, placing them with caregivers outside the family of origin. Placements include residence in institutions/group home facilities; with relatives of the family of origin (i.e., kinship care); or with other adult guardians, the latter of which is often referred to as foster care (US Department of Health and Human Services, henceforth DHHS, 2005, 2013). Alternative placements occur when children cannot live safely with their families of origin for various reasons, including direct threats to their well-being such as abuse, ongoing conflict, or physical or behavioral healthcare that "cannot be addressed in the family [of origin]" (DHHS, 2013). Worldwide, children who are abandoned or orphaned constitute a large group of youth residing in alternative placements, and the U.S. government emphasizes that abuse, neglect, and/or other safety concerns are crucial to the decision to remove a child from their family of origin (e.g., DHHS, 2013; Petrowski et al., 2017). Given the lack of consistent safety and associated upheaval, it is perhaps unsurprising that fostered youth around the world tend to face different, often greater, challenges than their non-fostered peers (e.g., Fernandez & Barth, 2010; Petrowski et al., 2017). In addition, families of origin report varying, often negative, experiences with the foster care system, and foster families play vital roles in the experiences and outcomes of (formerly) fostered youth (e.g., Colton & Williams, 1997; Höjer, 2011). Thus, much extant literature on foster care centers around understanding youth outcomes, examining factors that might improve the lives of fostered youth, and illuminating how foster care systems might better serve children, foster care providers, and families of origin. Undeniably, family communication scholars have contributed much to these conversations.

Foster Care and Foster Families: Existing Literature

Given that youth are placed in alternative care due to unsafe living conditions, it might be unsurprising that U.S. fostered youth "are the most vulnerable to poor health compared with any other children," often enduring negativity before, during, and after foster care (Kools & Kennedy, 2003, p. 39). Many fostered youth have experienced emotional, psychological, and/or sexual abuse (Leve et al., 2012; Oswald, Heil, & Goldbeck, 2010). Fostered youth bear heightened risk for developmental delays as well as negative physical, psychological, and social outcomes (see Kools & Kennedy, 2003; McWey et al., 2010; Schneiderman, Leslie, Arnold-Clark, McDaniel, & Xie, 2011). Even after care, young adults who age out of the foster care system experience victimization, incarceration, and homelessness at significantly greater rates than their peers (e.g., Courtney, Piliavin, Grogan-Kaylor, & Nesmith, 2001).

Prospects for fostered youth might look dim, but they are far from hopeless. Healthy relationships and membership in permanent, caring families bolster positive outcomes for fostered youth (e.g., Berrick, 2009; Luke & Coyne, 2008; Nelson & Colaner, 2020). Thus, foster families are tasked with providing children with basic care and support and can play a critical role for youth awaiting reunification or other permanent family arrangement. Furthermore, foster family members who provide care and love are often considered to be family—regardless of biology or legality—even after fostered youth exit the system (e.g., Nelson & Colaner, 2020; Thomas, Jackl, & Crowley, 2017). Nonetheless, not all perspectives of foster families are positive. Some youth report enduring ongoing negativity in foster homes (Thomas, 2014). In addition, members of the family of origin sometimes view the foster care system and foster families with skepticism, confusion, disdain, and/or outright anger (e.g., Thomas & Beier, 2018). Taken together, these dynamics create a complicated picture of foster families' place, purpose, and performance.

Foster Discourse and Ideology

Family communication scholars postulate that foster families rely heavily on communication to construct, maintain, negotiate, and/or deconstruct family identities, rendering them highly discourse-dependent (see Galvin, 2006, 2014; Miller-Ott, 2017; Nelson, 2017; Nelson & Colaner, 2020; Nelson & Horstman, 2017; Suter, Baxter, Seurer, & Thomas, 2014; Thomas, 2014). Given typical parameters of foster care (i.e., temporary placement, children enter foster families at older ages, social identity differences between children and caregivers, reunification goals) and foster families' discursive reliance, family communication scholars seek to understand how communication facilitates thriving relationships among those involved in the foster square (i.e., what Nelson [2017] has called the "foster care square" and Thomas [2015] labeled the "foster foursome") (Nelson, 2017; Patrick & Galvin, 2012; Thomas et al., 2017). Although more research on foster square communication is necessary, examining recent extant communication studies that forefront foster care highlights theoretical and practical progress and opportunities.

Scholars have begun illuminating communicative practices and cultural ideology central to foster experiences. Researchers contend that, for example, foster parents are vital to creating family belonging and solidarity (Miller-Ott, 2017; Nelson & Colaner, 2020). In regard to communicative practices, Miller-Ott found that foster parents utilized Galvin's (2006; 2014) internal discursive strategies (i.e., integrating biological and foster families; ritualizing) and external discursive strategies (i.e., explaining, labeling family roles, reframing) to create a sense of belonging and discursively labored to normalize the foster family form.

Much ideology-focused work has utilized Baxter's (2011) Relational Dialectics Theory (RDT)—which posits that multiple, competing discourses interplay in talk to create meaning. Early foster square-related RDT work examined how "family" was constructed in foster adoptive parents' narratives (Suter et al., 2014). The Discourse of Biological Normativity (DBN) emphasized biological families as more valid, legitimate, and authentic—resulting in preferences for visible similarity and reunification, whereas the Discourse of Constitutive Kinning (DCK) emphasized family as performative—dependent on members' care and love for one another (Suter et al.). Overall, foster adoptive parents' narratives acknowledged yet undermined the dominant discourse of family-as-biology by emphasizing love, care, and feeling like "family" as ultimately constituting family. Similarly, Thomas and colleagues (2017) examined discursive constructions of "family" among adult, formerly fostered youth. The Discourse of Family as Irreplaceable and Inescapable (Permanence), much like the DBN, reified normative understandings of what constituted family: biology and shared history. Contrarily, the Discourse of Family as Performative Kinning (Performance) manifested themes of role enactment, tolerance, and unconditional love. Performance competed with Permanence, demonstrating that Permanence is culturally pervasive and powerful, yet Performance, too, renders family meaningful (Thomas et al., 2017).

Scholars also employed RDT to explore how formerly fostered adults made meaning of the U.S. foster care system (Thomas & Scharp, 2018). The Discourse of System as Helpful (DSH) aligned with CWS goals and emphasized fostered youth protection and safety, stability, and "good" people in the system (e.g., social workers, foster parents). Conversely, the Discourse of System as Broken (DSB) emphasized harmful aspects of placement on children and families, inconsistency within the system, and under-support of foster care as an institution. The DSH and DSB compete to position the foster care system as a necessary good versus a necessary evil (Thomas & Scharp).

Scholars have also researched the discourses animating foster care globally. Today, the "best interest of the child" has often manifested as an ideology of bio-genetic support, whereby cases attend to families of origin, maintain biological links, and attempt reunification (Colton & Williams, 1997; DHHS, 2013). Support talk and practice permeates foster care internationally, with few exceptions. Argentina, Hungary, Australia, and Germany are largely opposed to reunification after a child's placement with a foster family for designated amounts of time (e.g., ranging from immediately [Hungary] to two years [Germany] after placement) (Colton & Williams, 1997). Colton and Williams note, "with respect to reunification, there seems to be some divergence between legislation and practice" such that Western countries support reunification in the abstract, but the tools and measures needed to implement reunification fall short in most cases (p. 45). Consequently, reunification rates are low, comprising 49% of U.S. foster care exits in 2017 (AFCARS, 2018).

Thus, while support ideology exists, understanding how communication might help solidify this into practice deserves focused scholarly attention.

Normalization, or understanding that fostered youth should be afforded opportunities to live life as ***normally*** as non-fostered youth, also pervades foster care talk (see Colton & Williams, 1997; Miller-Ott, 2017). Indeed, ideology currently constructing foster care as a place for family support and normalization has led to more children being placed in foster homes rather than facilities. An additional outcome of shifting ideology is the trend toward more diverse programs to account for varying ages and differing physical, emotional, and behavioral needs of foster children (Colton & Williams, 1997). Further exploration of ideologies that permeate talk within and about foster care holds promise for caseworkers and care providers, who might become better equipped to engage foster square members' positive and negative experiences related to foster care.

Narratives in and about Foster Care and Families

Foster care is a life course disruption that can be better understood by examining stories told by (former) foster youth and parents. Narrative research has gained momentum in the fields of communication and social work, examining unique facets of foster narratives, including: foster parent entrance narratives (Nelson & Horstman, 2017); foster child stigma (Michell, 2015); former foster children's identity construction (Thomas, 2014; 2015); and storytelling as therapy (Whiting, 2000). Taken together, this research underscores the importance of storytelling for identity, sense-making, and well-being and illuminates the ways in which narratives affect and reflect lived experiences of foster families.

In examining stories foster parents tell about a child's entrance into their care (i.e., foster entrance narratives), Nelson and Horstman (2017) found several themes linked with child well-being. When foster parents emphasized ***birth parent learning*** (i.e., birth parents were learning to become better parents), they reported that their foster child exhibited fewer peer relationship problems. However, when emphasizing ***temporary*** (i.e., the foster child's place in their home is temporary), foster parents reported that their foster child exhibited more peer relationship problems. Thus, while both themes emphasized ideology within the US child welfare system (i.e., parent rehabilitation; foster families as temporary), they are contradictory in terms of their effect on parents' perceptions of children's peer relationship issues. Future research should further examine storytelling effects on indicators of well-being, such as self-esteem and self-efficacy—from parents' as well as children's perspectives.

In addition to emergent research exploring parents' storytelling and perspectives, research examining narratives from children's perspectives has gained momentum. Outside of the communication discipline, scholars have examined how fostered youth reflect, perceive, and process via storytelling (see Michell, 2015; Whiting, 2000). Within the communication field, Thomas (2014) found that formerly fostered youth narratively construct three main identities: *victim*, *survivor*, and *victor*. Each identity emerges from a rupture narrative, whereby foster children recounted disruptive experiences of entering, living in, and exiting foster care (Thomas, 2014). Thomas, drawing on McAdams (1993), argued that the way former foster children integrate disruptive experiences—entering into foster care, transitioning between homes, and/or aging out of care—into their life stories has implications for their identity. Thus, narratives help scholars, practitioners, and policy makers to make better decisions by understanding how (former) foster youth make sense of their lives, identities, and cultures.

Belonging and Solidarity

Researchers have also employed Attachment Theory (Ainsworth & Bowlby, 1991) to elucidate communicative work that promotes foster family belonging and solidarity. Indeed, promoting multiple attachments—with birth and foster family members—might increase foster children's sense of shared family identity (Ellingsen, Shemmings, & Størksen, 2011). Further, Nelson and Colaner (2020) discovered that unrestrained foster parent-child communication can bolster shared family identity. Indeed, communication allows foster square members to nurture family solidarity and belonging. Long-term foster placements, in particular, might offer stability and secure attachment among fostered youth. In Sweden, goals underlying the foster care system advocate for family inclusivity, promoting dual attachment (i.e., connection to both one's family of origin and one's foster family). Ellingsen and colleagues (2011) note, "it is important for birth parents (*and* the foster parents) to recognize that they should avoid forcing the child to choose 'them or us'" (p. 314). When children are encouraged to develop secure bonds with members of both family structures, they tend to demonstrate more long-term resiliency. Future research should explore communicative constructions of family identity across the foster square, including foster siblings, extended (foster) family, birth parents, and even state employees/volunteers.

Future Theoretical Considerations

Because research examining foster families tends to be practice-oriented and outcome-based, we provide suggestions for future studies assessing foster communication dynamics and theoretical perspectives that might illuminate pertinent foster care topics. For example, foster care is rife with privacy concerns and implications. Members of the foster square must continuously manage boundaries around what information to reveal/conceal to children, foster/origin parents, extended family, and beyond. Thus, Communication Privacy Management theory (CPM: Petronio, 2002, 2013) holds promise for better understanding privacy ownership, control, and turbulence pertaining to information shared amongst the foster square. Because foster care is also plagued by uncertainty (e.g., where will children go and for how long, how might children predict/interpret interactions in placements, etc.), family communication scholars might also explore how members of the foster square communicatively manage uncertainty.

Additionally, scholars should examine the foster square from a systems perspective. Exploring relationships beyond the parent-child subsystem might deepen understandings of child, relational, and family outcomes (see Linares, Rhodes, & Montalto, 2010). Moreover, understanding foster family communication across the life course is imperative. Thus, the Foster Family Communication Model (Nelson, 2017) is a useful framework for examining foster narratives and fostered youth's information-seeking behaviors over time. Moving forward, we hope to see innovative research—from myriad theoretical perspectives—exploring the communication of the foster square.

Beyond the Family: Family Communication and Society

Foster care and the relationships within complicate sociocultural understandings of family. Structurally, "family" is often understood as shared biology, legal ties, and/or co-residence (see Baxter, 2014). Foster care troubles these norms, as fostered youth: (1) are removed from an often-biological family of origin; (2) are, at least initially, tied to a legal parent/guardian while also a ward of the State; and (3) reside with foster providers outside of the residence of the family of origin. In addition to structural understandings of family, U.S. Americans hold performative expectations of family members. In regard to parent-child relationships in particular, U.S. Americans carry cultural anticipations of support, care, and love; indeed, parents—especially mothers—are expected to provide children with care, safety, and unconditional love until, and even beyond, adulthood (see Thomas et al., 2017). These assumptions permeate understandings of the parent-child relationship, yet foster care draws attention to the conflation of biology and love. Given that children are placed in foster care when unable to live safely with their parent(s)/guardian(s), foster care represents a violation of both structural understandings and cultural assumptions surrounding family and its associated roles and performances.

Certainly, other family forms exist outside of biogenetic ties: scholars have studied the "adoption triad," of (legally) adoptive parent, child, and (biological) birthmother (see Hays, Horstman, Colaner, & Nelson, 2015). Foster care adds an additional layer of the State, thus creating links among four entities. In the foster square, fostered youth are tied in some way to three entities: the State (e.g., as represented through caseworkers and judges) garners legal custody of a child; foster providers are charged with caring for a child; and parents of origin maintain biological/legal ties even after a child's foster care placement. Interactions among any of these four entities hold opportunities to reify or resist ideological understandings of what family is and can be.

Given that child welfare cases often initially move forth with goals of reunification with the family of origin, foster parents are prepared to support multiple outcomes, including reunification. Case workers also frequently arrange visitations among children and family of origin members, to maintain and improve relationships. Thus, it might seem that foster care privileges biology-based ideology. However, because the goal of placement is "permanency with caring parents" (Children's Bureau, 2018, p. 4), case workers are foremost tasked with helping youth garner caring family membership in a timely manner. To better accomplish placement goals, case workers often implement concurrent planning, in which multiple permanency outcomes are considered and planned. Therefore, communication in and about foster care also resists assumptions that biological family is (always) best.

In addition to foster policies and procedures both resisting and reifying ideologies of family, those living and communicating in foster families also expand understandings of family. Perhaps unsurprisingly, given pervasive ideology of family-as-biology, both (formerly) fostered youth and foster parents speak to biological norms—the permanence and importance of biological ties—when making sense of family (see Suter et al., 2014; Thomas et al., 2017). In addition, shared history emerges as forever connecting family members in fostered youth's talk (Thomas et al.). Moreover, fostered youth and foster parents reference constitutive kinning, positioning familial role performance, care, and love as imperative to creating and maintaining family (Suter et al.; Thomas et al.). Given that constitutive kinning is often contrasted with biology in these narratives, foster family members' talk: (1) expands understandings of family by including relationships of care and love, even absent biology; and (2) shifts ideology by undermining the assumption that biological ties (always) equal relationships of care. Indeed, foster square communicative practices and meaning-making open discursive space to understand foster families—arguably, all families—as reliant on performances and feelings of support, care, and love. In turn, understanding families as supportive, caring, and loving not only transforms traditional non-familial ties into (potential) family (e.g., a foster relationship or close friend can be family), but also allows for relinquishing (i.e., deconstructing) unsupportive, uncaring, and/or unloving biological/legal relationships on the basis of not meeting requirements of family performance. Taken together, communication within and about foster care troubles cultural ideology, creating space for new, emergent understandings of family.

Implications for Scholars & Practitioners

We offer four primary avenues for future research on foster (family) communication—each of which holds practical insights for scholars, practitioners, and policy workers. First, understanding how social identities affect and reflect communication and solidarity deserves scholarly attention. Second, we call for researchers to implement and assess evidence-based interventions. Third, researchers should examine multiple perspectives and experiences. Last, much can be gained from critically investigating foster square communication dynamics.

Communicating Identities in Foster Families

Family is often perceived as an "ingroup" due to shared values, means of communicating, customs, and rituals (Soliz & Rittenour, 2012); however, foster family members often have differing social identities (e.g., race/ethnicity, sexuality, religiosity, social class, etc.), which can create "outgroups" within the foster square. Differing social identities hold potential to create intergroup dynamics—whereby turmoil (e.g., "us" versus "them") might develop (Soliz & Rittenour, 2012). However, foster parents often perceive sharing family identity with foster children by engaging solidarity-affirming communication (Miller-Ott, 2017; Nelson & Colaner, 2020). Consequently, deeper explorations into foster family identity work is imperative.

Ethnic minorities are disproportionally represented in the US foster care system (Padilla, Vargas, & Chavez, 2010). Research has revealed that cultural dissimilarity between foster children and parents is typical and negatively impacts children's psychological adjustment (Anderson & Linares, 2012). Yet, little is known about how talk might help to navigate and legitimate individual and family identities and/or ameliorate negative outcomes. For example, gay and lesbian foster parents reported using "interactions as opportunities to teach their foster children if and how they should respond to questions about or challenges to their family identity" (Patrick & Palladino, 2009,

p. 340). Indeed, the inherent diversity in foster family structure positions communication as central to the construction, negotiation, and maintenance of shared family identity (Soliz & Rittenour, 2012). Thus, we urge family communication scholars to explore how foster parents and children communicatively navigate identities to better understand and promote practices that enhance family solidarity and positive outcomes.

Implementing and Assessing Evidence-Based Interventions

Child welfare agencies worldwide are addressing the need for systemic change by implementing programs and infrastructure aimed at preventing children from entering foster care (Jones & Kruk, 2005). Preventive programs, such as Family Group Conferencing (FGC), promote conversation among families of origin and social workers to plan for children's best interests. In New Zealand, FGC is mandatory, and feedback from participating families has been overwhelmingly positive (Jones & Kruk, 2005). In addition, in-care interventions seek to normalize stress responses (see Dozier, Peloso, Lewis, Laurenceau, & Levine, 2008), reduce child emotional and behavior problems (see Chamberlain et al., 2008; Smith, Leve, & Chamberlain, 2011), encourage prosocial behavior (Smith et al., 2011), promote secure attachment (see Fisher & Kim, 2007; Dozier et al., 2008; Nelson et al., 2017), and combat caregiver stress (Fisher & Stoolmiller, 2008). The Incredible Years intervention even promotes healthy communication among foster square members, promoting co-parenting between parents of origin and foster parents, highlighting that communication scholars have much to contribute to these conversations (see Linares, Montalto, Li, & Oza, 2006).

To date, communication scholars have yet to create evidence-based foster care practice interventions—a testament to the need for more communication-focused work to improve outcomes for those in the foster square. Suggestions for existing communication-focused interventions that might translate to foster contexts include: (1) the expressive writing intervention (Pennebaker, 1997), which positions writing about emotional experiences as therapeutic and (2) the resilience and coping intervention (Houston et al., 2017), a group-based intervention that encourages members to share thoughts, feelings, and experiences about a problem and to identify promising coping strategies as part of an action plan. Beyond applying existing interventions, findings from communication studies could be implemented into family communication-focused training/coaching programs. For example, establishing training/coaching programs for foster parents, educational professionals, and/or community members to focus on trauma-informed care is imperative, given that fostered youth bear higher prevalence rates of traumatic experiences than their non-fostered peers (Beyerlein & Bloch, 2014). Indeed, trauma that is not addressed and treated is associated with long-term behavioral, emotional, and mental health challenges (Kinniburgh, Blaustein, Spinazzola, & van der Kolk, 2017); foster family communication researchers have much to contribute, as unpacking and treating trauma is a largely communicative venture. Bolstering understanding among parents, educators, and community members of how to recognize and communicatively respond to youth with complex trauma might strengthen support and improve outcomes for foster children with histories of abuse, neglect, and attachment disruption. Thus, we implore foster family researchers to continue to assess and address training and coaching programs focused on issues of trauma.

Ultimately, it is imperative that family communication scholars and practitioners: (1) understand vulnerabilities plaguing members of the foster square and the existing evidence-based interventions and programs that might provide some relief, (2) work to create and implement evidence-based interventions and training programs no matter how complex and difficult, and (3) assess and address the usefulness of these interventions and programs internationally. We implore family communication researchers to increasingly invest in this applied and practical work. In addition to examining what has been done *to/within* these families, our focus ought to shift to what we can do *for* these families.

Absent Voices: Current Fostered Youth and Fathers

Largely missing from extant foster family communication literature are voices of current fostered youth and fathers. Although numerous studies assess the experiences of former fostered youth in the U.S. (see Michell, 2015; Thomas, 2014; Thomas et al., 2017; Thomas & Scharp, 2018), attention to the communicative lives of children currently in care has been addressed minimally. This is due, in part, to legal constraints complicating access to fostered youth. Ethical considerations abound when researching children in care. In the U.S., researchers often must gain access to youth through the DHHS; although birth parent consent is not legally required, many researchers believe soliciting birth parent consent an ethical imperative, arguing "parents have a fiduciary relationship with children," and are still ultimately responsible for the child's best interests (Bogolub & Thomas, 2005, p. 276). This ethical preference results in relying on difficult and time-consuming attempts to garner the assistance of birth parents, overburdened caseworkers, and foster parents in accessing fostered youth, resulting in an understanding that foster children are largely inaccessible to researchers. Nonetheless, research assessing current foster children's perspectives does exist inside (see Johnson, Yoken, & Voss, 1995) and outside of the U.S. (see Andersson, 1999; 2009; Ellingsen et al., 2011; Ellingsen, Stephens, & Størksen, 2012; Jones & Kruk, 2005).

Studies assessing current foster children have largely examined children's perspectives and how experiences could be improved. Specifically, youth sought to learn about the circumstances of their placements to improve placement transitions (Johnson et al., 1995). Research shows that listening to youth leads to increased self-efficacy and self-esteem, both of which are linked to resilience (Ellingsen et al., 2011, p. 316). Indeed, fostered youth described desire to share their stories to encourage policy change and system improvement (Whiting, 2000). Other studies have focused on current foster children's impressions of family membership and permanency (see Andersson, 1999; Ellingsen et al., 2012). Andersson found that, absent a legal permanency option, many Swedish foster children between 10–11 years old perceived their foster homes as permanent and, consequently, regarded their foster family members as family. Fostered youth in Norway conceived of family in one of three ways, perceiving birth family, foster family, or both birth and foster families as their family (Ellingsen et al.). Research suggests that as the number of placements increases, so too does fostered youths' disconnection from birth, foster, and other (e.g., friends, caseworkers) family systems (Jones & Kruk, 2005). Thus, future communication research should garner current fostered youth's perspectives to illuminate suggestions and best practices for cultivating family belonging during a time that is often rife with uncertainty, trauma, and loss.

Another absent voice in foster communication literature is that of foster fathers. Research illustrates that mothers often serve as family gatekeepers (Hays et al., 2015) and kin keepers (Stone, 2004). Mothers are family storytellers; consequently, an overwhelming majority of research participants are foster mothers (see Miller-Ott, 2017; Nelson & Horstman, 2017; Nelson & Colaner, 2020; 72.2%, 93.1%, and 94.8%, respectively). Future research should solicit foster fathers' perspectives to better understand foster family dynamics.

A Call for Critical/Cultural Foster Square Scholarship

Extant studies examining foster family communication have largely been post-positivist (see Nelson & Colaner, 2020) or interpretive (see Miller-Ott, 2017; Thomas, 2014), although some critical work exists (see Suter et al., 2014; Thomas et al., 2017). The foster care context is ripe for critical interrogation, as marginalized identities, stigma, privilege, and oppression permeate the foster square. Much room exists for studies assessing foster family communication dynamics, cultural ideologies, and class-, race-, gender-, and ability-laden dimensions of foster care. Further, given that those in the foster square must communicatively manage marginalized relationships and identities, critical (postmodern) work is needed to better understand how identity (de)construction is ideologically saturated. Critical explorations of foster communication provide more holistic understandings of how culture and communication enable, constrain, and (de)construct experiences, identities, relationships, and sense-making for those in the foster square.

Conclusion

Throughout this chapter, we have elucidated the current status of foster care and foster family dynamics, overviewed extant foster-focused and communication-related literature from an international perspective, offered insights into the ways in which communication in and about foster families influences broader society and culture, and provided suggestions for future foster care-related communication research and practice. We invite communication scholars to join us on our quest to better understand foster care and foster family communication dynamics and practices.

References

Adoption and Foster Care Analysis Reporting System (AFCARS). (2018). Preliminary FY 2017 estimates as of August 2018. Adoption and foster care analysis and reporting system. Retrieved from: https://www.acf.hhs.gov/sites/default/files/cb/afcarsreport25.pdf.

Ainsworth, M. D. S., & Bowlby, J. (1991). An ethological approach to personality development. *American Psychologist*, *46*, 333–341. doi:10.1037/0003-066X.46.4.333

Anderson, M., & Linares, L. O. (2012). The role of cultural dissimilarity factors on child adjustment following foster placement. *Children and Youth Services Review*, *34*, 597–601. doi:10.1016/j.childyouth.2011.11.016

Andersson, G. (1999). Children in permanent foster care in Sweden. *Child and Family Social Work*, *4*, 175–186. Retrieved from http://lup.lub.lu.se/record/1472147.

Andersson, G. (2009). Foster children: A longitudinal study of placements and family relationships. *International Journal of Social Welfare*, *18*, 13–26. doi:10.1111/j.1468-2397.2008.00570.x

Baxter, L. A. (2011). *Voicing relationships*. Thousand Oaks, CA: Sage.

Baxter, L. A. (2014). Introduction to the volume. In L. A. Baxter (Ed.), *Remaking "family" communicatively* (pp. 3–16). New York, NY: Peter Lang Publishing.

Berrick, J. D. (2009). *Take me home: Protecting America's vulnerable children and families.* New York, NY: Oxford University Press.

Beyerlein, B. A. & Bloch, E. (2014). Need for trauma-informed care within the foster care system: A policy issue. *Child Welfare, 93,* 7–21.

Bogolub, E. B., & Thomas, N. (2005). Parental consent and the ethics of research with foster children: Beginning a cross-cultural dialogue. *Qualitative Social Work, 4,* 271–292. doi:10.1177/1473325005055592

Chamberlain, P., Price, J., Leve, L. D., Laurent, H., Landsverk, J. A., & Reid, J. B. (2008). Prevention of behavior problems for children in foster care: Outcomes and mediation effects. *Prevention Science, 9,* 17–27. doi:10.1007/s11121-007-0080-7

Children's Bureau of the US Department of Health and Human Services. (2018). Child welfare information gateway: Foster care statistics 2016. Retrieved from http://www.childwelfare.gov/pubs/factsheets/foster.pdf

Colton, M., & Williams, M. (1997). The nature of foster care international trends. *Adoption & Fostering, 21,* 44–49. doi:10.1177/030857599702100108

Courtney, M. E., Piliavin, I., Grogan-Kaylor, A., & Nesmith, A. (2001). Foster youth transitions to adulthood: A longitudinal view of youth leaving care. *Child Welfare,* 80, 685–717. PMID:11817658

Dozier, M., Peloso, E., Lewis, E., Laurenceau, J., & Levine, S. (2008). Effects of an attachment-based intervention on the cortisol production of infants and toddlers in foster care. *Development and Psychopathology, 20,* 845–859. PMID: 18606034

Ellingsen, I. T., Shemmings, D., & Størksen, I. (2011). The concept of 'family' among Norwegian adolescents in long-term foster care. *Child and Adolescents Social Work, 28,* 301–318. doi:10.1007/s10560-011-0234-0

Ellingsen, I. T., Stephens, P., & Størksen, I. (2012). Congruence and incongruence in the perception of 'family' among foster parents, birth parents and their adolescent (foster) children. *Child & Family Social Work, 17,* 427–437. doi:10.1111/j.1365-2206.2011.00796.x

Fernandez, E., & Barth, R. P. (Eds.). (2010). *How does foster care work? International evidence on outcomes.* London, UK: Jessica Kingsley Publishers.

Fisher, P. A., & Kim, H. K. (2007). Intervention effects on foster preschoolers' attachment-related behaviors from a randomized trial. *Prevention Science, 8,* 161–170. doi:10.1007/s11121-007-0066-5

Fisher, P. A., & Stoolmiller, M. (2008). Intervention effects on foster parent stress: Associations with child cortisol levels. *Development and Psychopathology, 20,* 1003–1021. doi:10.1017/S0954579408000473

Galvin, K. M. (2006). Diversity's impact on defining the family: Discourse-dependence and identity. In L. H. Turner & R. West (Eds.), *The family communication sourcebook* (pp. 3–20). Thousand Oaks, CA: Sage.

Galvin, K. M. (2014). Blood, law, and discourse: Constructing and managing family identity. In L. A. Baxter (Ed.), *Remaking family communicatively* (pp. 17–32). New York: Peter Lang.

Hays, A., Horstman, H. K., Colaner, C. W., & Nelson, L. R. (2015). "She chose us to be your parents": Exploring the content and process of adoption entrance narratives told in families formed through open adoption. *Journal of Social and Personal Relationships, 33*, 917–937. doi:10.1177/0265407515611494

Höjer, I. (2011). Parents with children in foster care—How do they perceive their contact with social workers? *Practice: Social Work in Action, 23*, 111–123. doi:10.1080/09503153.2011.557149

Houston, J. B., First, J., Spialek, M. L., Sorenson, M. E., Mills-Sandoval, T., Lockett, M., ... Pfefferbaum, B. (2017). Randomized controlled trial of the resilience and coping intervention (RCI) with undergraduate university students. *Journal of American College Health, 65*, 1–9. doi:10.1080/07448481. 2016.1227826

Johnson, P. R., Yoken, C., & Voss, R. (1995). Family foster care placement: The child's perspective. *Child Welfare, 74*, 959–974.

Jones, L., & Kruk, E. (2005). Life in government care: The connection of youth to family. *Child and Youth Care Forum, 34*, 405–421. doi:10.1007/s10566-005-7754-8

Kinniburgh, K. J., Blaustein, M., Spinazzola, J., & Van der Kolk, B. A. (2017). Attachment, self-regulation, and competency: A comprehensive intervention framework for children with complex trauma. *Psychiatric Annals, 35*, 424–430. doi:10.3928/00485713-20050501-08

Kools, S., & Kennedy, C. (2003). Foster child health and development: Implications for primary care. *Pediatric Nursing, 29*, 29–44. PMID:12630505

Leve, L. D., Harold, G. T., Chamberlain, P., Landsverk, J. A., Fisher, P. A., & Vostanis, P. (2012). Practitioner review: Children in foster care—vulnerabilities and evidence-based interventions that promote resilience processes. *Journal of Child Psychology and Psychiatry, 53*, 1197–1211. doi:10.1111/j.1469-7610.2012.02594.x

Linares, L. O., Montalto, D., Li, M. M., & Oza, V. (2006). A promising parenting intervention in foster care. *Journal of Consulting and Clinical Psychology, 74*, 32–41. doi:10.1037/0022-006X.74.1.32

Linares, L. O., Rhodes, J., & Montalto, D. (2010). Perceptions of coparenting in foster care. *Family Process, 49*, 530–542. doi:10.1111/j.1545-5300.2010.01338.x

Luke, N., & Coyne, S. M. (2008). Fostering self-esteem: Exploring adult recollections on the influence of foster parents. *Child and Family Social Work, 13*, 402–410. doi:10.1111/j.1365-2206.2008.00565.x

McAdams, D. P. (1993). *The stories we live by: Personal myths and the making of the self.* New York, NY: Guilford.

McWey, L. M., Acock, A., & Porter, B. E. (2010). The impact of continued contact with biological parents upon the mental health of children in foster care. *Children and Youth Services Review, 32*, 1338–1345. doi:10.1016/j.childyouth.2010.05.003

Michell, D. (2015). Foster care, stigma and the sturdy, unkillable children of the very poor. Continuum: Journal of Media & Cultural Studies, 29, 663–676. doi: 10.1080/10304312.2015.1025361

Miller-Ott, A. E. (2017). Developing and maintaining foster family identity through foster parents' identity work. *Journal of Family Communication, 17*, 208–222. doi:10.1080/15267431.2017.1293061

Nelson, L. R. (2017). The evolving nature and process of foster family communication: An application and adaptation of the Family Adoption Communication Model. *Journal of Family Theory & Review, 9*, 366–381. doi:10.1111/jftr.12204

Nelson, L. R., & Colaner, C. W. (2020). Fostering "family": Communication orientations in the foster parent-child relationship. *Western Journal of Communication*. doi: 10.1080/10570314.2020.1734231

Nelson, L. R., & Horstman, H. K. (2017). Communicated meaning-making in foster families: Relationships between foster parents' entrance narratives and foster child well-being. *Communication Quarterly, 65*, 144–166. doi:10.1080/01463373.2016.1215337

Oswald, S. H., Heil, K., & Goldbeck, L. (2010). History of maltreatment and mental health problems in foster children: A review of literature. *Journal of Pediatric Psychology, 35*, 462–472. doi:10.1093/jpepsy/jsp114

Padilla, J. B., Vargas, J. H., & Chavez, H. L. (2010). Influence of age on transracial foster adoptions and its relation to ethnic identity development. *Adoption Quarterly, 13*, 50–73. doi:10.1080/10926751003662598

Patrick, D., & Galvin, K. M. (2012). *Family communication and the foster care experience: The next frontier*. Paper presented at the 2012 National Communication Association Conference, Orlando.

Patrick, D., & Palladino, J. (2009). The community interactions of gay and lesbian foster parents. In T. J. Socha & G. H. Stamp (Eds.), *Parents and children communicating with society: Managing relationships outside of home* (pp. 323–342). New York, NY: Routledge.

Pennebaker, J. W. (1997). Writing about emotional experiences as a therapeutic process. *Psychological Science, 8*, 162–169. doi:10.1111/j.1467-9280.1997.tb00403.x

Petronio, S. (2002). *Boundaries of privacy: Dialectics of disclosure*. Albany, NY: New York Press.

Petronio, S. (2013). Brief status report on communication privacy management theory. *Journal of Family Communication, 13*, 6–14. doi:10.1080/15267431.2013.743426

Petrowski, N., Cappa, C., & Gross, P. (2017). Estimating the number of children in formal alternative care: Challenges and results. *Child Abuse & Neglect, 70*, 388–398. doi:10.1016/j.chiabu.2016.11.026

Schneiderman, J. U., Leslie, L. K., Arnold-Clark, J. S., McDaniel, D., & Xie, B. (2011). Pediatric health assessments of young children in child welfare by placement type. *Child Abuse & Neglect, 35*, 29–39. doi:10.1016/j.chiabu.2010.06.007

Smith, D. K., Leve, L. D., & Chamberlain, P. (2011). Preventing internalizing and externalizing problems in girls in foster care as they enter middle school: Impact of an intervention. *Prevention Science, 12*, 269–277. doi:10.1007/s11121-011-0211-z

Soliz, J., & Rittenour, C. E. (2012). Family as an intergroup arena. In H. Giles (Ed.), *Handbook of intergroup communication*. New York: Routledge.

Stone, E. (2004). *Black sheep and kissing cousins: How our family stories shape us*. London, England: Transaction Publishers.

Suter, E. A., Baxter, L. A., Seurer, L., & Thomas, L. J. (2014). Discursive constructions of the meaning of "family" in online narratives of foster adoptive parents. *Communication Monographs*, *81*, 59–78. doi:10.1080/03637751.2014.880791

Thomas, L. J. (2014). "Once a foster child ...": Identity construction in former foster children's narratives. *Qualitative Research Report in Communication*, *15*, 84–91. doi:10.1080/ 17459435.2014.955596

Thomas, L. J. (2015). *Fostering resilience: Exploring former foster children's narratives* (Doctoral dissertation). Retrieved from http://ir.uiowa.edu/etd/1775

Thomas, L. J., & Beier, I. P. (2018). *When foster care fosters conspiracy theory: A textual analysis of the FightCPS website*. Paper presented at the 2018 National Communication Association Conference, Salt Lake City.

Thomas, L. J., Jackl, J. A., & Crowley, J. L. (2017). "Family? ... not just blood": Discursive constructions of "family" in adult, former foster children's narratives. *Journal of Family Communication*, *17*, 238–253. doi:10.1080/15267431.2017.1310728

Thomas, L. J., & Scharp, K. M. (2018). *Voicing the system: How formerly fostered adults make meaning of the US foster care system*. Paper presented at the 2018 International Communication Association Conference, Prague.

US Department of Health and Human Services. (2005). A report to congress on adoption and other permanency outcomes for children in foster care: Focus on older children. Washington, DC: Children's Bureau. Retrieved from http://www.acf.hhs.gov/programs/cb/pubs/congress_adopt/congress_adopt.pdf.

US Department of Health and Human Services. (2013). Child welfare information gateway: Out-of-home care overview. Retrieved from http://www.childwelfare.gov/outofhome/overview.cfm.

Whiting, J. B. (2000). The view from down here: Foster children's stories. *Child and Youth Care Forum*, *29*, 79–95. doi:10.1023/A:1009497110958

12. *Communicatively Managing In-Law Relationships*

SYLVIA L. MIKUCKI-ENYART AND SARAH R. HEISDORF

In the United States, approximately two million marriages occur annually (Center for Disease Control and Prevention, 2017). Accompanying these unions is the formation of in-law relationships. Some quick calculus reveals that, on average, 8 million in-law relationships stem from these nuptials, not accounting for step in-law relationships or other "in-law-esque" configurations (e.g., cohabiting parents, long-term parental dating relationships). Despite the ubiquitous nature of in-law bonds, in-laws occupy a liminal space both in family life and academic scholarship. Within families, in-laws are often seen as "insiders" and "outsiders" simultaneously (Fischer, 1983; Mikucki-Enyart, 2016), resulting in in-law bonds being conceived of as "family lite." In other words, despite in-law's legal family membership status, they often do not have full membership privileges such as access to private information (e.g., wills/trusts, family secrets) or input in critical decision-making (e.g., parenting, health care). The precarious nature of in-law bonds is rooted in the enduring, negative, and gendered stereotypes that characterize this relationship, such as the possessive, jealous, and meddling mother-in-law or the conniving daughter-in-law looking to "steal" her husband from his family, especially his mother (Cotterill, 1994; Duvall, 1954; Morr Serewicz & Hosmer, 2011). These depictions likely taint the development of in-law bonds and serve as self-fulfilling prophecies. That is, cultural tropes serve as lenses though which in-laws observe and interpret each other's behavior. These negative portrayals often lead to more reactive and biased interpretations of one another's behavior, including communication (e.g., Mikucki-Enyart, 2018b, 2019). Pessimistic evaluations of in-law's behaviors result in problematic, conflictual, and dissatisfying in-law relationships (Bryant, Conger, & Meehan, 2001; Mikucki-Enyart, 2018b; Rittenour & Koenig

Kellas, 2015) and overlook their supportive possibilities (Chong, Gordon, & Don, 2016; Goetting, 1990).

Within the scholarly domain, Western cultural considerations such as individualism, autonomy, and prioritizing the marital unit over other family ties (Altman, Brown, Staples, & Werner, 1992) relegate in-law relationships to the fringe of the family system. As such, limited empirical attention has been given to in-law ties. Research that has focused exclusively on in-law relationships, however, demonstrates their pervasive and important impact on family functioning. In fact, researchers have documented direct associations between qualities of the in-law relationship (e.g., communication, family connection) and children-in-law's marital satisfaction and stability (Bryant et al., 2001; Mikucki-Enyart, 2019; Morr Serewicz, Hosmer, Ballard, & Griffin, 2008), parents-in-law's closeness with their adult children (Cao, Fine, Fang, & Zhou, 2018; Golish, 2000), and grandchildren-grandparent relationships (Chan & Elder, 2000; Fingerman, 2004). Research reflecting an Eastern cultural perspective, such as Korean or Indian in-law relationships, highlight how cultural values, such as filial piety and familism, versus individual factors (e.g., communication, satisfaction) correspond with caregiving, shared decision-making, support provisions, and the maintenance of intergenerational bonds (Goa & Ting-Toomey, 1998; Simkhada, Porter, & Teijlingen, 2010; Song & Zhang, 2012).

Despite divergent cultural orientations and scholarly approaches towards the study of in-law relationships, a common theme is clear: in-law relationships are important family system ties. Before advancements can be made in the study of in-law relationships, it is necessary to contextualize our understanding within the knowledge base that has been accrued to this point. As such, our goal in this chapter is to provide an overview of in-law scholarship which can serve as a jumping off point for continued research that increases our understanding of this complex, yet significant family bond. We begin by synthetizing current in-law scholarship, including relevant theoretical frameworks and broad findings from these programs of study. Next, we discuss how the theoretical and practical insight garnered from scholarship can transcend the walls of the family system and inform understanding of non-kin relationships. We conclude by recommending future directions of inquiry for in-law researchers and advancing important considerations for clinicians working with couples and families as they navigate the formation and maintenance of in-law bonds.

The Landscape of In-Law Scholarship: Theoretical Frameworks and Major Findings

Whether testing assumptions and propositions underlying "grand theories" or "theorizing" about the associations between (and among) related constructs, across disciplines, scholars apply diverse theoretical perspectives to study in-law relationships. The richness of these varied lenses is illustrated through the broad patterns of findings that have emerged from this body of scholarship. In the following sections, we discuss prominent theories utilized in contemporary in-law scholarship and resultant patterns of findings.

Theorizing on In-Law Relationships

Theories and models utilized to understand in-law bonds range from post-positivist lenses, aimed at hypothesis testing, to interpretivist frameworks, which are intended to develop theory emerging from in-law's situated and lived experiences. Some theories forefront the structural considerations that shape in-law bonds, whereas others focus on key communicative processes. Together, the application of these theories and models have provided foundational knowledge and inspired additional questions in need of answers. We discuss these frameworks next.

Triangular theory. In their simplest form, in-law relationships are triadic in nature, comprised of a linchpin (spouse/adult child), linchpin's relative (parent-in-law), and spouse (child-in-law), with the linchpin bonding the spouse and relative in a non-voluntary relationship (Morr Serewicz, 2008). Morr Serewicz (2008) unified these principals in her triangular theory of the communication and relationships of in-laws, which outlines four assumptions and three propositions that elucidate how the triadic, non-voluntary, and interdependent nature of in-law bonds shape the development and maintenance of these ties. The theory's assumptions assert that, in addition to the defining structural characteristics (i.e., triadic and non-voluntary), the in-law relationship is typically the weakest side of the in-law triangle, in-law bonds are in constant flux adapting to normative and non-normative lifespan stressors, and communication between and among members of the trio have consequences for the entire triad (Morr Serewicz, 2008). Scholars have utilized this theory and adjacent theorizing (e.g., linchpin theory; Bowen, 1993; Duck, Foley, & Kirkpatrick, 2006) to understand disclosure (Morr Serewicz, 2008), closeness (Woolley & Greif, 2018), and conflict (Song & Zhang, 2012) within the in-law triad.

Intergenerational Ambivalence. Intergenerational ambivalence is defined as "the simultaneous co-existence and opposition of harmony and conflict in intergenerational relations" (Lüscher, 2002, p. 591). Moreover, intergenerational ambivalence reflects experienced contradictions about structural norms and roles and individual emotions and cognitions within intergenerational relationships (Luescher & Pillemer, 1998; Pillemer & Suitor, 2002; Wilson, Shuey, & Elder, 2003). That is, parents- and children-in-law may recognize yet resent their structural obligations to one another (e.g., caregiving) or experience both positive and negative emotions toward one another (e.g., love-dislike), concurrently. Children-in-law, for instance, often report desiring both autonomy from and connection with their parents-in-law (Cotterill, 1994; Prentice, 2009); parents-in-law report enjoying grandparenting but also being burdened by this expectation (Low & Goh, 2015). Across disciplines (e.g., sociology, psychology, and communication), scholars have employed this perspective to examine how intergenerational ambivalence (Shih & Pyke, 2010; Wilson et al., 2003) influences in-law relationship development (Greif & Woolley, 2018; Turner, Young, & Black, 2006) and children-in-law's marital relationship (Beaton, Norris, & Pratt, 2003). Collectively, theorizing on intergenerational ambivalence helps illuminate the complexity and contradictions inherent within in-law bonds.

Communication Privacy Management Theory. Communication privacy management theory (Petronio, 2002) has been utilized to understand how in-law's use of metaphorical boundaries allows them to oversee access, ownership, and control of their private information through communicative practices such as self-disclosure, topic avoidance, or secrets. In addition to the practical functions of boundary management, disclosing or withholding private information is a symbolic way of granting or denying membership into the family's boundary system. That is, privacy management helps designate family "insiders" from "outsiders" (Petronio, 2002) and often reflects in-law's perceptions of family connection (Mikucki-Enyart, 2011; Mikucki-Enyart, 2018b; Morr Serewicz & Canary, 2008). Moreover, in-laws must negotiate boundary management against a backdrop of either congruent or incongruent privacy orientations, such as their willingness to be open with those inside (interior privacy orientations) and outside (exterior privacy orientations) the family system (Petronio, 2002). In-laws holding compatible privacy orientations, such as highly permeable interior boundaries, may share information freely and be satisfied with their boundary coordination. Conversely, in-laws with divergent orientations (e.g., impermeable vs. permeable interior boundary) may be dissatisfied with their privacy management and subsequently their relationship (Morr Serewicz & Canary, 2008). Scholars have employed this perspective to examine how in-law privacy management influences relational outcomes between in-laws (Mikucki-Enyart, 2011; Morr Serewicz & Canary, 2008) and within the in-law triad (Morr Serewicz & Canary, 2008).

The In-Law Uncertainty and Avoidance Model. The in-law uncertainty and avoidance model (IUAM; Mikucki-Enyart, 2018a; 2019) has been employed to understand how uncertainty, conceptualized as ambiguous, complex, or unclear situations, rules, or norms (Brashers, 2001; Morr Serewicz,

2006) can be a primary source of relational and communicative difficulty for in-laws. The IUAM tailors theorizing on uncertainty and communication to the in-law context and draws on a multiple goals theory of personal relationships (Caughlin, 2010) to illuminate the role of interaction goals (and goal inferences) as a crucial mechanism linking ambiguity, communication, and relational consequences.

Broadly, as depicted in Figure 12.1, the IUAM elucidates how uncertainty shapes in-law's message production and message processing via interaction goals (and goal inferences), which in turn shape in-law's avoidant communication (or perceptions of avoidance), and subsequent relational well-being within the in-law triad (e.g., parent-adult child dyad, marital dyad; Mikucki-Enyart, 2018b, 2019; Mikucki-Enyart & Caughlin, 2018). In addition to *relational uncertainty*, or questions about involvement in the relationship (Knobloch & Solomon, 1999), the IAUM identifies *family uncertainty*, referring to questions about the interdependent nature of in-law bonds, as a mechanism that corresponds with goals, communication, and relational well-being. Parents- and children-in-law experience discrete doubts. Parents-in-law primarily worry about how the child-in-law will impact the parent-child relationship, family rituals, and adjacent family ties, such as sibling and extended family bonds. Children-in-law's questions revolve around in-law's role in the couple's life (e.g., decision-making, meddling), their influence on the spouse/adult child, and balancing membership and intergenerational ties across two family systems (extended family and family-in-law). Despite divergent uncertainties, family uncertainty is a more portent predictor of communicative and relational outcomes than relational uncertainty, highlighting the significance of interdependence on in-law bonds.

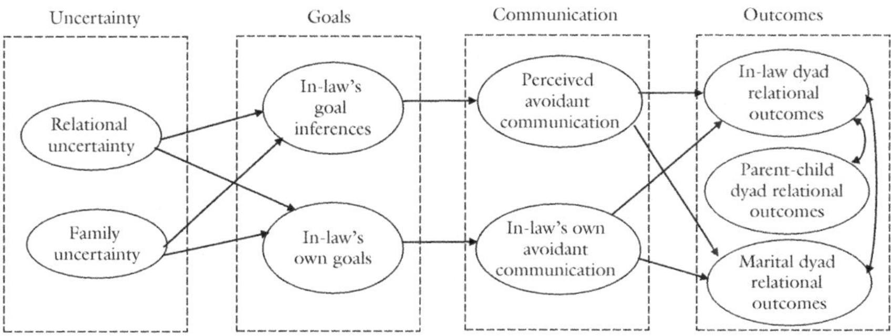

Figure 12.1: In-law uncertainty and avoidance model (IUAM)

Additionally, the IUAM identifies two distinct types of in-law relevant topic avoidance: tangential topic avoidance and in-law relevant topic avoidance. *Tangential topic avoidance* references topics outlined by Guerrero and Afifi (1995) and Caughlin and Golish (2002) that in-laws prefer to avoid, such as negative life experiences or past failures. *In-law relevant topic avoidance* reflects topics in-laws feel they *should* discuss, such as family planning or family-of-origin relationships (Mikucki-Enyart, 2018a, 2018b). This framework has been utilized to study in-law message production and processing under conditions of uncertainty and resultant relational implications.

Broad Trends from In-Law Scholarship

Similar to the diverse theoretical frameworks employed to study in-law bonds, findings from this body of scholarship are myriad. We organize our discussion of contemporary in-law research around three major themes that reflect social and structural considerations as well as illuminate key cognitive and behavioral processes that impact in-law relationships. Although these broad trends are presented separately, findings from this body of research are often woven together, with constructs working collaboratively to influence in-law relationships. Moreover, these results highlight the interwoven and consequential nature of in-law relationships not just for parents-in-law and children-in-law, but the broader family network.

Relational Expectations. Both parents- and children-in-law enter the in-law bond with a set of expectations, either positive or negative, derived from personal experience, culture tropes, or media portrayals (Doreen, Lumumba, & Kafu, 2017; Merrill, 2007). Daughters-in-law, for instance, report internalizing negative cultural tropes and media depictions of in-law bonds (Nganase & Basson, 2018), whereas mothers-in-law's experiences with their own mothers-in-law often guide their approach to the in-law relationship (Prentice, 2008). The bulk of research suggests that daughters-in-law often hold more negative expectations than their mothers-in-law (Merrill, 2007). Nganase and Basson (2018), for instance, found that South African daughters-in-law anticipated challenging and difficult relationships which stemmed from societal stereotypes. Conversely, their mothers-in-law forecasted positive and supportive relationships marked by mutual respect and love. Turner et al. (2006) found similar results, with U.S. daughters-in-law's recounting negative expectations for their formalized in-law relationship based on their interactions during courtship and the engagement period. In contrast, mothers-in-laws often reflected on a close or warm relationship, often stemming from their shared love of the linchpin.

Additionally, daughters-in-law, especially within Western cultures, often hold unrealistic and contradictory expectations for their mother-in-law's behaviors. U.S. daughters-in-law, for instance, report that "good" mothers-in-law welcome their daughters-in-law into the family fold with open arms (Merrill, 2007), often signaled through supportive and open communication, such as empathetic listening and disclosing acceptance and family history (Morr Serewicz & Canary, 2008; Rittenour & Soliz, 2009), while simultaneously staying out of the way and open to being held at arm's length. A daughter-in-law in Merrill's (2007) study, noted "You [mothers-in-law] have to walk the line between being supportive and being unobtrusive. Knowing when to butt out and when to provide that support and what that support should be" (p. 51). Cotterill's (1994) study of in-laws in Great Britain produced similar findings, resulting in Cotterill surmising that it is essential for mothers-in-law to have "extremely sensitive antenna" allowing them to "respond positively and at the right time" (p. 145). Expectations often set the tone for in-law relationships, serving as self-fulfilling prophecies (Markus & Nurius, 1986) or lenses through which in-laws make-sense of one another's behavior (e.g., Rittenour, 2012; Rittneour & Koenig Kellas, 2015). Negative or unmet expectations correspond with negative relational outcomes (Fingerman, Gilligan, Vanderdrift, & Prizter, 2012; Rittenour, 2012). Rittenour (2012), for instance, found that when mothers-in-law's behaviors deviated from daughters-in-law's expectations (or standards) for supportive and open communication, it negatively impacted family satisfaction and shared family identity. Fingerman et al. (2012) revealed that children-in-law's negative, pre-wedding expectations, such as balancing family membership, were negatively associated with in-law's post-wedding relational quality. Furthermore, although in-law bonds can change, for better or worse, over the relationship's lifespan (e.g., Turner et al., 2006; Nganase & Bassan, 2018), the bulk of research reveals continuity in pre- versus post-wedding in-law relational quality (Sprecher & Felmlee, 2000; Turner et al., 2006), which highlights the profound role of expectations on in-law bonds.

Interestingly, more formalized cultural scripts about in-law relationships may contribute to more congruent expectations between parents- and children-in-law. The joint family system in Pariwarbasti, India, for example, encourages positive expectations from both mothers- and daughters-in-law (Allendorf, 2017). Specifically, culture outlines that in-laws will love one another as their own family as well as accept and support them as they would a member bound by blood. However, just because cultural ideals offer unwavering guidelines for how in-law relationships *should* be, it does not necessarily mean that in-laws uphold these expectations (Allendorf, 2017). In Delhi, for instance, Hinduism upholds gendered norms reflecting patriarchal ideology, resulting in expectations that daughters-in-law love, serve, and obey their mothers-in-law as if they were their own (Datta, Poortinga, & Marcoen, 2003). However, these ideals do not translate into positive relational quality. In fact, compared to Belgian daughters-in-law, who are not bound by rigid expectations of obedience and prioritizing their mothers-in-law over their own mothers, Indian daughters-in-law reported lower attachment and closeness to their mothers-in-law (Datta et al., 2003). Collectively, research across cultures highlights the profound impact expectations have on the development and maintenance of in-law bonds.

Family connection. Although labeled differently across studies (e.g., shared family identity; Rittenour & Soliz, 2009; family in-group status; Morr Serewicz & Canary; and family connection; Mikucki-Enyart, 2018b, 2019), family connection has important repercussions on in-law's communication and relational health. Some studies focus on in-law's *own family connection*, in which they bestow family status to the other (e.g., "I consider my in-law to be a member of my family"; Mikucki-Enyart, 2011) and self-identify as a member of the in-law's family (e.g., "I am proud to be in the same family as my mother-in-law"; Rittenour, 2012). Additionally, in-laws report on *perceived family connection*, or the extent to which they believe their in-law has granted them family standing (e.g., "My in-law considers me to be a family member"; Mikucki-Enyart, 2019; Morr Sereweicz & Canary, 2008). As noted above, children-in-law expect to be welcomed into the family fold (e.g., Merrill, 2007). However, desiring family status is not just the purview of children-in-law. Parents-in-law also want to feel included in their children and children-in-law's new family unit (Cotterill, 1994; Merrill, 2007; Turner et al., 2006).

Family membership is often indicated (or perceived) through communicative behaviors. Open, inclusive, and supportive messages (e.g., Rittenour & Soliz, 2009; Morr Serewicz & Canary, 2008), for instance, are often markers of family status, whereas non-accommodative (e.g., emphasizing divergent values) and avoidant communication typically suggest a lack of family membership (Rittenour & Soliz, 2009; Mikucki-Enyart, 2011, 2018b, 2019).

In-law's degree of family connection also has important relational, communicative, and instrumental consequences. Across studies and cultures, findings indicate that family connection unequivocally impacts in-law's relational satisfaction. In-law's own and perceived family connection consistently shares a positive association with relationship satisfaction (e.g., Morr Serewicz & Canary, 2008; Rittenour & Soliz, 2009; Song & Zhang, 2012). Additionally, daughters-in-law's own family connection influences their conflict communication with their mothers-in-law (Song & Zhang, 2012) and corresponds with their intention to provide care to aging or ailing mothers-in-law (Rittenour & Soliz, 2009). Moreover, family connection influences adjacent family bonds, including the parent-child and marital dyad. Parents and children-in-law who did not feel welcome into the family fold often distance themselves from each other, which has ramifications for the parent-child relationship, and the child-in-law's relationship with the extended family-in-law and his/her spouse (e.g., Turner et al., 2006). Furthermore, children-in-law's lack of perceived family connection is indirectly associated with their marital satisfaction. More precisely, Mikucki-Enyart (2019) found that children-in-law's lack of perceived family connection corresponds with decreased in-law satisfaction, which is linked to dissatisfaction with their spouse. Thus, communicatively granting and perceiving family connection is crucial to the success of in-law relationships and adjacent family system ties.

Family Uncertainty. The ambiguous and scriptless nature of in-law bonds has long been acknowledged as creating difficult in-law relationships (Fischer, 1983; Morr Serewicz, 2006). As previously noted, the IAUM has illuminated the pathways linking uncertainty to in-law's goals, communication, and relational outcomes. Under conditions of doubt, for instance, in-laws are more apt to avoid communicating with one another either directly via topic avoidance (Mikucki-Enyart, 2011; Mikucki-Enyart & Caughlin, 2018) or indirectly by engaging in linchpin mediated communication (Mikucki-Enyart & Reed, 2020. These results reflect the paradox of uncertainty, such that those most in need of discussing ambiguity are least likely to engage in direct communication (Knobloch & Satterlee, 2009). Additionally, uncertainty corresponds with in-law's relational outcomes. For both parents- and children-in-law, uncertainty diminishes their own sense of family connection, (e.g., "I have let my in-law into the family circle;" Mikucki-Enyart, 2011), and the extent they believe their in-law has accepted them into the family fold (Mikucki-Enyart, 2019; Morr Serewicz & Canary, 2008) as well as their satisfaction with the in-law relationship (Mikucki-Enyart, 2011; Mikucki-Enyart & Caughlin, 2018). For children-in-law, uncertainty within the in-law dyad also has direct bearing on their marital satisfaction (Mikucki-Enyart et al., 2015).

Additionally, research utilizing the IAUM has revealed a more nuanced understanding of uncertainty's role in influencing in-law dynamics. More precisely, uncertainty is linked to in-law's communication and relational troubles indirectly through interaction goals (or goal inferences). Mikucki-Enyart and Caughlin (2018) found that children-in-law's uncertainty was positively associated with their desire to maintain uncertainty, but negatively associated with the aim of fostering a positive in-law identity or maintaining the in-law relationship. Similarly, Mikucki-Enyart (2018a) found that parents-in-law's uncertainty colored their interaction goals, such that uncertainty was positively associated with anti-social goals, like creating relational distance, and negatively associated with relationship enhancing aims, such as relationship protection. Uncertainty's impact on goals is significant, as in-law's aims shape their communication. In-laws wishing to maintain their current level of doubt or create relational distance, for instance, engage in more topic avoidance compared to those seeking pro-social aims (Mikucki-Enyart, 2018; Mikucki-Enyart & Caughlin, 2018). Unfortunately, in-law's use of topic avoidance is linked with relational dissatisfaction with the in-law relationship (see Figure 12.1). Uncertainty also influences message processing, or how children-in-law make sense of one another's communication (Mikucki-Enyart, 2019). In fact, children-in-law's uncertainty corresponds with perceptions that in-laws engage in topic avoidance to achieve maleficent aims. Moreover, goal inferences were indirectly linked to marital satisfaction. That is, biased goal inferences (e.g., boundary fortification) reduced children-in-law's perceptions of family connection, which in turn corresponded with dissatisfaction with the in-law, and ultimately dissatisfaction with their marriage. Thus, in-law uncertainty corresponds with relational outcomes through its impact on cognitive and communicative processes.

Beyond the Family: Family Communication and Society

At their core, family systems, including in-law triads, are small groups (Socha, 1997; Stafford & Dainton, 1995). As such, family members learn to manage multiple relationships, competing communication orientations, and diverse perspectives within the broader family unit. The ability to attend to multiple and conflicting demands is a skill that is applicable to small group dynamics outside of the family context (Socha, 1999), such as organizational working groups, friendships, and voluntary kin. For instance, similar to in-laws, co-workers are often placed in non-voluntary relationships with interdependent consequences. The difficulties experienced by in-laws, such as uncertainty or discrepant orientations toward communication (e.g., privacy orientation; Morr Serewicz & Canary, 2008), may reflect difficulties among non-voluntary and interdependent working relationships. Workers may, for instance, wonder how their colleague's performance will impact perceptions of their work, for better or worse. Or, they may struggle with identifying and adapting to communication norms of the work group. Prentice (2008), for instance, suggested that similar to in-laws, working groups may make initial attempts at assimilation, but then expect new members to adapt to established rules and routines not leaving room for disagreement or change.

Armed with knowledge about the interdependent consequences associated with communication and relational outcomes within triadic or small group structures, employers can work to facilitate a climate that encourages open communication versus topic avoidance when confronting uncertainty or integrating new members. Additionally, given that the involuntary tie in a triad is the weakest link, employers can work to strengthen their or a group leader's relationship with group members in an effort to capitalize on the spillover effect resulting from strong ties on one side of the triangle.

Relatedly, findings on in-law relationships can help friendship trios, specifically when two friends are woven into one another's life due to their relationship with a linchpin, as well as those balancing supplemental voluntary kin and non-voluntary kin bonds. Like in-law triangles, indirect, triadic friendships appear to suffer from drawbacks including hierarchies in which one friendship, or side of the triangle, is privileged over another (Frank, Muller, & Mueller, 2013). However, knowing that this bond may be the weakest link of the triad, friends can work together to ensure all relationships are strong to ensure the stability of the friendship trio. Additionally, knowing that negative disclosures result in unfavorable relationship perceptions and these perceptions are interdependent, friends should be mindful to not gossip about another member of the triangle to help buffer the entire triad. Similarly, research reveals that supplemental voluntary kin (VK) and biological families (BLF) are triadic in nature and can be brought together or kept apart by the linchpin (Braithwaite, Abetz, Moore, & Brockhage, 2016). Findings from in-law scholarship can help linchpins balancing VK and BLF relationships manage uncertainty, relationship expectations, and divergent communication needs to help successfully navigate these complex bonds.

Implications for Scholars and Practitioners

Based on the reviewed scholarship, we suggest several important lines of future inquiry along with practical applications derived from the extant body of in-law research.

Future Directions

While most research has investigated the bond between mothers-in-law and daughters-in-law (Rittenour & Soliz, 2009), there is a limited amount of research looking into the father-in-law and son-in-law relationship. Although some scholars have attempted to gain an initial understanding of this dynamic (Greif & Woolley, 2018), it is unclear how similar (or dissimilar) the bonds between fathers and sons-in-law are to mothers- and daughters-in-law. Future studies should target this duo in an effort to enhance theoretical understanding of this overlooked in-law pair. Further, most studies surrounding in-law relationships have focused the negative aspects and outcomes (e.g., Rittenour & Koenig Kellas, 2015; Merrill, 2007; Mikucki-Enyart, 2011). However, future research should investigate the positive aspects of the in-law relationship, including mutual support provision (Goetting, 1990) or facilitation of daily and family-level aims (Mikucki-Enyart, 2018a) to identify "best practices" to guide in-laws as they traverse this relationship.

Moreover, the prevalence of divorce for both parents and children-in-law undoubtedly effects the in-law bond and adjacent family relationships, such as the grandparent-grandchild bond (Greif & Woolley, 2018). Given the rise of gray divorce, referring to divorce over the age of 50 (Brown & Lin, 2012), children-in-law may be tasked with forming relationships with multiple parents-in-law (e.g., biological and step), which likely influences communication and closeness within the in-law triad. Additionally, little is known about in-law's post-divorce bonds absent grandchildren. Research should explore if and how childfree children-in-law maintain bonds with parents-in-law and the role these ties play in the child-in-law's and adult child's (ex-spouse) future romantic relationships. Lastly, although same-sex couples gained the legal right to marry in the United States in 2015, in-law research largely reflects a heteronormative bias. In one of the few studies that have explicitly examined gay and lesbian family relationships, Reczek (2016) found that ambivalence was salient. Relatedly, same-sex couples may experience uncertainty regarding acceptance and support from in-laws (and the larger family system), which influences communication and relational quality. As such, future research should attend to same-sex couples in an effort to provide guidance for a relationship ensconced in an additional layer of contextual ambiguity.

Practical Applications

Practitioners can utilize the findings in this chapter to bolster marriage preparation curricula to explicitly address in-law bonds. Importantly, clinicians should help in-laws dismantle negative stereotypes as these are often detrimental to the relational health of the in-law dyad and in-law triad. Moreover, normalizing the experience of intergenerational ambivalence (Greif & Woolley, 2018) and family uncertainty (Mikucki-Enyart, 2018a, 2018b) can help in-laws recognize that positive and negative emotions as well as doubts are natural when merging family system. Additionally, counselors working with couples and parents-in-law can provide scaffolding to facilitate discussions aimed at managing these queries. Relatedly, practitioners can help in-laws utilize appropriate and relationally enhancing communication topics, such as acceptance and family history. In addition, children-in-law often provide care to parents-in-law in old age or failing health (Pinquart & Sorensen, 2011). Healthcare professionals should ensure children-in-law caretakers remain informed, but also balance respect for parents-in-law's and the extended family's preferences regarding privacy boundaries and decision-making roles.

Concluding Thoughts

Despite or perhaps due to their ubiquitous nature, in-law bonds can be challenging to navigate. Uncertainty and divergent relational expectations present obstacles to creating a family connection, a consequence that reverberates throughout the family system. However, scholars have identified communication as a key resource for forging and maintaining in-law bonds. Balancing open and avoidant communication, communicating acceptance and inclusion, and effectively managing uncertainties can help in-laws foster a positive relationship and capitalize on the supportive potential of this important family tie.

References

Allendorf, K. (2017). Like her own: Ideals and experiences of the mother-in-law/daughter-in-law relationship. *Journal of Family Issues, 38*, 2102–2127. doi:10.1177/0192513X15590685

Altman, I., Brown, B. B., Staples, B., & Werner, C. M. (1992). A transactional approach to close relationships: Courtship, weddings, and placemaking. In W. B. Walsh, K. H. Craik, & R. H. Price (Eds.), *Person–environment psychology: Models and perspectives* (pp. 193–241). Hillsdale, NJ: Lawrence Erlbaum Associates, Inc.

Beaton, J. M., Norris, J. E., & Pratt, M. W. (2003). Unresolved issues in adult children's marital relationships involving intergenerational problems. *Family Relations, 52*, 143–153. doi:10.1111/j.1741-3729.2003.00143.x

Berger, C. R. (2002). Goals and knowledge structures in social interaction. In M. L. Knapp & J. A. Daly (Eds.), *Handbook of interpersonal communication* (pp. 181–212). Thousand Oaks, CA: Sage.

Braithwaite, B. O., Abetz, J. S., Moore, J., & Bockhage, K. (2016). Communicating structures of supplemental voluntary kin networks. *Family Relations, 65*, 616–630. doi:10.1111/fare.12215

Brashers, D. E. (2001). Communication and uncertainty management. *Journal of Communication, 51*, 477–497. doi:10.1093/joc/51.3.477

Bowen, M. B. (1993). Family therapy in clinical practice. Oxford, UK: Rowman & Littlefield.

Brown, S. L., & Lin, I. F., (2012). The gray divorce revolution: Rising divorce among middle-aged and older adults, 1990–2010. *Journals of Gerontology Series B: Psychological Sciences and Social Sciences, 67,* 731–741, doi:10.1093/geronb/gbs089

Bryant, C. M., Conger, R. D., & Meehan, J. M. (2001). The influence of in-laws on change in marital success. *Journal of Marriage & Family, 63,* 614–626. doi:10.1111/j.1741-3737.2001.00614.x

Cao, H., Fine, M., Fang, X., & Zhou, N. (2018). Chinese adult children's perceived parents' satisfaction with adult children's marriage, in-law relationship quality, and adult children's marital satisfaction. *Journal of Social and Personal Relationships.* Advance online publication. doi:10.1177/0265407518755319

Caughlin, J. P. (2010). A multiple goals theory of personal relationships: Conceptual integration and program overview. *Journal of Social and Personal Relationships, 27,* 824–848. doi:10.1177/0265407510373262

Caughlin, J. P., & Golish, T. D. (2002). An analysis of the association between topic avoidance and dissatisfaction: Comparing perceptual and interpersonal explanations. *Communication Monographs, 69,* 275–295. doi:10.1080/03637750216546

Center for Prevention and Disease Control. (2017). Marriage and divorce. Retrieved from https://www.cdc.gov/nchs/fastats/marriage-divorce.htm.

Chan, C. G., & Elder, G. H. (2000). Matrilineal advantage in grandchild–grandparent relations. *The Gerontologist, 40,* 179–190. doi:10.1093/geront/40.2.179

Chong, A., Gordon, A. E., & Don, B. P. (2016). Emotional support from parents and in-laws: The roles of gender and contact. *Sex Roles, 76,* 369–379. doi:10.1007/s11199-016-0587-0

Cotterill, P. (1994). *Friendly relations: Mothers and their daughters-in-law.* Bristol, PA: Taylor & Francis.

Datta, P., Poortinga, Y. H., & Marcoen, A. (2003). Parent care by Indian and Belgian caregivers in their roles of daughter/daughter-in-law. *Journal of Cross-Cultural Psychology, 34,* 736–749. doi:10.1177/0022022103258589

Doreen, O. A., Lumumba, K. P, & Kafu, J. (2017). Factors that determine the nature of relationship between mothers and their daughters in-law: A content analysis of the 'Mother-In-Law' TV drama series. *African Journal of Education, Science and Technology, 4,* 165–176.

Duck, S., Foley, M. K., & Kirkpatrick, D. C. (2006). Relating difficulty in a triangular world. In D. C. Kirkpatrick, S. Duck, & M. Foley (Eds.), *Relating difficulty: The process of constructing and managing difficult interaction* (pp. 225–232). Mahwah, NJ: Erlbaum.

Duvall, E. R. M. (1954). *In-laws, pro and con: An original study of inter-personal relations.* New York, New York: Associated Press.

Fingerman, K. L. (2004). The role of offspring and in-laws in grandparents' tie to their grandchildren. *Journal of Family Issues, 25,* 1026–1049. doi:10.1177/0192513X04265941

Fingerman, K. L., Gilligan, M., Vanderdrift, L., & Pitzer, L. (2012). In-law relationships before and after marriage. *Research in Human Development, 9*, 106–125. doi:10.1080/15427609.2012.680843

Fischer, L. R. (1983). Mothers and mothers-in-law. *Journal of Marriage and the Family, 45*, 187–192. doi:10.2307/351307

Frank, K. A., Muller, C., & Mueller, A. S. (2013). The embeddedness of adolescent friendship nominations: The formation of social capital in emergent network structures. *American Journal of Sociology, 119*, 216–253. doi:10.1086/672081

Gao, G., & Ting–Toomey, S. (1998). Communicating effectively with the Chinese. London: Sage.

Goetting, A. (1990). Patterns of support among in-laws in the United States. *Journal of Family Issues, 11*, 67–90. doi:10.1177/019251390011001005

Golish, T. D. (2000). Changes in closeness between adult children and their parents: A turning point analysis. *Communication Reports, 13*, 79–97. doi:10.1080/08934210009367727

Greif, G. L., & Woolley, M. (2018). Sons-in-law and their fathers-in-law: Gaining a preliminary understanding of an understudied family relationship. *Journal of Family Social Work*, 1–20. doi:10.1080/10522158.2018.1496509

Guerrero, L. K., & Afifi, W. A. (1995). Some things are better left unsaid: Topic avoidance in family relationships. *Communication Quarterly, 43*, 276–296. doi:10.1080/01463379509369977

Knobloch, L. K., & Satterlee, K. L. (2009). Relational uncertainty: Theory and application. In T.D. Afifi & W. A. Afifi (Eds.), *Uncertainty, information management, and disclosure decisions: Theories and applications* (pp. 106–127). New York, NY: Routledge/Taylor & Francis Group.

Knobloch, L. K., & Solomon, D. H. (1999). Measuring the sources and content of relational uncertainty. *Communication Studies, 50*, 261–278. doi:10.1080/10510979909388499

Low, S. S. H., & Goh, E. C. L. (2015). Granny as nanny: Positive outcomes for grandparents providing childcare for dual-income families. Fact or myth? *Journal of Intergenerational Relationships, 13*, 302–319. doi:10.1080/15350770.2015.1111003

Luescher, K., & Pillemer, K. (1998). Intergenerational ambivalence: A new approach to the study of parent-child relations in later life. *Journal of Marriage and the Family, 60*, 413. doi:10.2307/353858

Lüscher, K. (2002). Intergenerational ambivalence: Further steps in theory and research. *Journal of Marriage and Family, 64*, 585–593. doi:10.1111/j.1741-3737.2002.00585.x

Markus, H., & Nurius, P. (1986). Possible selves. *American Psychologist, 41*, 954–969. doi:10.1037/0003-066x.41.9.954

Merrill, D. H. (2007). *Mothers-in-law and daughters-in-law: Understanding the relationship and what makes them friends or foe.* Westport, CT: Praeger.

Mikucki-Enyart, S. L. (2011). Parent-in-law privacy management: An examination of the links among relational uncertainty, topic avoidance, in-group status, and in-law satisfaction. *Journal of Family Communication, 11*, 237–263. doi:10.1080/15267431.2010.544633

Mikucki-Enyart, S. L. (2016). Communication among in-laws. In C. Berger & M. Roloff (Eds.), *International encyclopedia of interpersonal communication*. Malden, MA: Blackwell.

Mikucki-Enyart, S. L. (2018a). Parents-in-law's topic avoidance: Understanding the role of interaction goals and relational characteristics. *Personal Relationships, 25*, 433–457. doi:10.1111/pere.12252

Mikucki-Enyart, S. L. (2018b). In-laws' perceptions of topic avoidance, goal inferences, and relational outcomes. *Journal of Family Communication, 18*, 317–333. doi:10.1080/15267431.2018.1492411

Mikucki-Enyart, S. L. (2019). Children-in-law's message processing: Associations among uncertainty, perceptions of topic avoidance, goal inferences, and marital satisfaction. *Journal of Social and Personal Relationships*. Advance online publication. doi:10.1177/0265407519841724

Mikucki-Enyart, S. L., & Caughlin, J. P. (2018). Integrating the relational turbulence model and a multiple goals approach to understand topic avoidance during the transition to extended family. *Communication Research, 45*, 262–296. doi:10.1177/0093650215595075

Mikucki-Enyart, S. L., & Reed, J.M. (2020). Understanding parents-in-law's uncertainty management through a relational turbulence lens.Communication Studies. Advance online publication.

Morr Serewicz, M. C. (2006). The difficulties of in-law relationships. In D. C. Kirkpatrick, S. Duck, & M. Foley (Eds.), *Relating difficulty: The process of constructing and managing difficult interaction* (pp. 101–118). Mahwah, NJ: Erlbaum.

Morr Serewicz, M. C. (2008). Toward a triangular theory of the communication and relationships of in-laws: Theoretical proposal and social relations analysis of relational satisfaction and private disclosures in in-law triads. *Journal of Family Communication, 8*, 264–292. doi:10.1080/15267430802397161

Morr Serewicz, M. C., & Canary, D. J. (2008). Assessments of disclosures from in-laws: Links among disclosure topics, family privacy orientations, and relational quality. *Journal of Social and Personal Relationships, 25*, 333–357. doi:10.1177/026540750708796

Morr-Serewicz, M. C., & Hosmer, R. A. (2011). Inlaws or outlaws?. In W. R. Cupach & B. H. Spitzberg (Eds.), *The darkside of close relationships* (2nd ed., pp 224–242). New York: Routledge.

Morr Serewicz, M. C., Hosmer, R., Ballard, R. L., & Griffin, R. A. (2008). Disclosures from in laws and the quality of in-law and marital relationships. *Communication Quarterly, 56*, 427–444. doi:10.1080/01463370802453642

Nganase, T. R., & Basson, W. J. (2018). Makoti and mamazala: Dynamics of the relationship between mothers- and daughters-in-law within a South African context. *South African Journal of Psychology*, 008124631879011. doi:10.1177/0081246318790118

Petronio, S. (2002). *Boundaries of privacy: Dialectics of disclosure.* Albany, NY: State University of New York Press.

Pillemer, K., & Suitor, J. J. (2002). Explaining mothers' ambivalence toward their adult children. *Journal of Marriage and Family, 64*, 602–613. doi:10.1111/j.1741-3737.2002.00602.x

Pinquart, M., & Sörensen, S. (2011). Spouses, adult children, and children-in-law as caregivers of older adults: A meta-analytic comparison. *Psychology and Aging, 26*, 1–14. doi:10.1037/a0021863

Prentice, C. (2009). Relational dialectics among in-laws. *Journal of Family Communication, 9*, 67–89. doi:10.1080/15267430802561667

Prentice, C. M. (2008). The assimilation of in-laws: The impact of newcomers on the communication routines of families. *Journal of Applied Communication Research, 36*, 74–97. doi:10.1080/00909880701799311

Reczek, C. (2016). Parental disapproval and gay and lesbian relationship quality. Journal of Family Issues, 37, 2189–2212. https://doi.org/10.1177/0192513X14566638

Rittenour, C. E. (2012). Daughter-in-law standards for mother-in-law communication: Associations with daughter-in-law perceptions of relational satisfaction and shared family identity. *Journal of Family Communication, 12*, 93–110. doi:10.1080/15267431.2010.537240

Rittenour, C. E., & Koenig Kellas, J. (2015). Making sense of hurtful mother-in-law messages: Applying attribution theory to the in-law triad. *Communication Quarterly, 63*, 62–80. doi:10.1080/0146337.2014.965837

Rittenour, C., & Soliz, J. (2009). Communicative and relational dimensions of shared family identity and relational intentions in mother-in-law/daughter-in-law relationships: Developing a conceptual model for mother-in-law/daughter-in-law research. *Western Journal of Communication, 73*, 67–90. doi:10.1080/10570310802636334

Shih, K. Y., & Pyke, K. (2010). Power, resistance, and emotional economies in women's relationships with mothers-in-law in Chinese immigrant families. Journal of Family Issues, 31, 333–357. doi: 10.1177/0192513X09350875

Simkhada, B., Porter, M. A., & van Teijlingen, E. R. (2010). The role of mothers-in-law in antenatal care decision-making in Nepal: A qualitative study. *BMC Pregnancy and Childbirth, 10.* doi:10.1186/1471-2393-10-34

Socha, T. (1997). *Group communication across the life span* (pp. 3–28). Boston, MA: Houghton Mifflin.

Socha, T. J. (1999). Communication in family units: Studying the first "group." In L. Frey (Ed.), *The handbook of group communication theory and research* (pp. 475–492). Thousand Oaks, CA: Sage.

Song, Y., & Zhang, Y. B. (2012). Husbands' conflict styles in Chinese mother/daughter-in-law conflicts: Daughters-in-law's perspectives. *Journal of Family Communication, 12*, 57–74, doi:10.1080/15267431.2011.629968

Sprecher, S., & Felmlee, D. (2000). Romantic partners' perceptions of social network attributes with the passage of time and relationship transitions. *Personal Relationships, 7*, 325–340. doi:10.1111/j.1475-6811.2000.tb00020.x

Stafford, L., & Dainton, M. (1995). Parent–child communication within the family system. In T. J. Socha & G. H. Stamp (Eds.), *LEA's communication series. Parents, children, and communication: Frontiers of theory and research* (pp. 3–21). Hillsdale, NJ: Lawrence Erlbaum Associates, Inc.

Turner, J. M., Young, C. R., & Black, K. I. (2006). Daughters-in-law and mothers-in-law seeking their place within the family: A qualitative study of differing viewpoints. *Family Relations*, *55*, 588–600. doi:10.1111/j.1741-3729.2006.00428.x

Wilson, A., Shuey, K., & Elder, G. (2003). Ambivalence in the relationship of adult children to aging parents and in-laws. *Journal of Marriage and Family*, *65*, 1055–1072. doi:10.1111/j.1741-3737.2003.01055.x

Woolley, M. E., & Greif, G. L. (2018). Mother-in-law reports of closeness to daughter-in-law: The determinant triangle with the son and husband. *Social Work*, *64*, 73–82. doi:10.1093/sw/swy055

13. *Identity, Relational Solidarity, and Stepfamily Communication*

Paul Schrodt

Across the landscape of family forms that fill households in the United States and in other nations around the world, few have created more challenges and opportunities for understanding of how family members communicate to create, negotiate, and alter individual and collective identities than the stepfamily. Broadly defined as a family in which "at least one of the adults has a child (or children) from a previous relationship" (Ganong & Coleman, 2018, p. 8), stepfamilies involve a plethora of personal relationships that vary considerably in form, structure, and complexity. In 2013, for example, 40% of U.S. marriages represented a remarriage for one or both partners (Lewis & Kreider, 2015), and 15% of American children lived with a stepparent and parent (Pew Research Center, 2015). Using data from more than 9,000 households in the U.S., Wiemers, Seltzer, Schoeni, Hotz, and Bianchi (2018) reported that 20% of households have at least one stepparent, and nearly 30% of households have a step-kin tie among either parents or adult children. Not only do stepfamilies exist in some form in nearly every country in the world (Ganong & Coleman, 2017), but cohabiting stepfamilies, specifically, constitute a large proportion of stepfamilies in Europe, New Zealand, and Australia (Beier, Hofacker, Marchese, & Rupp, 2010). Consequently, research on stepfamilies has grown from less than a dozen U.S. studies in the 1970s (Espinoza & Newman, 1979) to thousands of published investigations by scholars from nearly two dozen countries (Ganong & Coleman, 2017).

All families form and negotiate identities via interaction, and are thus, discourse dependent (Galvin, 2006). Families that depart from cultural norms (e.g., stepfamilies), however, are even more dependent on interaction to define and legitimate themselves as family as they negotiate boundaries and expectations for those inside and outside of the family (Schrodt, 2014). Likewise, family members experience greater or lesser degrees of solidarity through their interactions with each other, yet stepfamilies represent unique communicative contexts for examining relational solidarity given that they most often form in the wake of a romantic breakup, a divorce, or a parent's death. Achieving *solidarity*, or a sense of community and fellowship that arises from shared responsibilities and interests, can be challenging in stepfamilies given the lack of relational history among family members, the absence of relational norms to guide communication and relational development, and ambiguous family boundaries (Cherlin, 1978; Schrodt, 2014). In fact, as custody arrangements trend further and further toward joint custody and residence arrangements, and as the complexities of multiple (re)marriages and (step)children blur in-group/out-group distinctions and boundaries of family membership, feelings of solidarity and shared family identity can become increasingly nebulous. All families depend on boundary identification and management processes, yet for stepfamilies, the ambiguity of family membership grows as the number and complexity of stepfamily relationships expand. Nevertheless, researchers have identified several strengths (Golish, 2003), relational processes (Jensen, 2017; Jensen & Lippold, 2018), and communication behaviors (Braithwaite et al., 2018; Ganong, Coleman, Fine, & Martin, 1999; Schrodt, 2006a, 2006b, 2016; Waldron, Braithwaite, Oliver, Kloeber, & Marsh, 2018) that promote resiliency, health, and relational solidarity in stepfamilies.

In this chapter, I review stepfamily scholarship that speaks to the larger question of how stepfamilies communicatively manage the competing interests, tensions, loyalty divides, and developmental pathways that characterize stepfamily relationships. My goal is not to provide a comprehensive and exhaustive review of the stepfamily literature that exists elsewhere (e.g., Braithwaite & Schrodt, 2012; Ganong & Coleman, 2018), but to identify and describe communication phenomena that enhance (or inhibit) a sense of identity and relational solidarity in stepfamilies. First, I examine specific challenges and opportunities for stepfamily members to enact personal, relational, and familial identities that promote wellness. Second, I discuss how family communication in this particular family form can influence attitudes, behaviors, and societal discourses outside of the stepfamily. Finally, I conclude with some important thoughts for future researchers and family practitioners to consider.

Three Questions of Identity and Relational Solidarity in Stepfamilies

Personal Identity: Who Am I in This Stepfamily?

There is a growing consensus among family scholars that many of the challenges facing members of stepfamilies revolve around the roles of different family members, and particularly, the stepparent (Fine, Coleman, & Ganong, 1998; Fine, Ganong, & Coleman, 1997; Ganong et al., 1999; Schrodt, 2006c). In essence, the basic question concerns whether or not the stepparent should have an active or inactive role in the stepchildren's lives (Fine et al., 1998). Some scholars and clinicians contend that the stepparent should do no more than try to build a friendship with the stepchild(ren) (e.g., Papernow, 2018), whereas others (e.g., Hetherington, 1999) have found that the long-term benefits of having the stepparent act as a parent outweigh the short-term benefits of having the stepparent simply act as a friend. In their program of research, Fine et al. (1997, 1998) found different perceptions of the stepparent role between adults and children in the stepfamily system. Children were more likely than parents and stepparents to indicate that they preferred the stepparent to function as a friend rather than as a parental figure. However, adults were generally more likely to discuss the stepparent role with each other than they were to discuss this role with their stepchildren. This, in turn, led to little consistency in perceptions of parenting behaviors (i.e., warmth and control behaviors) for stepparents among family members, an unfortunate consequence given that consistency in perceptions of the stepparent role was positively associated with stepfamily members' interpersonal adjustment (Fine et al., 1998).

Schrodt (2006c) argued that viewing the stepparent relationship in terms of the positive regard that stepparents establish with their stepchildren, the parental authority that stepchildren grant their stepparents (if at all), and the degree to which stepparents and stepchildren discuss their feelings and their relationships with each other may be more useful in the long run than trying to fit the stepparent into some pre-existing role or label, such as "parent" or "friend." Consistent with this claim, researchers have identified specific communication behaviors that may help stepparents negotiate their personal identities within the stepfamily system and enhance relational solidarity. For example, Ganong et al. (1999) found three relatively distinct patterns of affinity-seeking and affinity-maintaining strategies among stepparents in their sample: *nonseeking* stepparents, *early affinity-seeking* stepparents, and *continuous affinity-seeking* stepparents. Not surprisingly, stepparents who were genuinely interested in establishing and maintaining close relationships with their stepchildren and continued their efforts well beyond the formation of the stepfamily (i.e., continuous affinity-seeking stepparents) were more likely to have stepchildren who reciprocated affinity-seeking efforts and developed close stepparent-stepchild bonds.

More recently, scholars have identified turning points (Braithwaite et al., 2018), discourses of forgiveness (Waldron et al., 2018), and everyday talk (Schrodt, 2016) as communication phenomena that enhance resiliency and strengthen stepparent-stepchild bonds. For instance, some of the most common turning points that create positive bonds with a stepchild include: (a) a stepparent's *prosocial actions* of gift-giving, friendly gestures, and/or acts of kindness, (b) *quality time* that the stepparent invests in the stepchild, including leisure time, time away from others, and relationship talks not focused on problems, and (c) *rituals*, such as holiday celebrations and special events such as birthdays, graduations, or weddings (Braithwaite et al., 2018). Schrodt (2016) found that stepparents who engaged in more everyday talk with their stepchildren were more likely to have stepchildren who held them in high esteem, which in turn, enhanced stepchildren's relational satisfaction. Likewise, opportunities to voice feelings of resentment and misunderstanding are important in developing positive stepparent-stepchild relationships (Braithwaite et al., 2018), as are processes of forgiveness that heal family connections, encourage relational growth, and enhance relational solidarity (Waldron et al., 2018).

Although the stepparent role has received the lion's share of scholarly attention, the issue of whether or not the stepparent should function as a "parent" is not the only issue facing stepfamily members. (Non)residential parents and (step)children must also navigate their own role uncertainties, ambiguities, and ambivalence during the process of becoming a stepfamily. For instance, Coleman, Fine, Ganong, Downs, and Pauk (2001) found that residential parents (e.g., residential mothers) often wrestle with a "guard and protect" ideology with their new spouse or partner, in which the biological parent errs on the side of guarding and protecting their children's interests in any disputes that may arise with the stepparent. Non-residential parents, on the other hand, are perhaps even more likely to experience tension and ambivalence as they negotiate access and coordinate visitations with their ex-spouses and their ex-spouses' new partners (i.e., the stepparents).

In a similar vein, stepchildren navigate tremendous role ambiguity and ambivalence in their relationships with other members of the family system, including stepparents, non-residential parents, and/or stepsiblings. For stepchildren living in multiple families/households, navigating the ambiguities, mixed emotions, and loyalty conflicts that so often characterize their interactions with other stepfamily members can be, at times, socially awkward and uncomfortable, and at other times, quite stressful and detrimental to their feelings of family and relational solidarity. For instance, a common, yet taken for granted symbolic activity that holds tremendous implications for the individual and relational identities of stepfamily members is the use of address terms. Koenig Kellas, LeClair-Underberg, and Normand (2008) found that nearly two-thirds of the stepchildren in their sample varied the terms of address they used to identify their stepfamily members depending on context, audience, and/or relationship. Whether using *formal* address terms that defined the person in reference to a third party (e.g., "my dad's wife"), *familiar* terms that included stepparents' first names or included the word "step" in reference to the parent or sibling, or *familial* terms that dropped the prefix "step" (e.g., using "mom" instead of "stepmom"), stepchildren engaged in both internal and external code-switching. Such code-switching functioned to communicate solidarity at times, to communicate separateness at other times, and to manage the balance of stepfamily life.

Finally, Speer, Giles, and Denes (2013) reported that perceptions of stepparents' communication accommodation enhanced stepchildren's feelings of shared family identity with their stepparent, which in turn positively predicted their satisfaction with stepfamily life. Although these researchers did not examine indicators of adjustment and well-being, when coupled with Ganong et al.'s (1999) findings on stepparents' affinity-seeking behaviors, their results suggest that role clarity in the stepparent-stepchild relationship is negotiated communicatively between both family members and may hold promise for furthering the well-being of individual family members and the stepfamily as a whole.

Relational Identity: Who Are We to Each Other in This Stepfamily?

The second question of identity that permeates the ebb and flow of stepfamily development involves the various dyads that comprise the stepfamily system. Specifically, the question of relational identity has prompted stepfamily scholars to examine the dialectical tensions and feelings of being caught that animate communication and conflict among different stepfamily dyads, as well as patterns of coparental communication that facilitate greater or lesser degrees of relational solidarity and satisfaction. First, relational dialectics theory (RDT) views relating as a dialogic process; a communicative process characterized by the intersection of oppositional discourses that constitute a relationship (Baxter, 2011). Cissna, Cox, and Bochner (1990) conducted the first investigation of stepfamily relationships from a communication perspective, one that revealed a "relationship dialectic" between the voluntary remarriage relationship and the involuntary stepparent relationship. In an effort to manage the tension between their marital and parental roles, Cissna et al. found that remarried couples attempted to accomplish two relational tasks: (1) establish the solidarity of the marriage in the minds of their children, in essence, communicating a "unified front" to the kids, and (2) use the marital solidarity to establish the credibility of the stepparent as an authority in relationship with the stepchildren. Their results provided preliminary insight into the relational tensions that animated the remarried couples' discourse, as couples sought to (re)negotiate their relationships with each other and with their (step)children in an effort to build family solidarity.

In more contemporary research using RDT, Baxter, Braithwaite, Bryant, and Wagner (2004) identified three underlying contradictions that permeated the discourse of stepparent-stepchild relationships. First, stepchildren wanted emotional closeness and a relationship with their stepparent. At the same time, their discourse reflected the desire for emotional distance out of feelings of loyalty to their old family, particularly the nonresidential parent. Second, stepchildren wanted communication that reflected openness with the stepparent and, at the same time, they eschewed such open communication. Third, stepchildren's discourse revealed a dialectical tension of desiring parental authority to rest only in the residential parent, yet at the same time, they often wanted discipline from their stepparent as well. Consequently, these competing discourses created tremendous ambivalence in the stepchild-stepparent relationship (Baxter et al., 2004).

Communication scholars have also used RDT to explore the relationships of nonresidential parents and their children. For example, Braithwaite and Baxter (2006) interviewed young adult stepchildren and identified interrelated discourses of parenting and nonparenting, coupled with openness and closedness. Although it seems reasonable to expect that most children would want a close parent-child relationship with their nonresidential parent (usually a father), the children in their sample were quite ambivalent when their nonresidential father or mother tried to parent them. At times, they perceived that the nonresidential parent did not have the experience or background in the child's daily life to be helpful to them. Moreover, stepchildren's discourse reflected the desire for intimate and open communication with their nonresidential parent, while at the same time they often found openness difficult.

These are but a few of the studies employing RDT to examine the discourses that reflect dialectical tensions in stepfamily relationships. They illustrate the idea that dialectical tensions animate communication processes in stepfamilies, and thus, constitute an important form of identity formation and negotiation in this complex family form. Dialectical tensions are not the only kind of tensions experienced in stepfamilies, however, as researchers have also examined the tension of triangulation in stepfamilies.

Most of the communication research on triangulation and loyalty binds in stepfamilies has relied on the general principles of family systems theory (Minuchin, 1974). For instance, Afifi and Schrodt (Afifi, 2003; Afifi & Schrodt, 2003; Schrodt & Afifi, 2007) conducted a series of studies identifying the antecedents and outcomes associated with "feeling caught" in stepfamilies. Children who feel caught between their parents often feel "put in the middle," "torn," or forced to defend their loyalty to each of their parents. Such feelings typically emerge when children become privy to their parents' disputes, are the recipients of negative or inappropriate disclosures, and when they become messengers or mediators of information between their parents (Afifi, 2003). Importantly, feeling caught typically induces a level of stress that reduces mental health and well-being. For example, Schrodt and Afifi (2007) found that interparental aggression, demand/withdraw patterns, and negative disclosures all positively predicted young adults' feelings of being caught between their parents, which in turn negatively predicted family satisfaction and mental health.

Of course, family systems theory is not the only lens useful for understanding how discourse activates and animates feelings of being caught in stepfamily relationships. Case in point, Braithwaite, Toller, Daas, Durham, and Jones (2008) used RDT to analyze focus-group discussions with young adult stepchildren on what it meant to feel caught between parents. These scholars heard competing discourses wherein children wanted to be centered in the attention of their parents, and at the same time wanted to avoid being caught in the middle, as illustrated by one young adult stepchild who talked about feeling "like a bone between two dogs."

Finally, Schrodt, Braithwaite, and their colleagues (i.e., Braithwaite, McBride, & Schrodt, 2003; Schrodt, 2010, 2011; Schrodt, Baxter, McBride, Braithwaite, & Fine, 2006; Schrodt & Braithwaite, 2011) have investigated the coparental communication patterns that enhance (or inhibit) relational identities and solidarity among different adults within the stepfamily system. *Coparental communication* refers not to the individual attempts of a parent to guide and direct the behaviors and activities of his or her child, but to the interaction patterns that emerge as one coparent supports and/or undermines the parenting attempts of his or her partner (Schrodt, 2010, 2011). Coparenting in stepfamilies presents its own unique set of challenges given that the coparental relationship between parents and their new partners co-occurs and even, at times, precedes the development of the remarried relationship (Schrodt & Braithwaite, 2011).

Illustrating the importance of coparental communication to the successful adaptation of stepfamily systems, this body of work has demonstrated that: (a) most of the interactions that occur between ex-spouses and between parents and their ex-spouse's new partner (i.e., the stepparent) are very brief, very business-like, and focused almost exclusively on the welfare of the children (Braithwaite et al., 2003); (b) coparents often discuss how the divorce decree provides a guide for informal coparenting decisions and cooperation unless (or until) one of the parents perceives that the other parent is taking advantage of their goodwill, at which point the decree is invoked as a more formal, legal resolution to their parenting disputes (Schrodt et al., 2006); (c) residential parents' and stepparents' coparental communication quality (i.e., supportive and cooperative) positively predicts their own (but not their partner's) satisfaction and mental health (Schrodt & Braithwaite, 2011); (d) residential parents experience stress and ambivalence as they manage the tensions associated with having their current relational partner (i.e., the stepparent) coparent with their ex-spouse (Schrodt, 2010); and (e) nonresidential parents' coparental communication with their ex-spouses (i.e., with residential parents) predicts meaningful variance in stepparents' satisfaction with the nonresidential parent (Schrodt, 2011). Clearly, coparental communication patterns reflect varying degrees of interdependence, stress, and ambivalence that facilitate (or inhibit) the negotiation of relational identities and solidarity in stepfamilies.

Familial Identity: Who Are We as a Family?

Whereas questions of personal identity focus on individuals and questions of relational identity focus on dyads, questions of familial identity focus on stepfamily members as groups (or systems). Here, scholars have looked primarily at the developmental pathways that stepfamilies take to achieve family solidarity (Baxter, Braithwaite, & Nicholson, 1999; Braithwaite, Olson, Golish, Soukup, & Turman, 2001), the communication strengths that differentiate strong stepfamilies from those struggling with the developmental process (Golish, 2003), and different types of stepfamilies based on family members' perceptions of family functioning (Schrodt, 2006c) and relational quality (Jensen, 2017; Jensen & Lippold, 2018). First, one of the more pressing concerns for stepfamily members, and the practitioners who work with them, is how best to communicate during times of transition and adapt to the changes in relationships and routines that occur when a stepfamily forms. Baxter et al. (1999) interviewed stepfamily members about key turning points that produced important changes in "feeling like a family" during the first four years of stepfamily development. They identified five developmental pathways found in the first four years of stepfamily development: (a) accelerated pathways (i.e., a pattern of quick movement toward 100% feeling like a family), (b) prolonged pathways (i.e., stepfamilies that progressed to higher levels of feeling like a family, although not as quickly as accelerated pathways), (c) stagnant pathways (i.e., stepfamilies that "never took off"), (d) declining pathways (i.e., stepfamilies that began with a high level of feeling like a family, then declined to zero), and (e) high-amplitude turbulent pathways (i.e., stepfamilies who experienced dramatic up and down shifts in feeling like a family).

As a follow-up to Baxter et al.'s (1999) research, Braithwaite et al. (2001) investigated how stepfamily members in the five trajectories interact and adapt during the process of becoming a family. They found that issues of boundary management, solidarity, and adaptation were central to the enactment of the different pathways of becoming a family. With respect to solidarity, for instance, most of the participants expressed a sense of optimism about becoming a family and wanting to feel like a family, even though many of them also expressed a sense of loss regarding their "old" family. Their results underscored the omnipresent nature of change in stepfamilies, as struggles often ensued when family members attempted to replicate traditional family roles and norms in an effort to live the myth of "instant family." Consequently, Braithwaite et al. concluded that stepfamily identity takes time to develop through periods of change as family members communicate in ways that facilitate flexibility and encourage solidarity.

Researchers have also devoted attention to the various communication processes that facilitate coping and resiliency in stepfamilies. For example, Golish (2003) identified the communication strengths that differentiate strong stepfamilies from those struggling with the developmental process. First, she identified seven primary challenges facing stepfamilies regardless of their strength: (1) "feeling caught," (2) regulating boundaries with a noncustodial family, (3) ambiguity of parental roles, (4) "traumatic bonding," (5) vying for resources, (6) discrepancies in conflict management styles, and (7) building solidarity as a family unit. In order to manage these challenges, however, strong stepfamilies were more likely than struggling stepfamilies to use a variety of communication behaviors, including more everyday talk among family members, greater levels of disclosure and openness, communicating clear rules and boundaries, engaging in family problem solving, spending time together as a family, and promoting a positive image of the noncustodial parent (Golish, 2003).

Finally, researchers have identified different types of stepfamilies using either stepchildren's perceptions of family functioning (Schrodt, 2006a), or their perceptions of relational closeness and involvement with different adults in the stepfamily system (Jensen, 2017; Jensen & Lippold, 2018). For instance, Schrodt (2006a) identified five different types of stepfamilies based on stepchildren's perceptions of stepfamily life (Schrodt, 2006b) and relationships with stepparents (Schrodt, 2006c). Whereas *bonded* and *functional* stepfamilies were characterized by low levels of dissension and avoidance and relatively high levels of stepfamily involvement, flexibility, and expressiveness, *evasive* and *conflictual* stepfamilies were both characterized by relatively high levels of dissension and avoidance and moderately low levels of involvement, flexibility, and expressiveness. Intriguingly, *ambivalent* stepfamilies described the experiences of nearly a fourth of the stepchildren included in Schrodt's (2006a) sample. These stepfamilies were characterized by slightly above-average levels of stepfamily dissension and avoidance and slightly below-average levels of involvement, flexibility, and expressiveness.

Recently, Jensen (2017; Jensen & Lippold, 2018) used a nationally representative sample of adolescents to identify four distinct patterns of stepfamily relationship quality that predict meaningful differences in adolescent health. Although the *residence-centered* and *inclusive* patterns both were marked by above-average mother-child closeness, stepfather-child closeness, and stepcouple-relationship quality, what distinguished them was the level of nonresident father-child involvement, with below-average levels of nonresident father-child involvement in *residence-centered* stepfamilies but particularly high levels of nonresident father-child involvement in *inclusive* stepfamilies. The *unhappy-couple* pattern displayed above-average mother-child closeness, near-average stepfather-child closeness and nonresident father-child involvement, and very low levels of stepcouple-relationship quality. The *parent-child disconnection* pattern possessed low mother-child and stepfather-child closeness, below-average nonresident father-child involvement, and slightly above-average stepcouple-relationship quality. Importantly, Jensen and Lippold (2018) found that adolescent adjustment over time is optimized when youth are living in residence-centered or inclusive stepfamilies, as compared with youth living in unhappy-couple or parent-child disconnection stepfamilies.

Taken as a whole, researchers have identified a litany of communication behaviors and family processes that enhance (or inhibit) the enactment of personal, relational, and familial identities in stepfamilies. As members communicate to negotiate their identities, they achieve greater or lesser degrees of relational solidarity, and in so doing, testify not only to the challenges that are inherent to stepfamily life, but to the opportunities that exist for expanding and changing larger societal discourses about the stepfamily.

Beyond the Family: Stepfamily Communication and Society

Although stepfamilies have existed throughout most of human history, the "discovery" of stepfamilies by social scientists is a relatively recent phenomenon, prompted largely by clinicians and policy-makers who found little information to guide their work when turning to research for answers about stepfamily dynamics (Ganong & Coleman, 2018). Four decades ago, Cherlin

(1978) identified the stepfamily as an incomplete institution, given the lack of guidance from social norms on familial roles and much needed but missing social support from societal institutions such as schools, legal systems, faith communities, and healthcare systems. For example, legal practices often inhibit stepfamily development, as under U.S. law, stepfathers or stepmothers who wish to adopt stepchildren under the age of 18 must convince the original father or mother to relinquish parental rights (Papernow, 2018). Although British law allows stepparents to adopt without requiring the parent of the same sex to relinquish parental rights (Malia, 2008), in Japan, divorce law gives custody to only one parent (usually the mother), making it difficult for children to have post-divorce connections with their nonresidential parent (Nozawa, 2015). Moreover, research on the legal and societal implications of LGBT divorce and remarriage remains almost nonexistent (Johnson, O'Connor, & Tornello, 2016).

Cultural norms create additional challenges to stepfamilies that members may not fully understand. Whereas Anglo-European family norms draw firm boundaries around the nuclear family and create contexts for interparental competition, African-American traditions of "child keeping" and "informal adoption" support cooperative coparenting across family boundaries (Papernow, 2018). Not only have some scholars argued that a paucity of language exists for describing and defining stepfamily relationships (Cherlin, 1978), but the prefix "step," when placed before "parent" or "family," is meant to convey "substitute"—a term that has historically carried connotative meanings of inferiority for members of U.S. society. Furthermore, one of the most common pop culture references to stepfamilies is the "wicked stepmother" myth, a "stigma that places a significant strain on a stepmother's self-esteem and role enactment" (Christian, 2005, p. 28). As a result of such stigmatization, stepmothers often face greater challenges in developing satisfying stepparent-stepchild bonds than stepfathers, with such challenges emerging as particularly salient for nonresidential stepmothers (Weaver & Coleman, 2005).

Given these challenges, how might stepfamily members influence the attitudes, behaviors, and discourses of those who live outside of the stepfamily? One answer lies in the abilities of stepfamilies to embrace the functional ambivalence that characterizes the emotional landscape of stepfamily relationships. One of the defining characteristics that distinguishes stepfamilies from other family forms is the (dys)functional ambivalence inherent to stepfamily life (Schrodt & Braithwaite, 2010). Although some scholars have framed this ambivalence as problematic and dysfunctional, it can, and often does, serve very functional purposes. For example, embracing the ambivalence of stepfamily relationships acknowledges the unique challenges associated with stepfamily development, which in turn, allows family members to craft their own relationships independent of the nuclear family model, a model that lacks the flexibility necessary for accommodating the fluid and permeable boundaries of the stepfamily. By releasing themselves from the unrealistic expectations of closeness and solidarity that come from clinging too tightly to traditional models of first-marriage family relationships, stepfamily members can create new spaces and new opportunities to relate to each other in ways that facilitate healthier forms of adaptation to stepfamily life. In effect, this view of stepfamilies encourages researchers and practitioners to view stepfamilies in their own right, rather than as a "lesser cousin" to the traditional nuclear family form.

A second answer lies in the ability of stepfamilies to find creative and innovative ways to tell their stories (e.g., Koenig Kellas et al., 2014), particularly when those stories convey a sense of strength, resiliency, and solidarity while overcoming developmental challenges in the process of becoming a family. In the 1990s, for example, popular movies (e.g., *The Stepmom*) and U.S. television series (e.g., *Once and Again*) helped portray stepfamily relationships to the general population. During this time period, the ubiquity of stepfamilies became more apparent in the highly-publicized lives of celebrities and American Presidents, as half of the individuals who occupied the office of the President during the last quarter of the 20th century had been or were members of stepfamilies (Ganong & Coleman, 2018). Although stepfamilies are still not completely institutionalized, like other marginalized family forms, there is evidence that new norms are being created, as it is now more common for schools and other societal institutions to view children who have three or more adults as parental figures as "normal" (Ganong & Coleman, 2018). Indeed, as public education and health officials become more and more aware of the tremendous variability that exists in families today, subtle changes in societal understandings of post-divorce and remarried family life should expand the opportunities that individuals have to navigate the complexities of stepfamily life. Consequently, as stepfamilies tell their stories and help normalize these new cultural values, they can help change larger societal discourses surrounding the stepfamily and create new opportunities for scholars and practitioners alike.

Implications for Scholars and Practitioners

Despite the tremendous growth in stepfamily scholarship that has occurred over the last 40 years, two persistent problems continue to plague this body of work. First, the deficit-comparison approach continues to permeate the literature, particularly in the family sciences, as some scholars (a) emphasize between-group comparisons using the first-marriage, nuclear family as the ideal standard, and (b) problematize stepfamily structures and experiences via theories employed, questions addressed, and interpretations of findings (Ganong & Coleman, 2018). Hence, communication scholars have a tremendous opportunity to help change the scholarly narrative on stepfamilies by incorporating more communication-as-constitutive (e.g., Baxter, 2011) and discourse-dependent perspectives (e.g., Galvin, 2006) into existing bodies of work that fail to capture the interactional nuances and complexities of stepfamily life. Indeed, an important direction that future researchers should continue to take is to investigate stepfamilies in their own right to identify and describe those communication behaviors that promote successful adaptation, family solidarity, and resiliency across different types of stepfamilies.

Second, stepfamily researchers and clinicians continue to operate in very separate spheres, although a relatively newer wave of stepfamily clinicians are prompting new forms of scientific inquiry into stepfamily relationships (Ganong & Coleman, 2018). For example, as a leading pioneer in stepfamily therapy and clinical work, Patricia Papernow (2013, 2018) identified five major challenges that stepfamilies face that differentiate them from first-time families: (1) Insider/outsider positions are intense and fixed; (2) Children struggle with losses, loyalty binds, and change; (3) Issues of parenting, stepparenting, and discipline often divide the couple; (4) Stepcouples must build a new family culture while navigating previously established family cultures; and (5) Ex-spouses (and other parents outside the household) are part of the family. In response to these challenges, Papernow (2018) advanced a three-level model of clinical intervention that seeks to help family practitioners address these concerns: (a) at the *psychoeducational* level (i.e., the "what" level), practitioners can offer information about what is normal, what works, and what does not work, to meet stepfamily challenges; (b) at the *interpersonal connection* level (i.e., the "how" level), practitioners can invite stepfamily members into important conversations that help them work together to meet their challenges; and (c) at the *intrapsychic family-of-origin* level (i.e., the "why" level), practitioners can unpack and explore individual family-of-origin wounds and intergenerational legacies that may be thwarting the therapeutic processes occurring at the psychoeducational and interpersonal connection levels. Each of these levels hold tremendous promise for guiding family practitioners as they seek to help both adults and children adjust to stepfamily life. Likewise, communication scholars have contributed greatly to the psychoeducational level of Papernow's model by identifying communication strengths that differentiate strong stepfamilies from those struggling with the developmental process (e.g., Golish, 2003), as well as to the interpersonal connection level by illuminating communication processes that enhance the personal and relational well-being of stepfamily members (e.g., Braithwaite et al., 2001, 2008, 2018; Koenig Kellas et al., 2014; Schrodt, 2006a, 2010, 2011; Schrodt & Braithwaite, 2011).

Finally, future researchers should expand their inquiry to include stepsiblings and extended stepfamily members, such as step-grandparents. With a few notable exceptions (e.g., Soliz, 2007), researchers have generally neglected the communication processes that facilitate identity formation and enactment, as well as relational solidarity, among stepsiblings and step-grandparents. Yet, how resources are allocated among these extended family relationships and the various coalitions that form within and between them carry tremendous implications for familial identity and the sense of community (or lack thereof) that forms among stepfamily members. Although some scholars have begun to examine stepfamily relationships post stepfamily dissolution (e.g., Coleman, Ganong, Russell, & Frye, 2015), researchers also need to more adequately account for time and transitions in the development of relational solidarity among stepfamily members. How does the communication of ex-stepparents with their ex-stepchildren contribute to feelings of solidarity among both adults and children? How might serial marriages among adult partners and the various ways in which they talk about the "on-again/off-again" nature of their relationships alter stepchildren's understandings of relational solidarity and marriage? Finally, how are societal and cultural understandings and discussions of stepfamily relationships changing our understanding of what it means to be a "normal" family, if at all? By investigating these types of questions and many more, scholars can expand our understanding how stepfamilies communicatively manage the individual, familial, societal, and cultural differences that promote relational solidarity while enabling individuality and well-being.

References

Afifi, T. D. (2003). 'Feeling caught' in stepfamilies: Managing boundary turbulence through appropriate communication privacy rules. *Journal of Social and Personal Relationships*, *20*, 729–755. doi:10.1177/0265407503206002

Afifi, T. D., & Schrodt, P. (2003). "Feeling caught" as a mediator of adolescents' and young adults' avoidance and satisfaction with their parents in divorced and non-divorced households. *Communication Monographs*, *70*, 142–173. doi:10.1080/0363775032000133791

Baxter, L. A. (2011). *Voicing relationships: A dialogic approach.* Thousand Oaks, CA: Sage.

Baxter, L. A., Braithwaite, D. O., Bryant, L., & Wagner, A. (2004). Stepchildren's perceptions of the contradictions in communication with stepparents. *Journal of Social and Personal Relationships, 21*, 447–467. doi:10.1177/0265407504044841

Baxter, L. A., Braithwaite, D. O., & Nicholson, J. H. (1999). Turning points in the development of blended families. *Journal of Social and Personal Relationships, 16*, 291–313. doi:10.1177/0265407599163002

Beier, L., Hofacker, D., Marchese, E., & Rupp, M. (2010). Family structures and family forms—An overview of major trends and developments working report. *European Commission's Seventh Framework Programme.* University of Bamberg

Braithwaite, D. O., & Baxter, L. A. (2006). "You're my parent but you're not": Dialectical tensions in stepchildren's perceptions about communicating with the nonresidential parent. *Journal of Applied Communication Research, 34*, 30–48. doi:10.1080/00909880500420200

Braithwaite, D. O., McBride, M. C., & Schrodt, P. (2003). "Parent teams" and the everyday interactions of co-parenting in stepfamilies. *Communication Reports, 16*, 93–111. doi:10.1080/08934210309384493

Braithwaite, D. O., Olson, L., Golish, T., Soukup, C., & Turman, P. (2001). Developmental communication patterns of blended families: Exploring the different trajectories of blended families. *Journal of Applied Communication Research, 29*, 221–247. doi:10.1080/00909880128112

Braithwaite, D. O., & Schrodt, P. (2012). Stepfamily communication. In A. L. Vangelisti's (Ed.), *Routledge handbook of family communication* (2nd ed., pp. 161–175). New York, NY: Routledge.

Braithwaite, D. O., Toller, P., Daas, K., Durham, W., & Jones, A. (2008). Centered but not caught in the middle: Stepchildren's perceptions of dialectical contradictions in the communication of co-parents. *Journal of Applied Communication Research, 36*, 33–55. doi:10.1080/00909880701799337

Braithwaite, D. O., Waldron, V. R., Allen, J., Oliver, B., Bergquist, G., Storck, K., ... Tschampl-Diesing, C. (2018). "Feeling warmth and close to her": Communication and resilience reflected in turning points in positive adult stepchild-stepparent relationships. *Journal of Family Communication, 18*, 92–109. doi:10.1080/15267431.2017.1415902

Cherlin, A. (1978). Remarriage as an incomplete institution. *American Journal of Sociology, 84*, 634–650. doi:10.1086/226830

Christian, A. (2005). Contesting the myth of the 'wicked stepmother': Narrative analysis of an online support group. *Western Journal of Communication, 69*, 27–47. doi:10.1080/10570310500034030

Cissna, K. N., Cox, D. E., & Bochner, A. P. (1990). The dialectic of marital and parental relationships within the stepfamily. *Communication Monographs, 57*, 44–61. doi:10.1080/03637759009376184

Coleman, M., Fine, M. A., Ganong, L. H., Downs, K., & Pauk, N. (2001). When you're not the Brady Bunch: Identifying perceived conflicts and resolution strategies in stepfamilies. *Personal Relationships, 8*, 55–73. doi:10.1111/j.1475-6811.2001.tb00028.x

Coleman, M., Ganong, L., & Russell, L., & Frye, N. (2015). Stepchildren's views about former steprelationships following stepfamily dissolution. *Journal of Marriage and Family, 77*, 775–790. doi:10.1111/jomf.12182

Espinoza, R., & Newman, Y. (1979). *Stepparenting (DHEW Publication #48-579)*. Rockville, MD: U.S. Department of Health, Education, & Welfare.

Fine, M. A., Coleman, M., & Ganong, L. H. (1998). Consistency in perceptions of the step-parent role among step-parents, parents, and stepchildren. *Journal of Social and Personal Relationships, 15*, 811–829. doi:10.1177/0265407598156006

Fine, M. A., Ganong, L. H., & Coleman, M. (1997). The relation between role constructions and adjustment among stepfathers. *Journal of Family Issues, 18*, 503–525. doi:10.1177/019251397018005003

Galvin, K. (2006). Diversity's impact on defining the family: Discourse-dependence and identity. In L. H. Turner & R. West (Eds.), *The family communication sourcebook* (pp. 3–19). Thousand Oaks, CA: Sage.

Ganong, L., & Coleman, M. (2017). *Stepfamily relationships: Development, dynamics, and interventions* (2nd ed.). New York, NY: Springer.

Ganong, L., & Coleman, M. (2018). Studying stepfamilies: Four eras of family scholarship. *Family Process, 57*, 7–24. doi:10.1111/famp.12307

Ganong, L., Coleman, M., Fine, M., & Martin, P. (1999). Stepparents' affinity-seeking and affinity-maintaining strategies with stepchildren. *Journal of Family Issues, 20*, 299–327. doi:10.1177/019251399020003001

Golish, T. D. (2003). Stepfamily communication strengths: Understanding the ties that bind. *Human Communication Research, 29*, 41–80. doi:10.1111/j.1468-2958.2003.tb00831.x

Hetherington, E. M. (1999). Family functioning and the adjustment of adolescent siblings in diverse types of families. *Monographs of the Society for Research in Child Development, 64*(4, Serial No. 259), 1–25. doi:10.1111/1540-5834.00045

Jensen, T. M. (2017). Constellations of dyadic relationship quality in stepfamilies: A factor mixture model. *Journal of Family Psychology, 31*, 1051–1062. doi:10.1037/fam0000355

Jensen, T. M., & Lippold, M. A. (2018). Patterns of stepfamily relationship quality and adolescents' short-term and long-term adjustment. *Journal of Family Psychology*. Advance online publication retrieved from http://dx.doi.org/10.1037/fam0000442

Johnson, S. M., O'Connor, E., & Tornello, S. L. (2016). Gay and lesbian parents and their children. In L. Drozd, M. Saini, & N. Oleson (Eds.), *Parenting plan evaluations: Applied research for the family court* (2nd ed., pp. 514–532). New York, NY: Oxford Press.

Koenig Kellas, J., Baxter, L. A., LeClair-Underberg, C., Thatcher, M., Routsong, T., Normand, E. L., & Braithwaite, D. O. (2014). Telling the story of stepfamily beginnings: The relationship between young-adult stepchildren's stepfamily origin stories and their satisfaction with the stepfamily. *Journal of Family Communication, 14*, 149–166. doi:10.1080/15267431.2013.864294

Koenig Kellas, J., LeClair-Underberg, C., & Normand, E. L. (2008). Stepfamily address terms: "Sometimes they mean something and sometimes they don't." *Journal of Family Communication, 8*, 238–263. doi:10.1080/15267430802397153

Lewis, J. M., & Kreider, R. (2015). *Remarriage in the United States.* Washington, DC: U.S. Census Bureau, American Community Survey Reports, ACS-30.

Malia, S. E. C. (2008). How relevant are U.S. family and probate laws to stepfamilies? In J. Pryor (Ed.), *International handbook of stepfamilies: Policy and practice in legal, research, and clinical environments* (pp. 545–572). Hoboken, NJ: Wiley.

Minuchin, S. (1974). *Families and family therapy.* Cambridge, MA: Harvard University Press.

Nozawa, S. (2015). Remarriage and stepfamilies. In S. R. Quah (Ed.), *The Routledge handbook of families in Asia* (pp. 345–358). London, UK: Routledge.

Papernow, P. (2013). *Surviving and thriving in stepfamily relationships: What works and what doesn't.* New York, NY: Routledge.

Papernow, P. (2018). Clinical guidelines for working with stepfamilies: What family, couple, individual, and child therapists need to know. *Family Process, 57*, 25–51. doi:10.1111/famp.12321

Pew Research Center. (2015). *The American family today* [Data file and code book]. Retrieved from http://www.pewsocialtrends.org/2015/12/17/1-the-american-family-today/

Schrodt, P. (2006a). A typological examination of communication competence and mental health in stepchildren. *Communication Monographs, 73*, 309–333. doi:10.1080/03637750600873728

Schrodt, P. (2006b). Development and validation of the Stepfamily Life Index. *Journal of Social and Personal Relationships, 23*, 427–444. doi:10.1177/0265407506064210

Schrodt, P. (2006c). The stepparent relationship index: Development, validation, and associations with stepchildren's perceptions of stepparent communication competence and closeness. *Personal Relationships, 13*, 167–182. doi:10.1111/j.1475-6811.2006.00111.x

Schrodt, P. (2010). Coparental communication with nonresidential parents as a predictor of couples' relational satisfaction and mental health in stepfamilies. *Western Journal of Communication, 74*, 484–503. doi:10.1080/10570314.2010.512282

Schrodt, P. (2011). Stepparents' and nonresidential parents' relational satisfaction as a function of coparental communication in stepfamilies. *Journal of Social and Personal Relationships, 28*, 983–1004. doi:10.1177/0265407510397990

Schrodt, P. (2014). Discourse-dependence, relational ambivalence, and the social construction of stepfamily relationships. In L. A. Baxter (Ed.), *Remaking "family" communicatively* (pp. 157–174). New York, NY: Peter Lang.

Schrodt, P. (2016). Relational frames as mediators of everyday talk and relational satisfaction in stepparent-stepchild relationships. *Journal of Social and Personal Relationships, 33*, 217–236. doi:10.1177/0265407514568751

Schrodt, P., & Afifi, T. D. (2007). Communication processes that predict young adults' feelings of being caught and their associations with mental health and family satisfaction. *Communication Monographs, 74*, 200–228. doi:10.1080/03637750701390085

Schrodt, P., Baxter, L. A., McBride, M. C., Braithwaite, D. O., & Fine, M. (2006). The divorce decree, communication, and the structuration of co-parenting relationships in stepfamilies. *Journal of Social and Personal Relationships, 23*, 741–759. doi:10.1177/0265407506068261

Schrodt, P., & Braithwaite, D. O. (2010). Dark clouds with silver linings: The (dys)functional ambivalence of stepfamily relationships. In W. R. Cupach & B. H. Spitzberg (Eds.), *The dark side of close relationships II* (pp. 243–268). New York: Routledge.

Schrodt, P., & Braithwaite, D. O. (2011). Coparental communication, relational satisfaction, and mental health in stepfamilies. *Personal Relationships, 18*, 352–369. doi:10.1111/j.1475-6811.2010.01295.x

Soliz, J. (2007). Communicative predictors of a shared family identity: Comparisons of grandchildren's perceptions of family-of-origin grandparents and step-grandparents. *Journal of Family Communication, 7*, 177–194. doi:10.1080/15267430701221636

Speer, R. B., Giles, H., & Denes, A. (2013). Investigating stepparent-stepchild interactions: The role of communication accommodation. *Journal of Family Communication, 13*, 218–241. doi:10.1080/15267431.2013.768248

Waldron, V. R., Braithwaite, D. O., Oliver, B. M., Kloeber, D. N., & Marsh, J. (2018). Discourses of forgiveness and resilience in stepchild-stepparent relationships. *Journal of Applied Communication Research, 46*, 561–582. doi:10.1080/00909882.2018.1530447

Weaver, S. E., & Coleman, M. (2005). A mothering but not a mother role: A grounded theory study of the nonresidential stepmother role. *Journal of Social and Personal Relationships, 22*, 477–497. doi:10.1177/0265407505054519

Wiemers, E. E., Seltzer, J. A., Schoeni, R. F., Hotz, V. J., & Bianchi, S. M. (2018). Stepfamily structure and transfers between generations in U.S. families. *Demography*. Advance online publication retrieved from https://link.springer.com/article/10.1007/s13524-018-0740-1

14. *Family Socialization of "Otherness"*

CHRISTINE E. RITTENOUR

World peace begins at home, and so our final chapter on family difference explores how universal harmony is nurtured, squelched, or squandered through family communication surrounding "otherness." Literature commonly addresses narratives around various social identities (i.e., Bradford & Syed, 2019), or assesses non-familial means of socializing outgroup attitudes (i.e., Solomon & Kurtz-Costes, 2018), yet family's socialization power remains comparatively under researched. This "ultimate ingroup" is our first socializer of prejudice (Allport, 1954), and the available scholarship on family communication *about* difference begins painting a picture of practices parents employ to produce more prosocial orientations toward outgroups. These trends, and the limited findings about children's role in family socialization, are summarized. After reviewing the known and largely negative trends of seemingly simple attitude transmission, I address how parents teach children to appreciate their *own* identities, and conclude with evidence and suggestions for future inquiry.

Transmitting Negative and Positive Attitudes Toward Others

Attitudes about different social groups tend to be taught or "caught" from older-to-younger generations. While some claim that parent messages are less effective then self-derived attitudes about difference (Bigler & Liben, 2006), strong empirical evidence reveals family's sizeable impact, especially during pre-adolescence. Much of parent-child prejudice research confirms Allport's assertions about family's primacy in children's earliest feelings about outsiders. Messages are reaffirmed and continuously activated such that children can employ them once they can distinguish social group differences (around age three for visible and consistently salient social distinctions such as race and gender). Devine theorized that the seeking and sense-making behaviors of the child of prejudiced parents often strengthens negative outgroup attitudes around age seven (1989). Even if their self-reports show otherwise, seven-year olds presume that their parents and their own attitudes are alike (Gniewosz & Noack, 2006), and around age twelve, a child of prejudiced parents cues their "otherness attitudes" as their own (e.g., Bigler & Liben, 2006).

The potency of parental attitudes about difference is lasting. In their meta-analysis, Degner and Dalege (2013) demonstrated that children's prejudice moderately correlates with parent prejudice—a trend that far exceeds minimal effectiveness. But these frequently assessed negative attitudes are one component of transmitted ideas about difference. Positive ideas about difference are often put under an umbrella term of "tolerance." While tolerance and prejudice are distinct, they are also related to each other (van Zalk & Kerr, 2014), as anti-prejudicial attitudes are a necessary but insufficient condition for a pro-difference position, suggesting some similarity in the processes through which these are inherited. The nature of socialization is such that verbal/nonverbal, intentional/unintentional messages about otherness can dually inform transference of *both* of these phenomena within the family.

Positively Positioning our Ingroup

Just as exists within macro-cultures, families are micro-cultures whose messages culminate to teach members how to believe and behave. Allport and Devine asserted that parents construct environments of positive "versus" negative feelings toward outgroups. Illuminating principles moldable to many—and possibly any—outgroup, parental-ethnic racial socialization (PERS) is a realm of family scholarship that offers hope for how families foster positivity toward difference. Focusing on how parents talk about social difference surrounding their own social group, Hughes identified the PERS as the process of parent-to-child transmission of values and ideals surrounding racial, religious, cultural, and ethnic groups, as well as the transmission of the intergroup dynamics presumed to exist across these social categories (Hughes et al., 2008). This socialization is enacted directly and indirectly across four realms: cultural socialization, egalitarianism, preparation for bias, and promotion of outgroup mistrust, all of which are more likely to be employed *only* when the parents believe them necessary to children's functioning (2013).

The first parenting ethnic socialization strategy, ***cultural socialization***, is the transmission of values, practices, and important pieces of ingroup history. It is primarily enacted through taking children to cultural events that address and celebrate their racial/ethnic group. *Egalitarianism* includes messages about the equal abilities, merits, and deserved rights of those within and across all different groups. Egalitarianism sometimes includes messages about the benefits of diversity, an appreciative approach which Hughes and colleagues' refer to as "pro-diversity," that is synonymous with multiculturalism, the ideology that (racial and cultural) differences are existent, to be acknowledged, and to be celebrated (Holoien & Shelton, 2012). *Preparation for bias* represents parents' messages about society's unequal treatment of diverse/minority groups. This focuses on prejudice against the child's own racial/ethnic group, and its frequency is related to how much they have experienced bias in their own lives (Hughes, 2003). Finally, *promotion of (outgroup) mistrust* includes cautionary tales and/or explicit warnings about children's future interactions with outgroups. In the following section, the intergroup consequences of the PERS are brought to light through Van Bergen, Ruyter, and Pels' (2017) interviews with antagonistic and egalitarian college students in Turkey. Their results—focused on adult children's own and their parents' thoughts and communication about Muslims—are next reviewed in a way that reflects their likely emblematic conclusions for broader trends of adult parent-child communication about difference.

College-aged adult children labeled as antagonistic were those showing strong opposition to outgroups (van Bergen et al., 2017). Commonly manifest in hostile verbal and physical intergroup conflict, antagonistic interviewees conveyed an "us versus them" discourse and described their ingroup norms, artifacts, and history as superior. Non-natives referenced themselves as targets of prejudice and rationalized their (resultant) ingroup favoritism as being universal. Not to be confused with the *bias* component of parenting socialization that acknowledges the reality of intergroup dynamics, antagonistic student sentiments such as "people always give priority to their own race" proposes outgroup members would *always* biasedly treat them and serves as justification for reactive mistreatment.

Most antagonistic students reported that their parents emphasized ingroup superiority and outgroup-targeted mistrust (van Bergen et al., 2017). Parents warned of likely mistreatment by outgroup members but offered no support (e.g., advice, sympathy) for being targeted. Parents also warned of the negative consequences of outgroup association. Some parents were so adamant against befriending or dating outgroup members that they even threatened violent "discipline" should this occur. Parents in the majority compared Muslim behaviors as counter to the proper behaviors displayed by their own ingroups and instilled the importance of immigrants' assimilation into dominant culture. There were also sentiments of being ignored for having strong beliefs.

College students labeled as egalitarian held anti-antagonistic positions toward the target outgroup (van Bergen et al., 2017). They emphasized similarity across social groups, and did not emphasize their ingroup membership. Once prompted, they asserted strong disagreement with antagonists. While all the egalitarian students tended to think their parents were egalitarian, differences emerged between those with more pro-diversity socialization (again, reflective of multiculturalism) and those from "colorblind" households. Parents celebrating diversity often lived in neighborhoods with multicultural schools, were seen behaving in inclusive ways toward outgroup members, and were remembered as explicitly rationalizing their egalitarian views. Colorblind sentiments were conveyed through parents' understatement of prejudice. A father is remembered as "attach(ing) much more value to being a good person" (van Bergen et al., 2017, p. 570), which might be what underscores his and other sampled adult children's perception that difference is unimportant.

Unlike all of their antagonistic counterparts, egalitarian students had been supported by their parents in regard to experiencing and responding to discrimination. Their parents acknowledged, but did not always emphasize, discrimination. Some encouraged their children to speak out against injustice, or noted that they did so themselves, thus offering a legitimacy and validation to children's feelings they had been treated unjustly based on group membership.

Not all college students modeled parents' presumed antagonistic or egalitarian beliefs. Several antagonistic students perceived their parents as *non*-antagonistic (though not necessarily egalitarian), suggesting a flipping of values. One adult child took on a stronger negative stance than his parents and held the impression that both he and his father were stubborn in their stances, but in opposite socio-political ideologies. A few egalitarian students reported negative—and even antagonistic—views by their parents. Though not the purpose of their study, van Bergen and her colleagues' findings provide avenues for exploring children's modeling or compensation of "otherness" socialization (van Bergen et al., 2017, p. 576).

As just illuminated, parents face a challenge when it comes to socialization of discrimination. Of course, this challenge is disproportionately placed on minoritized groups. Many parents report directly talking about difference because their children *are* different, and so parental ethnic-racial socialization is likely more common and/or pronounced among minority groups (e.g., Lee, Grotevant, Hellerstedt, & Gunnar, 2006). Children trained to recognize discrimination are more likely to seek social support and employ problem solving techniques when it occurs (Daniel & Daniel, 1999). However, parents' promotion of mistrust in the outgroup can lead to negative intergroup attitudes among adult children (Stevenson & Arrington, 2009) and may need to be presented alongside other truthful messages about the presence of fairness (and general variability) in the general public's treatment of outgroups.

Given that social inequality differently affects different social groups, educating and warning children calls for parents of different social groups to speak differently when describing their and their children's (historical and present) role within that social hierarchy, and researchers have few clues except to note that this socialization is important for all. White children's parents who engage in PERS tend to do so when in response to an unfortunate event that requires explanation and support, but rarely do so proactively or preemptively (Tran, Mintert, & Jew, 2017). Alongside other taboo topics such as sex and death, social injustice might make parents squeamish. Perhaps parents think others can or should teach their children about these issues and/or fear they will inadequately address difference themselves. While the absence of messages about discrimination likely sends the incorrect message that they are non-existent or unimportant, parents may be correct about their ineptness to instruct. Some white children who deem social harmony as an unworthwhile pursuit have parents who frequently emphasized the presence of social injustice (Vittrup, 2018). This aversion to parents' professions about injustice may be the result of family communication incompetencies, which reminds us to draw from the broader family scholarship to inform our (re)thinking about parent-child communication of "otherness."

Family Communication Mediators and Moderators of Communication about Otherness

Communication regarding difference likely underscores broader messages about control and enforced homogeneity of values. Authoritarianism (Tran et al., 2017) and a strong conformity orientation are both directly linked to greater prejudice among parents and children (Meeusen & Dhont, 2015), perhaps due to their underlying theme that "people with power make the rules and those beneath them follow". However, parental control can complicate matters. A highly controlling mother can "turn" a low biased child into a more biased child over the pre-adolescent years. For more highly biased young children, a mother displaying little control assists with the child's gradual lessening of this anti-social attitude (Odenweller & Harris, 2018). General support of children may also play a role, as children's adherence to parents' outgroup attitudes (specifically toward immigrants) was enhanced when they felt highly supported by their parents (Jugert, Eckstein, Beelmann, & Noack, 2016).

Though rarely assessed, the meaningfulness of parents' messages must matter and is probably more important than the frequency of their communication about otherness, as has been noted by Miklikowska (2016) and van Bergen and colleagues (2017). This meaningfulness might manifest as child-to-parent identification. As suggested by several theorists including Bandura and Nesdale (1971, 2001), children likely come to adopt their ingroup's norms of prejudice when they identify with that group. This is evidenced by implicit racial bias scores, wherein low identification leads to non-correlated parent and child prejudice scores but a strong identification coincides with strongly correlated parent and child scores (Stevenson & Arrington, 2009).

Regarding explicit bias, those with low identification had significantly related scores, but this relationship was negative, meaning that a lack of parent-child identification coincided with children expressing the opposite feelings than those expressed by the parent (Sinclair, Dunn, & Lowerty, 2005). As seen in van Bergen and colleagues' study, *compensation* can take place among those who wish to *behave* dissimilarly from parents with whom they de-identify. Taken together, these trends suggest that family environments of connection promote open-mindedness toward those outside of the family and a relational-distancing function for parents who express negative views of outgroups.

Positively Positioning Otherness: Teaching Tolerance and Appreciation

Perhaps the most hopeful message of family socialization about otherness can be found within Samuel Oliner's (2003) work on bold altruism toward outgroups. Having survived the Holocaust due to the brave kindness of strangers, Oliner's fascination led him to uncover several core principles among them. Regardless of their societal position or occupation, they shared a devotion to equality, justice, and caring toward humans. These principles were ingrained in the norms of the primary groups to which they belonged since childhood, beginning with their families. From a young age, their parents instilled in them that *all* people were to be treated fairly as individuals, regardless of group membership. These altruistic individuals recalled parenting behaviors they later modeled. A soldier who saved Jews said this of his mother, "She would never look down on people. She would always appreciate what people were worth, and it didn't matter whether they were poor or whatever" (p. 143) and recalled that his father—the person with whom he said he most strongly identified in life—was insistent that his son never look down on others, even if they quite literally worked underneath him, for "all people are people" (Sinclair et al., 2005).

Although this soldier's orders were to exterminate Jews, he saw the true nature of his position—as a law upholder—was to maintain these core values that were taught by his parents and consistently communicated by the institution through which he became a soldier. In this way, care, justice, and equality were the compass that directed him, even when the norms and risks of his job, nationality, and broader society were pushing him to be biased (Oliner & Oliner, 1988, p. 143). Regarding the primacy of parenting socialization, Oliner agrees with family communication scholars and other developmental theorists in regard to the lasting impact of family values. He asserts that the strength, compassion, and bravery that is required of outgroup helping is found among those who had strong, healthy relationships with their parents from an early age. Summarizing principles of attachment theory, the Oliners explain how feeling love, protection, direction, and security in the parental relationship helps children grow into what could be considered a "secure attachment to humanity". It may also underlie the empathy these heroes displayed—an empathy that many did not talk about (this is logical, of course, as many who are empathic simply view it as a way of living), but that Oliner derived from their many statements and affect regarding the pain of others and the responsibility they felt to relieve that pain.

While it may require less bravery than that displayed by the rogue rescuing Nazi soldier, it is fair to assert that those displaying everyday acts of outgroup kindness are also brave. These acts may not be dangerous, but when society, and our arguably natural tendencies, tell us to categorize and then (mis)treat accordingly (Oakes, 2003), courage and conviction are necessary to lead a life in which "others" are treated as if they were part of our ingroup (Oliner & Oliner, 1988). To this end, some of these family characteristics uncovered in Oliner's work may emerge in what I refer to now as the "tolerance to appreciation" continuum.

The scope of positivity toward otherness spans from two proposed extremes: apathetic acceptance of otherness and enthusiastic embrace of otherness. The first of these extremes—what I identify here as *tolerance*—conceptually overlaps with positive attitudes toward outgroups. While tolerance has been used as a goal of sorts (Oakes, 2003), tolerant individuals take a watered down approach to difference and likely engage in more passive facilitation, such as cordial conversation or even friendship. Still anti-prejudiced, tolerant individuals do not actively go out of their way to assist outgroups as a whole or as individuals (Dursun-Bilgin, Çelik, & Kasımoğlu, 2018). Tolerance, which likely draws from the aforementioned colorblind ideology—as noted by van Bergen and colleagues—maintains the position that fairness across groups is important, and/but that it may already have occurred. In this way, those (merely) tolerant of otherness may quite literally tolerate complaints of social inequality and/or efforts to rectify these (e.g., affirmative action), but they would be unlikely to take actions like voting for the Equal Rights Amendment as they would see no need to do so.

At the other end of our presumed "tolerance to appreciation" continuum is a deep appreciation for and celebration of human difference, which is to be accompanied by recognition that society is far from sharing this perspective. As a result of embracing difference, appreciators strive to learn about and grow from the differences of others. Further, recognizing social inequality and desiring its demise, appreciators actively facilitate efforts for diverse groups to be treated fairly. Extending the "multiculturalism" mentality across contexts, Miville and colleagues use the term *universal-diverse orientation* for this awareness, acknowledgment, and appreciation of difference that I propose be promoted by parents (see Kegel & DeBlaere, 2014 for recent employment of the construct). There is recent evidence of adult children's adherence to the same ideology in which difference is deemed useful, and the differences of people are thought to coexist with their commonalities (Vittrup, 2018).

This "tolerance to appreciation" continuum is primarily conceptual, as it would be difficult to isolate cognitions and communication in order to accurately designate a family's position between these end points. After all, families may move back and forth from tolerance to acceptance. There may even be circumstances in which a family would "jump" out of this continuum to engage in prejudicial activities (e.g., passive harm). Still, if we recognize that family communication can be geared to various levels of positivity toward otherness, we might better understand and prescribe strategies for optimally mobilizing families as factories for social change.

Setting an Agenda of Appreciation: Best Practices for Parents

Agreeing with Samuel Oliner that such compassionate behavior deserves more attention (Liao, Spanierman, Harlow, & Neville, 2017), I propose that families abandon myths about social equity and attend to appreciating otherness through techniques of cross-cultural artifacts, cross-group friendships gathering within the home, outspokenness about injustice, and within-family intergroup contact.

The presence, praise, and rich descriptions of outgroups do not have to come from parents—they can come through other media materials such as books, documentaries, and fictional films about the history and culture of different groups. Parents can employ these materials in lieu of their own knowledge, and sharing these materials among the family is another way to connect home life to life outside of the home. Doing so teaches that humans are richly different and similar.

Difference is well introduced to the family by people who *are* different (and, of course, always, also similar) to the family members. By bringing different people into the home and hearts of family members, cross-group friendships reduce colorblind mentalities among adults (Soliz & Rittenour, 2012) and are also linked to children's prosocial thoughts toward outgroups (Langrehr, 2014). Those studied by Oliner (2003) said their parents had friends of various social/cultural/political identities, and they would laugh and learn about each other within each other's homes. This early intergroup contact maximizes the benefits of interpersonal relationships with outgroup members. Family-to-family visits involve trust, intimacy, and affection that exceed that of public life and are a means of instilling comfort and competence within future intergroup interactions (Meeusen, 2014).

Borrowing from the Common Ingroup Identity Model's propositions (Gaertner & Dovidio, 2000), we remind families that such inclusion does not have to come at the expense of ingroup pride. Early "pulling in" of otherness normalizes inclusive acts, makes them a part of the group identity, and can instill habits that young children might "catch" and continue into adulthood. Data supports this, as parents who encourage and express positivity toward outgroups have children who are more likely to opt into college classes, celebrations, and activities that focus upon race, gender, and other intergroup contexts.

In addition to relationships with outgroup members, difference is perhaps best embraced when outgroup members become family. Many of this book's chapters demonstrate how within-family differences cause tensions, discomfort, distance, and dissatisfaction. Their authors offer hope, though, by pinpointing this commonly shared ingroup identity as the mechanism through which family members saw each other more positively, *and* saw their "once outgroups" more positively. For instance, transracial adoptions lead to upward socialization in which parents' perspectives are expanded. These parents experience their own racial identity transformation and the racial identity transformation of their family unit (see Ch. 10, this volume), often leading them to help children cope with discrimination. This is particularly common when parents' colorblind mentality is low (Liao et al., 2017). This positivity can then be extended to non-family members who representing these diverse identities.

While race, religion, sexual orientation, and political affiliation are commonly studied as intergroup realms within the family, age and gender should not be overlooked. Age is addressed herein as a means of designating upward or downward socialization (see below), but gender assessments reveal a fascinating trend regarding outgroup attitudes: that gender actually has very little to do with this type of value transmission. Father and mother data are often collapsed for their similarities, and dyadic gender makeup of cross- or same-sex does not reveal differences. While boys/men do tend to report more negative other-attitudes than girls/women (e.g., Goodboy, Martin, & Rittenour, 2016), the gender of parent-child dyads reveals no differences. While this could be interpreted as evidence against gender schema theory, it may be that outgroup attitudes are not just a "male thing" or "female thing," despite the fact that women are likely taught to think and talk more sensitively in regard to these matters (Jugert et al., 2016), and fears of outgroup mistreatment are different for daughters than they are for sons. Researchers might consider how interpersonal (or intragroup) identification between family members is a more causal mechanism for value transfer, with gender unnecessary for teaching about otherness. Of course, additional discourse about feminism and its processes—while following similar trends of PERS—also benefits our understanding of the interplay between teaching children how to "do" social justice (Jugert et al., 2016).

While a family member of a social outgroup is shown to enhance members' feelings toward that social group, this method of prejudice-reduction is not a guarantee. Also, as noted elsewhere in this book, the same group-based exclusionary practices that exist outside of the family can often occur inside, especially when the family has strong norms against differentiation and/or the differentiating behavior is core to the family's values, as is often labeled the black sheep effect (Colaner & Rittenour, 2015; Few-Demo, Lloyd, & Allen, 2014). Still, family members that were once outgroup members can teach tolerance and inclusion of broader outgroups, but it is not the only means of improving family members' attitudes toward otherness.

Future Directions and Implications for Scholars and Practitioners

This review of literature on family communication leads to several suggestions for future scholarship: verbal and nonverbal channels and the role of (in) consistency, addressing more of the family system, addressing familial groups beyond the immediate family, the role of timing, and reciprocal socialization. Though nonverbal communication is noted to be important to PERS, there is little attention to verbal "versus" nonverbal communication of otherness within the family. Broadly, nonverbals are more heavily trusted for affective messages, yet are unable to capture verbal messages' depth. In broader family communication literature, ambiguity and inconsistency of parenting practices complicate or harm children's wellbeing and learning. As such, children may quickly associate a father's outgroup-targeted scoff with negative attitudes, but—even as "wise sponges"—children's learning about difference might be challenged when their father says that he "sees no color." Commonly uttered phrases of "my mom isn't racist, but …" (Fitness, 2005) speak to children's perception that their parents' behaviors and voiced ideologies do not always match. Such utterances may also speak to the cognitive dissonance experienced during children's sense-making of parents' prejudiced actions. The learning process is likely to effect and be effected by relational quality.

Beyond the dyad, the broader family system and surrounding culture teach intergroup attitudes, and the interdependence of these relationship surely carries consequences for outgroup socialization. Essentially, the family communication scholar of diversity faces the tough challenge of considering parents as pedagogical forces (e.g., Chen, Simmons, & Kang, 2015) and also accounting for the things that make families a separate—and quite complicated—realm of interconnections, nonsummativity, and complex interactions. Taking on family-like traits such as support and guidance, schools and religious institutions are known to influence attitudes toward outgroups, though their direct influence may be eclipsed by direct parent-child communication (e.g., Vozmediano, San-Juan, Vergara, & Alonso-Alberca, 2017). Perhaps more crucial are these groups' impact on the centrality children perceive of their racial and ethnic groups (Galvin, Dickson, & Marrow, 2006). Family socialization of otherness likely intersects with broader communities in crucial ways, the least of which is that parents often decide on their family's neighborhood, school, and religious affiliation.

Religion and political membership intersect with parental socialization about difference. Among Jewish Israeli parents observed communicating with their children, it was the nationalist religious parents—and not the secular parents—who were observed communicating more negative outgroup attitudes and specification of group membership (Stevenson & Arrington, 2009). It is likely that parents directly communicate verbal and nonverbal messages about outgroups *because* of their own religious norms, and it is also likely that they further socialize *through* creating an environment of like-minded and like-behaving individuals.

Broader still, nationalism has a hand in intergroup dynamics. As expected given tolerant "versus" appreciative approaches, a parent's political ideologies often indicates their prejudice; parent-child discourse *about* politics is responsible for heightened parent-child agreement on these ideals as well as their explicit prejudice (Stevenson & Arrington, 2009). According to Nesdale, the norms of the immediate socializing ingroup exist alongside two other contributors to anti-outgroup sentiments: immense intergroup conflict and great perceived threat from the outgroup(s). A family may not be able to maintain its members' positivity toward otherness in a hostile climate where an outgroup is placed at fault. Conversely, and as illuminated through the heroes in Oliner's (2003) research, intense intergroup conflict might be squelched if children highly identify with a group/family whose norms are of love and inclusion for all. To more precisely determine the potential of such a "humanity is my ingroup" obligation, researchers might be more purposeful in directly comparing the general population to those with high familial obligation to non-family/outgroups.

In addition to purposeful sampling and employment of experiments to assess cause/effect relationships, researchers might also attend to the role of timing. Across the broader literature on reducing prejudice and enhancing intergroup relations, timing emerges as paramount. For instance, intergroup contact's prosocial outcomes are likely optimized when the involved parties do not learn of their differing group memberships until after they have formed a positive interpersonal relationship (Hewstone et al., 2014). This is tricky for families, but it can occur. Are the results the same? Can the shared history of the group serve as an aid or hindrance to relationships? Given that theorization leads us to different conclusions (black sheep effect and intergroup sensitivity theory, respectively), we must assess these questions. Researchers might also consider the evolution of family communication about otherness. Segall and colleagues disputed the assumption that early processes of over-emphasizing categories is a "given" among all young children (Segall, Birnbaum, Deeb, & Diesendruck, 2015), finding that parents' sheer verbalizing of strangers' gender and ethnic categories was the greatest trigger of their 5-year-old children's ethnic essentialism (the belief that a person can never change the psychological and physical properties that are shared by *all* of their group members), and that this was more important than parents' social group membership or expressed negative attitudes. As this construct has been linked to intergroup bias, we might caution parents to wait until children are older before "marking" others' group membership.

In accordance with social learning theory and reliance on parents to do the teaching, researchers tend to take a downward socialization approach to understanding the teaching of otherness within the home. Just as children teach their parents and grandparents about technology and leisure activities, they likely teach them to value (or devalue) difference. Despite resurgences of hate crimes after an advancement among minority groups (e.g., Obama's election), American cohorts continue to be less bigoted over time, and—juxtaposed to stereotypes—older adults *grow* to be less prejudiced over time (Henry & Sears, 2009). Upward socialization may be a cause for this shift. Regarding attitudes toward immigrants, parent and child data revealed equivalent prejudice and tolerance shifts for *both* generations across a two year period (Miklikowska, 2016).

Building upon what we know about downward socialization, we might further address upward socialization such as (grand)children's and nieces/nephews' explicit messages to their older family member as well as younger family members' interpersonal relationships forming latent intergroup contact ties (e.g., granddaughter loving someone of a different race). As a communication scholar recognizing the transactional nature of communication, and as a family researcher recognizing that world peace begins in the home, I have a daydream of multiple generations discussing difference together, with warmth toward each other, in ways that challenge and progress each other's sophisticated thinking about otherness. If we can better understand and ultimately help families accomplish more of these prosocial exchanges, we might use this "haven from a heartless world" to *transform* this somewhat divided world into one of harmony.

Conclusion

As family is our first and foremost teacher of how to think and communicate about ourselves and others (Galvin, Braithwaite, & Bylund, 2014), parents take a front seat in driving children's feelings about "otherness." As feelings—and not accurate information—are what push people happily toward or fearfully away from difference, parents' promotion of otherness likely begins with their displayed positivity toward the topic. The summarized literature illuminates some best practices for doing so, and also addresses the nuances of family-based education *about* difference. While educating children as to the realities of broader "anti-difference" discourse and practices can be an empowering practice that enhances ingroup-linked esteem among minorities, it can also fuel hostility. As we expand and combine these trends, we might also incorporate upward/reciprocal and transactional communication processes of tolerance and appreciation. Recognizing the roles of broader familial groups such as church and national discourse, we might help parents teach children about prejudice in ways that maintain positive affect toward outgroups. We might also help them to teach children that processes of prejudice are universal, as *all* humans are privy to categorization and the biased practices that often follow (Segall et al., 2015). Talking openly about prejudice's pervasiveness can remind us to be vigilant as well as patient in our ongoing efforts to be more inclusive, hence expanding "family" to all of humanity.

References

Allport, G. W. (1954). *The nature of prejudice.* New York: Doubleday Books.

Bandura, A. (1971). *Social learning theory.* Morristown, NJ: General Learning Press.

Bigler, R. S., & Liben, L. S. (2006). A developmental intergroup theory of social stereotypes and prejudice. *Advances in child development and behavior* (Vol. 34, pp. 39–89). Amsterdam, Netherlands: Elsevier.

Bradford, N. J., & Syed, M. (2019). Transnormativity and transgender identity development: A master narrative approach. *Sex Roles.* doi:10.1007/s11199-018-0992-7

Chen, Y.-W., Simmons, N., & Kang, D. (2015). "My family isn't racist—However ...": Multiracial/multicultural Obama-ism as an ideological barrier to teaching intercultural communication. *Journal of International & Intercultural Communication, 8*(2), 167–186. doi:10.1080/17513057.2015.1025331

Colaner, C. W., & Rittenour, C. E. (2015). "Feminism begins at home": The influence of mother-daughter gender socialization on daughter career and motherhood aspirations as channeled through daughter feminist identification. *Communication Quarterly, 63*, 81–98. doi:10.1080/01463373.2014.965839

Daniel, J. L., & Daniel, J. E. (1999). African-American childrearing: The context of hot stove. In T. J. Socha & R. C. Diggs (Eds.), *Communication, race, and family* (pp. 25–43). Mahwah, NJ: Lawrence Erlbaum Associates.

Degner, J., & Dalege, J. (2013). The apple does not fall far from the tree, or does it? A meta-analysis of parent–child similarity in intergroup attitudes. *Psychological Bulletin, 139*(6), 1270–1304. doi:10.1037/a0031436

Devine, P. G. (1989). Stereotypes and prejudice: Their automatic and controlled components. *Journal of Personality and Social Psychology, 56*(1), 5.

Dursun-Bilgin, M., Çelik, M. U., & Kasımoğlu, E. S. (2018). The role of communication in tolerance education. *Quality & Quantity: International Journal of Methodology, 52*(Suppl 2), 1179–1186. doi:10.1007/s11135-017-0628-y

Few-Demo, A. L., Lloyd, S. A., & Allen, K. R. (2014). It's all about power: Integrating feminist family studies and family communication. *Journal of Family Communication, 14*(2), 85–94. doi:10.1080/15267431.2013.864295

Fitness, J. (2005). Bye bye, black sheep: The causes and consequences of rejection in family relationships *The social outcast: Ostracism, social exclusion, rejection, and bullying* (pp. 263–276). New York, NY: Psychology Press.

Gaertner, S. L., & Dovidio, J. (2000). *Reducing intergroup bias: The common ingroup identity model.* Ann Arbor, MI: Psychology Press.

Galvin, K. M., Braithwaite, D. O., & Bylund, C. L. (2014). *Family communication: Cohesion and change* (9 ed.). Milton Park, UK: Taylor & Francis.

Galvin, K. M., Dickson, F. C., & Marrow, S. R. (2006). Systems theory: Patterns and (w)holes in family communication. In D. O. Braithwaite & L. A. Baxter (Eds.), *Engaging theories in family communication* (pp. 309–324). Thousand Oaks, CA: Sage.

Gniewosz, B., & Noack, P. (2006). Intergenerationale Transmissions-und Projektionsprozesse intoleranter Einstellungen zu Ausländern in der Familie. *Zeitschrift für Entwicklungspsychologie und Pädagogische Psychologie, 38*(1), 33–42.

Goodboy, A. K., Martin, M. M., & Rittenour, C. E. (2016). Bullying as a display of social dominance orientation. *Communication Research Reports, 33*, 159–165.

Henry, P. J., & Sears, D. O. (2009). The crystallization of contemporary racial prejudice across the lifespan. *Political Psychology, 30*(4), 569–590. doi:10.1111/j.1467-9221.2009.00715.x

Hewstone, M., Lolliot, S., Swart, H., Myers, E., Voci, A., Al Ramiah, A., & Cairns, E. (2014). Intergroup contact and intergroup conflict. *Peace and Conflict: Journal of Peace Psychology, 20*(1), 39.

Holoien, D. S., & Shelton, J. N. (2012). You deplete me: The cognitive costs of colorblindness on ethnic minorities. *Journal of Experimental Social Psychology, 48*(2), 562–565.

Hughes, D. (2003). Correlates of African American and Latino parents' messages to children about ethnicity and race: A comparative study of racial socialization. *American Journal of Community Psychology, 31*(1–2), 15–33.

Hughes, D., Rivas, D., Foust, M., Hagelskamp, C., Gersick, S., & Way, N. (2008). How to catch a moonbeam: A mixed-methods approach to understanding ethnic socialization processes in ethnically diverse families. In *Handbook of race, racism, and the developing child* (pp. 226–277). Hoboken, NJ: Wiley.

Jugert, P., Eckstein, K., Beelmann, A., & Noack, P. (2016). Parents' influence on the development of their children's ethnic intergroup attitudes: A longitudinal analysis from middle childhood to early adolescence. *European Journal of Developmental Psychology, 13*(2), 213–230. doi:10.1080/17405629.2015.1084923

Kegel, K., & DeBlaere, C. (2014). Universal-diverse orientation in Asian international students: Confirmatory factor analysis of the Miville-Guzman universality-diversity scale, short form. *Cultural Diversity and Ethnic Minority Psychology, 20*(3), 469.

Langrehr, K. J. (2014). Transracially adoptive parents' color-blind attitudes and views toward socialization: Cross-racial friendships as a moderator. *Cultural Diversity and Ethnic Minority Psychology, 20*(4), 601–610. doi:10.1037/a0036528

Lee, R. M., Grotevant, H. D., Hellerstedt, W. L., & Gunnar, M. R. (2006). Cultural socialization in families with internationally adopted children. *Journal of Family Psychology, 20*(4), 571–580. doi:10.1037/0893-3200.20.4.571

Liao, H.-Y., Spanierman, L. B., Harlow, A. J., & Neville, H. A. (2017). Do parents matter? Examination of White college students' intergroup experiences and attitudes. *The Counseling Psychologist, 45*(2), 193–212. doi:10.1177/0011000017694337

Meeusen, C. (2014). The parent–child similarity in cross-group friendship and anti-immigrant prejudice: A study among 15-year old adolescents and both their parents in Belgium. *Journal of Research in Personality, 50,* 46–55. doi:10.1016/j.jrp.2014.03.001

Meeusen, C., & Dhont, K. (2015). Parent–child similarity in common and specific components of prejudice: The role of ideological attitudes and political discussion. *European Journal of Personality, 29*(6), 585–598. doi:10.1002/per.2011

Miklikowska, M. (2016). Like parent, like child? Development of prejudice and tolerance towards immigrants. *British Journal of Psychology, 107*(1), 95–116. doi:10.1111/bjop.12124

Nesdale, D. (2001). Language and the development of children's ethnic prejudice. *Journal of Language and Social Psychology, 20,* 90–111.

Oakes, P. (2003). The root of all evil in intergroup relations? Unearthing the categorization process. In R. Brown & S. Gaertner (Eds.), *Blackwell handbook of social psychology: Intergroup processes* (pp. 3–21). Malden, MA: Blackwell.

Odenweller, K. G., & Harris, T. M. (2018). Intergroup socialization: The influence of parents' family communication patterns on adult children's racial prejudice and tolerance. *Communication Quarterly, 5,* 1–21.

Oliner, S. P. (2003). Do unto others. Cambridge, MA: Westview Press.

Oliner, S. P., & Oliner, P. M. (1988). *The altruistic personality: Rescuers of Jews in Nazi Europe: What led ordinary men and women to risk their lives on behalf of others?* New York, NY: Free Press.

Segall, G., Birnbaum, D., Deeb, I., & Diesendruck, G. (2015). The intergenerational transmission of ethnic essentialism: How parents talk counts the most. *Developmental Science, 18*(4), 543–555.

Sinclair, S., Dunn, E., & Lowerty, B. S. (2005). The relationship between parental racial attitudes and children's implicit prejudice. *Journal of Experimental Social Psychology, 41,* 283–289. doi:10.1016/j.jesp.2004.06.003

Soliz, J., & Rittenour, C. E. (2012). Family as an intergroup arena. In H. Giles (Ed.), *The handbook of intergroup communication* (pp. 331–342). Thousand Oaks, CA: Routledge.

Solomon, H. E., & Kurtz-Costes, B. (2018). Media's influence on perceptions of trans women. *Sexuality Research and Social Policy, 15*(1), 34–47. doi:10.1007/s13178-017-0280-2

Stevenson, H. C., & Arrington, E. G. (2009). Racial/ethnic socialization mediates perceived racism and the racial identity of African American adolescents. *Cultural Diversity and Ethnic Minority Psychology,* 15(2), 125.

Tran, A. G. T. T., Mintert, J. S., & Jew, G. B. (2017). Parental ethnic-racial socialization and social attitudes among ethnic-racial minority and White American emerging adults. *American Journal of Orthopsychiatry, 87*(3), 347–356. doi:10.1037/ort0000204 van Bergen, D. D., de Ruyter, D. J., & Pels, T. V. M. (2017). 'Us against them' or 'all humans are equal': Intergroup attitudes and perceived parental socialization of Muslim immigrant and native Dutch youth. *Journal of Adolescent Research, 32*(5), 559–584. doi:10.1177/0743558416672007

van Zalk, M. H. W., & Kerr, M. (2014). Developmental trajectories of prejudice and tolerance toward immigrants from early to late adolescence. *Journal of Youth and Adolescence, 43*(10), 1658–1671.

Vittrup, B. (2018). Color blind or color conscious? White American Mothers' approaches to racial socialization. *Journal of Family Issues, 39*(3), 668–692. doi:10.1177/0192513x16676858

Vozmediano, L., San-Juan, C., Vergara, A. I., & Alonso-Alberca, N. (2017). 'Watch out, sweetie': The impact of gender and offence type on parents' altruistic fear of crime. *Sex Roles: A Journal of Research, 77*(9–10), 676–686. doi:10.1007/s11199-017-0758-7

About the Authors

Colleen Warner Colaner (Ph.D., University of Nebraska) is an Associate Professor of Communication at the University of Missouri. Her research examines how communication shapes and sustains relationships in complex, diverse, and modern family structures and experiences. In this work, she focuses on children's communication experiences and abilities, with an aim to understand children's unique perceptions of their family relationships. She takes an applied approach to scholarship by translating family communication research to families in the community. She serves as a family communication educator, partnering with mental health professionals to provide families with strategies for connecting and coping.

Monica Cornejo (M.A. University of California, Santa Barbara, 2019) is a doctoral student in the Department of Communication at University of California, Santa Barbara. She studies the privacy management, identity, and family communication of undocumented immigrants in the United States. Ultimately, Monica aims to utilize her research to create new resources and interventions that will benefit undocumented immigrants' social mobility and interpersonal relationships.

Debbie S. Dougherty (Ph.D. University of Nebraska, 2000) is Professor of Communication at University of Missouri and the Editor in Chief for the Journal of Applied Communication Research. Her research program explores the relationship between power and organizing, particularly as related to both sexual harassment and social class. She has authored a book on social class and communication, titled *The Reluctant Farmer: An Exploration of Work, Social Class, and the Production of Food.* Her research has been published in journals such as *Harvard Business Review, Human Relations, Journal of Communication, Human Communication Research, Communication Monographs, Management Communication Quarterly, Journal of Applied Communication Research, and Sex Roles.* She sits on the editorial board for seven scholarly journals. She has received numerous awards for her research and community projects including the National Communication Association 2019 *Applied Scholar Award*, 10 top paper awards, The *Jack Kay Award for Engaged Research, the Management Communication Quarterly Article of the Year Award, the Norman K. Denzin Qualitative Research Award, the Excellence in Education Award, and the Gold Chalk Award* for graduate student mentoring.

Hue T. Duong (Ph.D., University of Georgia) is an assistant professor at Georgia State University. His research focuses on health communication, social marketing, and development communication. Prior to acdemia, he worked in UNICEF projects for nine years to support children and disadvantaged communities in Southeast Asia. Hue is a former Fulbright scholar.

Marcus W. Ferguson Jr. (M.A. The University of Missouri- Columbia, 2017) is a Black male first-generation doctoral student in the Department of Communication at the University of Missouri-Columbia. He studies both organizational and family communication. His research interests focus on power, race, stigma, and diversity. Specifically, he takes an intersectional approach to uncovering the ways in which each of these areas function within the organizational and family communication context. His research takes a critical approach to addressing issues and uses this information to provide applied solutions/practices. His publications appear in *Management Communication Quarterly* and the *Journal of The Society for Social Work and Research.*

Craig Fowler (Ph.D., Pennsylvania State University) is an associate professor in the School of Communication, Journalism and Marketing at Massey University, New Zealand. His research interests focus on family communication, intergenerational relationships, and issues related to communication and successful aging.

Tina M. Harris (Ph.D., University of Kentucky) is the Manship-Maynard Endowed Chair of Race, Media, and Cultural Literacy in the Manship School of Mass Communication at Louisiana State University. Her primary research interest is interracial communication, with specific foci on critical communication pedagogy, race and identity, diversity and media representations, racial social justice, mentoring, and racial reconciliation, among others. She is a well-published and very active senior scholar with many accolades and awards for her longstanding history of making valuable contributions to the discipline, university, and department for her teaching, research, and service.

Aparna Hebbani (Ph.D., University of Memphis) is a Lecturer in the School of Communication & Arts, at The University of Queensland, Australia. She researches refugee and asylum seeker settlement in Australia, and the media representation of Muslims, asylum seekers, and refugees in Australia. Her ability to conduct high quality research and secure collaborations is evidenced through her grants and publications record. She has led a team which won a highly competitive Australian Research Council Linkage grant ($135,000) investigating refugee employment and intergenerational communication. Dr. Hebbani has served on the Multicultural Queensland Advisory Council, Queensland India Council, as well as boards of many NGOs in Australia and overseas.

Sarah R. Heisdorf (M.A., University of Nebraska-Lincoln) is a Ph.D. student in the Department of Communication Studies at The University of Iowa. Her research focuses on how families make sense of uncertainty surrounding health and transitions later in life, such as in the grandparent-grandchild relationship or with elderly family members. Her work has appeared in in *Journal of Applied Communication* and the *Journal of Divorce & Remarriage.*

Jennifer A. Kam (Ph.D., The Pennsylvania State University, 2009) is Associate Professor in the Department of Communication at University of California, Santa Barbara. She studies the ways in which stressors—stemming from racial/ethnic identification, immigration, and acculturation—relate to immigrant youth's academic, mental, and physical well-being. She utilizes a stress-resilience-thriving framework to identify psychological, individual action-oriented, and interpersonal communication processes that can attenuate the negative effects of stressors and/or directly promote academic, mental, and physical well-being. She has published over 40 journal articles and received the National Communication Association Interpersonal Communication Division's Early Scholar Award in 2016.

LaShawnda Kilgore (M.S., Illinois State University) is a doctoral student in the Department of Communication at the University of Missouri-Columbia. Her research seeks to understand the experiences of foster youth (former and current). Specifically, she seeks to understand how they communicatively process and cope with trauma and how to help families thrive when it is made up of individuals that have experienced childhood trauma. In this work, she presents literature on trauma and its lasting impact on the individual and their families. She offers insight in the healing nature of relationships and the role they play in providing safety and care to those recovering from trauma.

Mairead MacKinnon is a Ph.D. candidate and research assistant at the University of Queensland. Mairead's research is interested in understanding the way Australian media report on refugees and how journalists and editors make decisions when reporting on refugee-related issues. She is also interested in how former refugees perceive the impact of media coverage on their sense of belonging and how they are accepted by the larger Australian society. She has published in both the communication and journalism field. Mairead is also a Sessional Academic teaching various communication and journalism courses.

Jimmie Manning (Ph.D., University of Kansas) is Professor and Chair for Communication Studies at the University of Nevada, Reno. His research focuses on meaning-making in relationships. This research spans multiple contexts to understand how individuals, couples, families, organizations, and other cultural institutions attempt to define, support, control, limit, encourage, or otherwise negotiate relationships. He explores these ideas through three contexts: relational discourses, especially those about sexuality, gender, love, and identity; connections between relationships and efficacy in health and organizational contexts; and digitally mediated communication. His research has been supported by agencies including the National Science Foundation and has accrued over 70 publications in outlets including *Communication Monographs*, *Journal of Family Communication*, and *Journal of Computer-Mediated Communication*, among others. He also coauthored the book *Researching Interpersonal Relationships: Qualitative Methods, Research, and Analysis* (Sage Publications). Recent awards include the Central States Communication Association Warren Award and the National Communication Association Kibler Award.

Laura V. Martinez (M.A., California State University, Fullerton) is a doctoral student at the Hugh Downs School of Human Communication at Arizona State University. Her research interests include identity across a number of areas, namely in intercultural, interpersonal, and organizational communication. She is the recipient of the CSUF William Gudykunst Memorial

Scholarship and the Top Thesis Award in the Intercultural Communication Division of the National Communication Association for her research and interest in intercultural matters within the context of interfaith marital identity management and conflict negotiation.

Sylvia L. Mikucki-Enyart (Ph.D., University of Illinois at Urbana-Champaign) is an assistant professor in the Department of Communication Studies at The University of Iowa. Her research focuses on how uncertainty impacts family communication and relational outcomes during periods of anticipated and unexpected change, such as the transition to extended family and late-life parental divorce and stepfamily development. Her work has appeared in *Communication Monographs, Journal of Family Communication, Journal of Social and Personal Relationships,* and *Personal Relationships.*

Roselia Mendez Murillo (M.A., University of California, Santa Barbara, 2018) is a doctoral student in the Department of Communication at University of California, Santa Barbara. She studies the ways in which family members and mono-English speakers communicate support to Latinx language brokers. She is also interested in further exploring the experiences of immigrant families who have undergone stepwise migration. Ultimately, she aims to contribute to their well-being by exploring their mental health, stressors, and family functioning.

Leslie R. Nelson (Ph.D., University of Missouri) is an Assistant Professor of communication studies at California Polytechnic State University, San Luis Obispo. Her research focuses on illuminating how communication may: (1) create, maintain, and deconstruct personal, social, and familial identities, (2) promote sense-making during relational transitions, and (3) impact individual and relational well-being in diverse family forms. Currently, much of her research explores family communication processes in both foster and adoptive families.

Angela L. Palmer-Wackerly (Ph.D., The Ohio State University) is an Assistant Professor in the Department of Communication Studies at the University of Nebraska-Lincoln. She specializes in Health Communication and researches the ways in which identities and supportive communication from family, friends, and health care providers relate to patients' health and treatment decisions. She uses mixed methods and community-based participatory research (CBPR) principles to: (1) improve communication between families, patients, and providers to influence health and treatment decision-making in cancer, infertility, and the intersection between these two diseases; and (2) engage rural communities through communication to create sustainable, culturally competent solutions to community-defined health problems.

Jihye Park (M.S., University of Wisconsin–Milwaukee) is a doctoral student in the Department of Communication at the University of Missouri. Her research focuses on political polarization, social identity theory, social media, and computational approaches to digital trace data.

Christine E. Rittenour (Ph.D., University of Nebraska) researches communication between and about people belonging to different social, role-based, and value-based identities. Positioning family as the primary place for learning about difference, she addresses how being different within a family coincides with communication among members, and also addresses how families talk and teach about non-familial social groups. Some of her work is published in *Sex Roles* and the *Journal of Family Communication*, and future publications are currently formulating at West Virginia University where Rittenour is an associate professor in the Department of Communication Studies.

Paul Schrodt (Ph.D., University of Nebraska–Lincoln) is the Philip J. and Cheryl C. Burguières Professor of Communication Studies at Texas Christian University. He studies communication behaviors that facilitate family relationships, with a particular interest in stepfamily functioning. He is a former Chair of the Family Communication and Interpersonal Communication Divisions of the National Communication Association (NCA), and he currently serves as Editor of *Communication Monographs.* He has authored more than 100 journal articles and book chapters, and is the recipient of the NCA's Bernard J. Brommel Award for Family Communication and the Early Career Award in Interpersonal Communication.

Jordan Soliz (Ph.D., University of Kansas) is a Professor of Communication Studies at the University of Nebraska-Lincoln. His research centers on communication and intergroup processes focusing primarily on identity and difference in personal relationships, families, and communities with the goal of understanding how communication facilitates relational and community solidarity, development or changes in worldviews and social attitudes, and individual well-being. He also investigates processes and outcomes of intergroup contact and intergroup dialogue. Dr. Soliz is the past editor of the *Journal* *of Family Communication* and past Chair of the Intergroup Communication Interest Group of the International Communication Association.

Lindsey J. Thomas (Ph.D., University of Iowa) is an Assistant Professor of communication studies in the School of Communication at Illinois State University. Her merged-methods program of research explores intersections of postmodern families, health, and culture, primarily focusing on communicative processes of family (de)construction and (de)legitimacy. Much of her current research takes a critical/dialogic approach to examine the ways in which formerly fostered youth make sense of their lives and how experiences and sense-making processes might connect with well-being outcomes.

Stella Ting-Toomey (Ph.D., University of Washington) is Professor of Human Communication Studies at California State University, Fullerton (CSUF). Her teaching passions include intercultural communication theory and training and interpersonal conflict management. She is the author or editor of 18 books, and more than 120 articles and chapters in prestigious communication journals and handbooks. She has written extensively on the topics of cultural-ethnic identity negotiation processes and conflict face negotiation issues. She is a recipient of the system-wide CSU Wang Family Excellence Award and the CSUF Outstanding Professor Award in recognition for superlative teaching, research, and service.

Heather L. Voorhees (Ph.D., University of Nebraska) is a postdoctoral fellow at the University of Texas at Austin's Center for Health Communication. Using both qualitative and quantitative methods, her research examines the intersection between chronic illness, identity, and social support.

Benjamin R. Warner (Ph.D., University of Kansas) is an associate professor in the Department of Communication at the University of Missouri. His research interests include political polarization, the effects of partisan identities on message reception, and the effects of political campaign communication.

Natilie Williams (M.S., Illinois State University, 2016) is a doctoral student in the Department of Communication at the University of Missouri–Columbia while studying Communication: Identity & Diversity. Her research interests include interpersonal and family communication as related to Black men and women utilizing voluntary kin relationships for companionship and personal development. She often utilizes the Strong Black Woman Collective theory when analyzing platonic, yet familial-like relationships, that serves as a protective barrier in times of need for Black men and women.

Farrah Youn-Heil (B.A., University of South Florida) is currently pursuing an M.A. in Communication Studies at the University of Georgia. Her research interests are primarily in interracial communication and racial representations in media.

Andrea Zorn (PgDip, Massey University) is an assistant lecturer in the School of Communication, Journalism and Marketing at Massey University, New Zealand. Her Ph.D. research focuses on the meanings women entrepreneurs ascribe to their ventures, using critical approaches to focus particularly on women in precarious circumstances.

Index

Children, Families, and Aging

Thomas J. Socha, *General Editor*

From first words to final conversations, communication plays an integral and significant role in all aspects of human development and everyday living. The Lifespan Communication: Children, Families, and Aging series seeks to publish authored and edited scholarly volumes that focus on relational and group communication as they develop over the lifespan (infancy through later life). The series will include volumes on the communication development of children and adolescents, family communication, peer-group communication (among age cohorts), intergenerational communication, and later-life communication, as well as longitudinal studies of lifespan communication development, communication during lifespan transitions, and lifespan communication research methods. The series includes college textbooks as well as books for use in upper-level undergraduate and graduate courses.

Thomas J. Socha, Series Editor | *tsocha@odu.edu*
Erika Hendrix, Acquisitions Editor | *erika.hendrix@plang.com*

To order other books in this series, please contact our Customer Service Department at:

peterlang@presswarehouse.com (within the U.S.)
order@peterlang.com (outside the U.S.)

Or browse online by series at www.peterlang.com

Made in the USA
Monee, IL
24 April 2023